P9-CMF-371

The Lincoln Papers

THE STORY OF THE COLLECTION WITH SELECTIONS TO JULY 4, 1861

ABRAHAM LINCOLN ON HORSEBACK
Pencil sketch by Waud
Reproduced from the original in the Library of Congress

THE STORY OF THE COLLECTION

WITH SELECTIONS TO JULY 4, 1861

THE LINCOLN PAPERS

DAVID C. MEARNS

INTRODUCTION BY CARL SANDBURG

VOLUME II

DOUBLEDAY & COMPANY, INC.

GARDEN CITY, NEW YORK, 1948

PRINTED IN THE UNITED STATES
AT
THE COUNTRY LIFE PRESS, GARDEN CITY, N. Y.

FIRST EDITION

PART TWO—THE PAPERS

(CONTINUED)

New York, No. 207 East 23rd. St.
December, 10th. 1860.

Hon: Abraham Lincoln
President elect of the United States,
Dear Sir:

As a slight testimonial of my admiration of you as a man, a patriot and a statesman, allow me, an entire stranger, to present for your acceptance the accompanying two hats which I have caused to be manufactured expressly for this purpose.

Wishing you the amplest success in the Administration of the affairs of our beloved country (the exalted duties of which will soon devolve upon you by the voice of the American people) I have the honor to be, sincerely and truly,

Your friend &c
Mrs. Louisa Livingston Siemon

Cleveland, Dec. 11th. 1860.

To the Honorable A. Lincoln.—P. E. U. S.
Your Excellency!

I as a good Republican, I deem it my duty, to communicate the following facts:

In the dwelling in which I reside, a Young Girl lives, who is a singular rare phenomena. She is a Sonambulist, a Clairvoyant (not a Spiritualist), in a very highly developed State.

Last evening she requested my presence, I found her in a trance. She communicated to me the following circumstances and requested me, to warn Your Excellenzy.

"That a conspiracy existed, to murder Your Excellency—that it was resolved to employ poison, to effect your death, and if no other opportunity presented itself, to bribe your domestices, to consumate the deed. And that your arival at Washington was the period of time, agreed upon. She counsels complete secrecy and circumspection, and begs your Excellency, that You should on feeling the slightest indisposition, drink hot milk in Large quantities—in order to frustrate the diabolicol plot."

The undersigned is no Spiritualist, but is free from any similiar prejudice; but knows the absolute verity of many events foretold by this Sonambule,—and therefore in interest of Your Excellency, of the country and of the Republican party implores Your Excellency, not to disregard this Admonition.

Your v. y.
G. A. a Wide Awake

Clev.

W City 11th Decr. 1860.

Dear Sir

Yesterday I wrote you a short note, which was accompanied by a letter from Mr Gilmer of N.C. I should be obliged, (if you answer Mr. G.) that a copy should be sent to me at the same time. Our correspondence is to be confidential until yr. consent shall be given to make it otherwise

Many Southern men have expressed a great desire that you should come here *soon* that Southern men, who are sincere Union men might see & converse with you. Think of this & judge for yourself, whether any good could come of such a step just now

Our Com. met this morning. The sky is overcast. No one can foresee clearly what is in the future.

Yrs truly
Thos. Corwin

A Lincoln,

CONFIDENTIAL

Cairo Illinois Dec 11th. 1860

Dr Sir:

Immediately after your nomination for the Presidency I wrote you a short note informing you that "I had calculated your nativity" and that as certainly "as the day of your birth had been correctly reported to me just so certainly you would be elected President"—I also stated to you that "I would call on you in Washington"—

It is now Sir my pleasure to inform you that I have just completed a fuller and more accurate calculation of your nativity and I have now to inform you that about the end of the first year of your administration or at the begining of the second year you will encounter a most serious———which may possibly involve your life

By prudence however you may avoid the evil I cannot trust more to paper, but I say this much to put you on your guard, I refer you to *David J Baker Jr* of this place for my character &c I am no office seeker, but speak to you the words of truth & soberness

Respy
Richd. E Randolph

Washington, D. C.
Dec. 11. 1860.

My Dear Sir:

I thought I could advise you before this time how Seward feels about Cabinet matters, but I cannot, for he guards himself with such vigilance in regard to those matters that his most intimate friends are not able to ascertain his views or wishes. Whether he would like to go into the cabinet or go back to the Senate nobody knows. But one think is certain, *he dont want to go abroad.*

He expresses the greatest confidence in your wisdom and ability, and says he pays no attention to all this small talk about the cabinet—that you are acquainted with the public men of the Country and will undoubtedly make wise selections, regardless of cliques and factions and local interests.

I see no ray of light in the general gloom which surrounds us.

Yours Truly,
E B Washburne M C

Hon. A. Lincoln

ILLINOIS REPUBLICAN STATE CENTRAL COMMITTEE

Chicago, Dec 11 1860.

Hon A. Lincoln
Springfield Ill
My Dear Sir:

Perhaps you noticed a statement in the *Tribune* a day or two since to the effect that $40,000 had been subscribed in the St Charles Hotel, New Orleans, to procure the assassination of yourself & Hamlin. The gentleman who witnessed this unparliamentary proceeding was J. M. Richards Esq of this city, the President of our Fremont Club in 1856, & a young man of unimpeachable character in every way. He related the affair to me; and while he did not attach great importance to it, he thought it not wholly impossible that some fool or fanatic might attempt to claim the reward. He represents the state of feeling in Louisiana & Mississippi to be that of pure frenzy. I may remark in this connection that people are getting mad very fast in this latitude. War is deemed quite a probable event and if we are to have war, nine men out of ten, Republicans & Democrats alike, prefer to have it in defence of the Constitution & under the forms of law.

I have not written this for the purpose of alarming anybody on the subject of assassination, but because I thought you ought to know the authority for the published statement aforesaid.

Very Truly Your Friend
Horace White

December, the 11..18..60

My lincoln sir i this after Noon take the opertunit to rite A lettr to you I was very much pleased Whean I heard you was leced for our president for I don all I could to git you in to ofies I stude in the streats and hurade for you and waed in the mud sume the river to A Repubalican meeting and traveled a bout six weakes lectionneer for you and spent considerable pocet chane and yesterday I had a law sute with a democrat on presidence lection I bet 50 fifty dollars that you would be a lected and he bet the same a mount that you would Not so when we heard that you was leced I toled the Gentleman that I wanted the money and he refused paying it and one word brot on a nother tel at last I Nocked the gentleman down and so you see he tuck the law on me and it Cost Me 50 dollars so Mr lincoln I have don my part for you I think you ar in debt to me for my Cindness to you

pleas ancer this lettr
to Mr A lincoln

George. W. Wright
Sarah. E. Wright

Washington Dec 13/60

My dear Sir–

Since writing my longer letter, it occurs to me that you expressed a wish to know whether Gov. Chase's name was ever connected with the indorsement of the "Helper Book." In the course of my conversation with him, I asked him if he indorsed that book. And he replied, *no.* He said it was sent to him for an indorsement; but that, an examination convinced him that, while calculated to do much good, it contained some exceedingly injudicious sentiments; and that, for that cause, he withheld his indorsement.

Very truly,
Geo. G. Fogg

Hon. Ab. Lincoln
Illinois

To Mr. Raymond's letter of December 14, Mr. Lincoln replied four days later: "What a very mad man your correspondent Smedley is. Mr. Lincoln is not pledged to the ultimate extinction of slavery; does not hold the black man to be the equal of the white, unqualifiedly as Mr. S. states it; and never did stigmatize their white people as immoral and unchristian; and Mr. S. cannot prove one of his assertions true. . . . As to the pitcher story it is a forgery out and out. I never made but one speech in Cincinnati. . . . I have never yet seen Governor Chase. I was never in a meeting of negroes in my life; and never saw a pitcher presented by anybody to anybody."

Times Office
N.Y. Dec. 14, 1860.

My dear Sir:—

Although I know you are overwhelmed with letters from all quarters I venture to enclose for your perusal a letter just received from an able, wealthy, influential gentleman of Mississippi, Col. Smedley. I do this mainly to ask your attention to the concluding paragraph in which he speaks of an Address said to have been made by you when some Free Negros presented a silver pitcher to Gov. Chase.

I remember seeing during the canvas, something of this sort in the Herald, but set it down then as a forgery. I believe it to be so still. But it is evidently doing very great mischief, when so sensible a man as Col. Smedley is thus influenced by it.

The feeling in this city is improving. But the Union men at the South *stand in need of backing*. It is not worth while to attempt in any way to satisfy either the Disunionists there, or the party malignants here. But the Union men of the South must belong to our party,—and it seems to me important that we should open the door for them as wide as the hinges will let it swing.

Buchanan, as is clear, means to do all the harm he can,—and unfortunately he has the power to do a great deal. He will leave things in a very bad shape evidently for his successor. I am under great obligation for your attention in replying to the note which I took the liberty of writing you some days since. If you can find time to say a word about the *silver pitcher speech* it will be serviceable in my comments on these matters.

I am, Very truly, Your ob't serv't

Henry J. Raymond

Hon. A. Lincoln.

Alexander Hamilton Stephens, future Vice-President of the Confederacy, acknowledged Mr. Lincoln's request for a copy of his speech before the Georgia Assembly on secession.

Crawfordsville Ga
14. Dec. 1860.

My Dear Sir

Your short and polite note of the 3d. Ulto asking for a revised copy of the speech to which you referd. was not received until last night—The newspaper report of the speech has never been perused by me—The notes of the reporter were submitted to me and corrected to some extent before being published but not so thoroughly as I could have wished—The report was substantially correct—If I had had any idea that it would have been so extensively circulated as it has been and been republished in so many papers throughout the country as it has been I should have prepared a copy for the Press in the first instance—But I had no such thought and therefore let the report go as it did—There are several verbal inaccuracies in it but the main points appear sufficiently clear for all practical purposes—

The Country is certainly in great peril and no man ever had

heavier or greater responsibilities resting upon him than you have in the present momentous crisis—

Yours most respectfully
Alexander H. Stephens

Hon. Abraham Lincoln
Springfield
Ill.

Bank of Cleveland (Old Soldiers—1812—Head Quarters)
Cleveland, O. Decr 15 1860

Hon A Lincoln
Sir

The National Democrat of this City publishes a letter signed by you to Tom Eweing Soft Soapeing the South Your friends all pronounce it a forgery If it is not we are Sold Revolutions never go backwards The Cotton States are practically out of the Union There can be no cordial Union What folly to expect it Let them go as go they will and peace go with em Dont humble ourselves and ask pardon for doing right Stand up manfully with your friends I mean your true friends who stand on principle not the office seekers It is Bucannans want of principle that has ruined his administration We are certainly on the eve of great troubles and I fear blood shed Call around you men of Stamana and thoroughly died in the principles of freedom The world will be thankfull for the good fruits—

Youres
G F Lewis

The day you humble yourself before the South will be one that detaches your best friends from you We hope that day never will dawn A friend has just been in thinks the letter is genuine and feels indignant I am no way convinced

PRIVATE

New York December 15th 1860

Hon Abraham Lincoln
My dear Sir

Permit me to command a few moments of your valuable time, in order to express the sentiments and wishes of a *Large Class* here and else where.

Before going further allow me to introduce myself—I am twenty six years a resident of New York and during that time have formed a large acquaintance with our good citizens of my own sphere in society, and am well known to the Irish & German Catholic portion of the Lower or rather middle class, and with these Latter I have almost unbounded influence in consequence of having been at the head and the Directress of almost every public undertaking gotten up by them, which, through the blessing of God, has on all occasions been successful—It would seem egotistical to mention this but for the necessity in order to show you dear Sir, the means I have of understanding the feeling of *the people* here on public matters—therefore you will pardon me for speaking of myself—I must not allow you to imagine me a *Large virago-looking* woman-politician, who belongs to a class (*I detest*) *"woman's rights"*—I am small (not awe inspiring!) and the Mother of six daughters and two sons, all of whom I have educated myself, (and not by keeping a school but at home while attending to my daily domestic duties) My daughters are accomplished, musicians and linguists, and my oldest son in his fathers law office, has received all his instruction from my own lips except the tuition of eighteen months from a Tutor in German & Mathematics. I was forced to mention these facts to remove an impression from your mind that you might be in communication with a *"Strong minded* woman"! Now to business.

My husband, James W. White (one of the Judges of the Superior Court of our City) and myself are warm personal friends of Horace Greely, and to us, as well as yourself, dear Sir, his unwearied and faithful labors during this last campaigne is a subject of grateful appreciation. His friends here and elsewhere are looking for a place for him in the Cabinet, and it will cause *great disappointment* should he not receive a favor worthy of his acceptance. He is a man who will *never* approach or present the slightest claim himself, his sensitive, high minded pride will prevent him from doing so, but I do not know a man who better understands what should be recognised by the Higher powers as due to him.

You must pardon the suggestion of a doubt, that you will forget one from whom you have received such aid, but having heard it on all Sides rumored "that Horace Greely would of course be offered the office of Post Master General" I concluded to write *privately* on the subject to you. Mr Greely has not the remotest idea that I would do so, and I am sure he would object to it, feeling that no suggestion should be necessary. I was induced to write in consequence of a discussion on the subject that passed in my presence between a gentleman of New York & San Francisco.

This City is largely democratic in consequence of the prevailing prejudice among the ignorant class of Irish & German, that the Republican party are opposed to giving patronage to foreigners—Now if this can be removed by judicious appointments in our City thousands can be won over to the Republican party. No one in New York understands this better than Mr Greely and no one would be better calculated to direct or counsel with on the subject than he. I am writing entirely disinterestedly, but understandingly My husband was nominated by the Republican party for Judge of the Superior Court this fall.—With a majority of democratic voters of *twenty thousand,* opposed to him, and many, indeed most of these, his own Countrymen (Irish) it seemed to some, hopeless to expect success for him. But I knew my influence with these people and I took my carriage and like the ladies of Europe I went day & night among *the people* and found out their causes of prejudice against *"black republicans."* At first they would rail at my husband and denounce him for "being put up" by Such a party—I reasoned with them and never left *one* till I had won them over. The consequence was my husband was elected by over fifteen hundred majority *over the Democratic* Candidates who were Strong men. I am convinced that judicious appointments in this City will completely reverse the State of things. *I know the Irish well,* although I am an American.

Permit me to congratulate you dear Sir upon the honor paid you by your Country and also present my kind regards to your good lady whom it would give me much pleasure to know. When you come to our City it will afford my husband and myself great pleasure to see you at our own house No 53 East 34th St—

Please consider this letter entirely *confidential* and oblige me by a reply

With Sentiments of high regard
and esteem Yours
Rhoda E. White

St Louis Mo.
Dec 17/60

The Hon A Lincoln
Sir

I have to day received a letter from Major Hunter acceding gladly to my proposal to him to accompany you to Washington.—We are old officers, and old friends, and if any difficulty should arise, which is barely possible, I should hope that we might be of some service to you.—I am reading every thing I can find on the events of the day, and the more I study them, the more I am convinced that secession is treason, not in a state collectively, but in the individuals of a state who contravene the laws of the United States and who cannot be absolved from the obligation to obey these laws, by any State authority.—

I do not believe it would be necessary for the Genrl Government to *make war* upon the seceding states.—The collection of the revenue and the holding of the Forts, which would be indispensably necessary, would be to some extent coercion, but still they would be defensive measures, and I think the people of the South will pause some time, before they will *go to War* with the Genrl Govmt.

Has it occurred to you, Sir, that the white males of the Cotton

States are only about 1/10 of the white males of the whole country. —What would posterity think of us as a people, if we should let this 1/10 break up our glorious government.

It is evident that affairs are becoming more and more complicated every day, but the greater the difficulties, the greater the glory in overcoming them.—

Will you please let me know when you will leave for Washington, and in the mean time, if I can be of any service to you, I beg you to command me.

With high respect
Your Obt Servt
E V Sumner
Col U S A

[Endorsed:]

Mr. L is not forgetting him
Will let him know when determined

Washington, D. C.
Dec. 17. 1860.

My Dear Sir:

I have to-day had a long interview with Lt. General Scott. I saw a great deal of the General prior to his nomination in 1852, and was his strong supporter in the Baltimore Convention. I have kept up his acquaintance ever since and have received strong evidences of his friendship and confidence. I therefore felt authorized to call upon him, and felt inclined to do so, as in these troublous times public attention is called to him as the highest officer in the Army.

Though old, I was gratified to find him in so good health and his mind apparently as sound and vigorous as eight years ago. He talked to me very freely in regard to the present state of affairs, and his differences between himself and the President and the Secretary of War in regard to the re-inforcements of the Forts in the South, and particularly at Charleston. His recommendations to that end were made in October and had they been regarded he thinks a vast deal would have been accomplished towards averting the impending trouble. I was astonished to learn from him the precarious situation of Fort Moultrie. He says with the present force, it really offers no defence against surprise or sudden assault, and that 250 men could take it without the loss of five men, that Fort Sumpter is really the key to the harbor—that 100 men could hold that Fort for a long time and against any force that could be brought to bear upon it—that it really commands Fort Moultrie and could demolish it in a single day—that this Fort Sumpter has only five workmen in it—that the enemy could go right into it and turn its guns upon Moultrie. In fact, everything substantially is at the mercy of any enemy that might appear. None of his suggestions or recommendations have been acted upon, and of course he is powerless to do anything further, but his heart is sound and true. "I wish to God," said he, "that Mr. Lincoln was in office." He continued, "I do not know him, but I believe him a true, honest and *conservative* man." Then he asked earnestly, "Mr. Washburne, is he a *firm* man?" I answered that I had known you long and well, and that you would discharge your duty and your whole duty in the sight of the furnace seven times heated. He then said resolutely and hopefully, "all is not lost." But I could not tell you all of our talk even if it would interest you. It was of a confidential character, but he gave me permission to state what I pleased of the interview to you, with the same qualification. Wade's speech to-day is considered well timed and just what was needed. But enough.

Yrs. Truly,
E. B. Washburne

Edward Bates had been invited by Mr. Lincoln to join his cabinet.

St Louis, Dec 18/60

Hon. A. Lincoln
Springfield Ills:
D. Sir,

Since my return from Springfield, I have consulted with judicious friends, who express the opinion that a good effect might be produced on the public mind—especially in the border slave States—by letting the people know (substantially) the relations which now subsist between us. And, being now fully committed to the work, it is my opinion also; and I base that opinion, in part, upon several letters lately recd. from Md., Va. & Ky.

As to the *manner* of the communication—will you direct it yourself—or leave it to the discretion of friends here? If the latter, obeying, of course, your verbal directions to me, *not* to indicate the particular office.

Most respectfully
Edw. Bates

Fort Leavenworth,
Dec. 18th 1860

Dear Sir:

Last spring, you recollect, it first became public, that Gov. Wise, previous to the election of Mr. Buchanan, had sent a Circular to all the Southern Governors, requesting their co-operation; and stating that he had twenty thousand men ready, in case of Fremont's election, to march on Washington, and prevent his inauguration. On this occasion a Southern Democratic Army Officer, of high rank, made the following statement at this post.—

That "it was well understood at the time, among the leaders of the Democracy in Washington, that Fremont's inauguration was to have been prevented in this way—and that Gen. Pierce was to have co-operated with Wise, using the Army and Navy of the United

States for this purpose—he himself, Gen. Pierce, to *hold over,* and keep possession of the government.—

Now Sir, from Mr. Buchanan's Message, and from a careful study of the signs of the times, I am very much inclined to believe, that they intend to attempt the same game with you—to have the Old Public Functionary hold over, and thus demoralize your Administration, and bring about the same anarchy and confusion at the North, as they will have plunged into, at the South.—

Would it not be well, to have a hundred thousand Wide Awakes, wend their way quietly to Washington, during the first three days of March: taking with them their capes and caps? By a *coup-de-main* we could arm them in Washington.

The reins once in your hands, I can not doubt a triumphant result, and that you will preserve every Star on our flag.

I am much honored by your kind invitation, conveyed through Col. Sumner. I shall not fail to be on hand.

I have the honor to be,
Most Sincerely,
Your ob. serv.
David Hunter
U. S. Army.

Hon. A. Lincoln,
Springfield,
Illinois.—

Prior to Mr. Lincoln's inauguration the following states had seceded from the Union: South Carolina, December 20, 1860; Mississippi, January 9, 1861; Florida, January 10, 1861; Alabama, January 11, 1861; Georgia, January 19, 1861; Louisiana, January 26, 1861; Texas, February 1, 1861.

Batavia Kane Co Illinois
Dec 21, 1860

Sir

I beg most respectfully to ask you for an employment in your future Household in any Capacity in which you would require the services of a good English Servant

I may state that I have lived with Lord Talbot de Malahide as Footman and travelling servant with Rt Hon Judge Ball The Lady Louisa Tennison who is sister to Earl of Leichfield and also with the Earl of Dunreaven from all of whom I can produce Testamonials of the highest order

I may state I have a thorough knowledge of the routine of the dinner table and will undertake the care and polishing of Plate as well as an siver smith in this Country or Europe I also understand the care of Oil and Fluid Lamps as well as the management of gas

Sir Should you require my Services you will find me a sober honest and trustworthy man and fully equal to the duties which I undertake to perform

I Remain Sir
Your Most Obedient Humble
Servant
John Devoy

To The
Honbl
Abraham Lincoln
[Endorsed:]
Bateville Kane Co. Ill. December 21, 1860.

John Devoy wishes a place in the White House.

OFFICE OF THE TRIBUNE
New York, Decr. 22nd 1860

My dear Sir

I have yours of the 19th. Let me try to make my views a little more clear:

1. I do not believe that a State can secede at pleasure from the Union, any more than a stave may secede from a cask of which it is a component part.

2. I do believe that a people—a political community large and strong enough to maintain a National existence—have a right to form and modify their institutions in accordance with their own convictions of justice and policy. Hence if seven or eight contiguous States (not one small one) were to come to Washington saying, "We are tired of the Union—let us out!"—I should say, "There's the door —go!" and I think they would have a *right* to go, even though no one recognized it. If they should set to fighting and whip us, every one would say they had a right to govern themselves; and I do not see how their having a few more or less men, or a better or worse general than we, can make or mar their right of self-government.

3. If the seceding State or States go to fighting and defying the laws,—the Union being yet undissolved, save by their own say-so—I guess they will have to be made to behave themselves. I am sorry for this, for I would much sooner have them behave of their own accord; but if they wont, it must be fixed the other way.

4. We shall never have peace nor equality in the Union till the Free States shall say to the Slave, "If you want to go, go; we are willing." So long as they threaten secession and we deprecate it, they will always have us at a disadvantage.

5. The Cotton States *are going.* Nothing that we can offer will stop them. The Union-loving men are cowed and speechless; a Reign of Terror prevails from Cape Fear to the Rio Grande. Every suggestion of reason is drowned in a mad whirl of passion and faction. You will be President over no foot of the Cotton States not commanded by Federal Arms. Even your life is not safe, and it is your simple duty to be very careful of exposing it. I doubt whether you ought to go to Washington via Wheeling and the B. & O. Railroad unless you go with a very strong force. And it is not yet certain

that the Federal District will not be in the hands of a Pro-Slavery rebel array before the 4th of March.

6. I fear nothing, care for nothing, but another disgraceful back-down of the Free States. That is the only real danger. Let the Union slide—it may be reconstructed; let Presidents be assassinated—we can elect more; let the Republicans be defeated and crushed—we shall rise again; but another nasty compromise whereby everything is conceded and nothing secured will so thoroughly disgrace and humiliate us that we can never again raise our heads, and this country becomes a second edition of the Barbary States as they were sixty years ago. "Take any form but that!"

Excuse me fore boring you at such length, when you must be drowned in letters. I hope not to do so again.

Yours,
Horace Greeley.

Hon A. Lincoln, Springfield, Illinois

(So many people entertain a violent prejudice against my handwriting that I have had the above copied to save you trouble in deciffering it.)

H. G.

Seaford Sussex County Delaware
24th. December 1860 (Monday)

Dear Sir

In a letter I wrote you from Cincinnati about the middle of October I made certain statements concerning Mr. Secretary Floyd's conspiring with the southern secessionists

Time has proved the correctness of most of my allegations, but in the letter of "Occasional" published in the Philada Press of Saturday last the statements concerning the commanding offices of Fort Monroe Va. and of Fort Moultrie S.C. are I *believe* entirely erroneous. The Commandant of the former is not only a native of N. England, but so is his wife and until very recently Mrs. Dimick and the children have resided permanently at Portsmouth N.H. while the Colonel has seized every opportunity to revisit his family. Since the inauguration of Mr. Buchanan, Col. Dimick has suffered considerably from Mr. Floyd fondness for providing for his Virginia favorites. Col. Dimick is not a very bold man and will seek no unnecessary occasion to declare his attachment to northern institutions, but if he remains in command of Fort Monroe till your inauguration, the secessionists will get no foothold there.

Major Anderson the commander of Fort Moultrie is a native of Kentucky and a brother of Larz Anderson the son in law of Nicholas Longworth of Cin. and of Charles Anderson formerly [*of*] a lawyer of Cin. but now a stock raiser of Texas. Maj. Anderson's wife is a daughter of Gen. Clinch formerly of the Army, a southern man. Major Anderson claims his residence at Savannah Georgia; he has always been a hanger on around Head Quarters and has done scarcely any duty with his regiment. In the winter of '53 & 54 when the 3d Art'y. (to which he then belonged) sailed for California Maj Anderson got Mr. Secretary Davis to put him on nominal duty as Insp. of iron at Newark N.J. and he continued on this (living all the time at the celebrated New York Hotel in N.Y. City) until last winter when he was promoted to the 1st Arty. Mr. Floyd then ordered him to Old Point Comfort (Ft. Monroe) but before he joined this new station the Secretary of War put him on the mixed commission ordered by Congress to inspect the Mil'y Academy.

His friend Jefferson Davis was also on this commission and doubtless recommended Maj Anderson as his colleague. The hue and cry about Col. Gardner's sympathy with the fire eaters was raised to give the War Dept an excuse for removing him from Ft. Moultrie, and the rumors of Maj Anderson's devotion to the Union and of his wife's appeal to the President for reinforcements at Ft. Moultrie are all raised to blind the public. The only way Fort Moultrie can be retained three months is by the north showing so united a front against secession as to convince Maj Anderson (who is not deficient in powers of discernment) that the union shall remain "one and inseparable".

The Commander at Pensacola, Col. Winder is a rabid disunionist, but he has recently been promoted to a regiment in California, and the officer who ought to succeed to the command of Pensacola (Capt Eddy) is a native of R.I. and a safe man, but I presume Col. W. will be retained at Pensacola.

The Postmaster and Capt Martin (the father of the U.S. Consul to Matanzas Cuba) are the only professed disunionists in this community and they are not in earnest. The Chesapeake Bay not only separates this peninsula from the southern confederacy but a rail road which is to run down opposite Norfolk and which is nearly complete has transferred trade and travel from Baltimore to Philadelphia. At some few points having *steamboat* connection with Baltimore and no *rail road* facilities there is a slight display of southern feeling, but I will guarantee to keep the whole peninsula including the two counties of Virginia *in* the present Union with not exceeding five hundred men. This hundred (township) which contains more slaves than any other in the state gave ninety nine Lincoln votes at the presidential election and now twice as many can be obtained.

As to the city of Balt. I know it thoroughly and my wife's father is a Breckenridge merchant there. The present noise in favor of joining the south is merely for the sake of trade they having discovered that northern men are comparatively indifferent as to the political sentiments of those they trade with. Baltimore has a trade with Boston and also with Cincinnati and the west that she has not the slightest intention of sacrificing and when Ohio and Indiana announce that the federal Union shall be preserved, the Baltimore Sun will cork up its thunder.

If the liberties of this country ever are subverted it will not be by plug uglie's and dead rabbits but by our city merchants and manufacturers.

Respectfully yours
George W. Hazzard
Captain U. S. Army

DECEMBER 1860

Abraham Lincoln
Springfield
Illinois

[Endorsement below]

Capt. G.W. Hazzard
U.S.A.
1860

Advises of Sec Floyds conspiracy—

Washington, Dec. 24 1860

Hon. A. Lincoln,
My Dear Sir,

I am reluctantly compelled to believe that the President means to surrender up the fortifications at Charleston when demanded by the South Carolina Authorities— We are powerless in Congress, because a majority either sympathise with the treason in South Carolina, or are unwilling to do anything to put it down— If the facts turn out as I fear, it will involve the duty of hanging Buchanan, if we are ever in a condition to meet out justice to him— I think a majority of the Senate would vote against defending the forts by force— Such encouragement of course [*encourages*] strengthens the secessionists— I have now very little hope of Douglas. Pugh & Nicholson are both out against the use of force to execute the laws— The question is no longer about African Slavery, but whether we have a government capable of maintaining itself. The stealing of bonds from the Interior department is as bad as Matteson's fraud & of a piece with other transactions. If the people feel that constitutional liberty is worth preserving, they will now rally to its support. It is idle to talk about new constitutional guarantees, when those we have are violated with impunity by the secession of a state—

I have faith that in the end all will be right, though the treachery of the administration may involve the shedding of blood to accomplish it—

I suppose you have been informed of the meeting of the five Governors of Maine, Mass, (Conn) New York, Pa & Ohio in the City of New York a few days since— I understand they all agreed that the constitution must be maintained & the laws enforced at all hazards, & that they would so recommend to their respective Legislatures— Gov. Dennison told me he should write Gov. Yates, & he also suggested that the placing of Gov. Chase in the Cabinet would be quite acceptible to Ohioans— All our friends are delighted at your course as indicated from Springfield— Gov. Seward is back— He does not know that I am advised of your offer to him, & of course has said nothing to me about it. You probably know what he intends doing. Gov. Corwin has not yet delivered your letter to Mr. Gilmer—

Truly Yours
Lyman Trumbull

New York
Dec. 26, 1860.

Dear Sir:

The danger of compromise is nearly over; the peril of disunion is just rising into view. The Secessionists are now doing their utmost to coerce Gov. Hicks of Maryland into calling the Legislature (Democratic) which is to call a State convention. If they fail, I think the Legislature will be called irregularly—that is, will get together in something which will be made to pass for authority. If they can get Maryland into their clutches, *every Slave State but Delaware and perhaps Missouri will have seceded before the 4th of March, and Mr. Lincoln must fight for the possession of Washington City*. Of course, the plot may miscarry; but Yancey, Wise & Co. are pushing it with all their might, and the virtual dissolution of the Government gives them every facility. I tell you I think it today an even chance that Mr. Lincoln will *not* be inaugurated at Washington on the 4th of March.

I would have liked very much to talk peace and fraternity—begging the Secessionists to look toward a peaceable separation; but our friends will not listen to any thing but fight, so I shall have to let them have their own way. If Mr. L. were once in possession of the White House, this would all do; as it is, I think we mistake in not talking smoothly at least until we are in position to *use* daggers as well as *speak* them. However, let them have their way.

Yours
Horace Greeley

W. H. Herndon, Esq.
Springfield, Ill.

Washington Dec 26, 1860

CONFIDENTIAL
A Lincoln
My Dr Sir

The evidences of my ears and eyes are forcing me to believe that the sessionists are seriously contemplating resistance to your inauguration in this Capitol. There is certainly a secret organization in this city numbering several hundred members having that purpose in view—sworn armed men, and bunches or lodges affiliated with them in design, extend south to Richmond, Raleigh & Charleston. The malakoff in their way, is Baltimore and that fortress they have laid seige to. The Union & loyal sentiment of her citizens is gradually giving way, and the vicious rabble are getting control. If things go on there for the next 60 days as they have for the last 30, the city will be under the complete control of Disunion Vigilance Committees and a reign of terror will domineer over that city. When this key point is stormed by the enemy and in their hands, Maryland will go the same way. The city rules the State—the southern and central counties especially. It is the intention of the dis-unionists, if they get Baltimore on their side to prevent you reaching this city by force, and with the aid of the lodges here and in Virginia and south to "clear out" the Republicans here, take possession of the Capitol and proclaim the Southern Confederacy. It is whispered that they intend to proclaim Breckinridge President and Bell Vice P. or H. C. Johnson. At all events they will call a southern convention here to "reconstruct" the Constitution, as they term it.

There are other plans discovered such as to prevent the counting of the electoral votes in February, but this part of the scheme depends upon their ability to prevent your inauguration in the Capitol, and that depends, they admit (say), on the position that Maryland and Baltimore will take between now & then. In my candid judgement our friends in free states do not appreciate the "situation", or comprehend the actual danger ahead.

I am not writing to you as an alarmist, but still I would not be true to my duty to you, to fail to warn you of what the enemy *seems* to be doing.

In my judgement, Gov. Yates, and other Western Governors should urge their legislatures to put the militia in condition to move to the assistance of the Federal Government to enforce the laws and quell rebellion. It may be essentially necessary for a dozen or twenty of our Illinois Volunteer Companies to be fully prepared to start on a days notice for Baltimore and Washington. Whole regiments may be necessary. The secession epidemic is spreading with fearful rapidity and violence thro' the Slave States, and if Maryland gives way your friends will have to fight their way with the sword from the Pa. line to the Capitol. And rather than let the rebels hold possession of Washington and exclude the rightful Administration, it were better to lay wast Maryland to reach here. If the Capitol should fall into the hands of the insurgents the world will regard them as victorious, and their government will be recognized as among the powers of the earth.

I have thought that if Judge Davis could spend a week in Baltimore he could definitely ascertain the extent and speed of growth of the sessation movement. He could probably do much to make headway against it if authorized to give Winter Davis and the leading Union men the proper assurances as to the disposition of the Federal patronage of that city, with a score or two of clerkships in the departments here. Those things would go a great way. I throw them out as suggestions to consider The Republicans of Baltimore have done our cause much mischief by proclaiming that all the offices, fat and lean, will fall into their hands. If we can hold the Old Whigs of Maryland the dis-unionists will fail in their great conspirace to seize this Capitol and drive you away, at the point of the bayonet.

Yours Truly
J. Medill

[Envelope franked by O. Lovejoy]

Washington, Dec. 27 1860

Hon. A. Lincoln,
My Dear Sir,

We are all rejoiced at the noble conduct of Maj. Anderson in taking possession of Fort Sumpter as reported by telegraph— I understand that his force is sufficient to hold Sumpter which commands Moultrie— Anderson has probably acted without orders, which is all the better— This will probably bring matters to a crisis sooner than Mr. Buchanan expected— Matters will yet all come right I trust— Your true course I have no doubt is to remain quiet & not loose your equanimity let what will happen— This may be pretty difficult when treason reigns in high places— Mr. Seward accepts as I supposed he would— In making up your cabinet I trust you will not overlook Mr. Judd, in whom I personally feel more interest than in any other person named– Besides I think he is just such a man as would be most useful to you–

Yours truly
Lyman Trumbull

PRIVATE

Dec 28th 1860.

My dear Sir,

There is a feverish excitement here which awakens all kind of apprehensions of possible disturbance and disorders, connected with your assumption of the government. I do not entertain these apprehensions myself– But it is worth consideration in our peculiar circumstances that accidents elsewhere may aggravate opinion here.

Habit has accustomed the public to anticipate the arrival of the President elect in this city about the middle of February and evil minded persons would expect to organize their demonstrations for that time. I beg leave to suggest whether it would not be well for you, Keeping your own counsel) to be *prepared* to drop into the City a week or ten days earlier. The effect would probably be reaping and sowthing.

Very truly yours
William H. Seward

The Honorable
Abraham Lincoln
&c &c

If nothing should occur to seem to render it advisable to come so early, your preparation only would be hastened not lost.

we shall probably not go to
Washington unless previously
notified that we are wanted there

Hartford, Conn
Dec 30th 1860

Hon Abm Lincoln
Dr Sir

Having seen threats that you shall not be inaugurated on the 4th of March next & having this morning seen letters from Republicans at Washington which give a very dark picture I write to offer you my services.

If you say the word, I will be there with from twenty to one thousand men, or one hundred, (any reasonable number) *organized & armed*

A hint, or a wish expressed will bring to your side on that occasion a true delegation of *Hartford Wide Awakes,* not in uniform but ready for *duty*

Communicate with me if wanted

Geo P. Bissell

P.S. *We will go at our own charges*

I refer you to Hon Gideon Welles, Hartford or any Connecticut Republican of prominence

Baltimore. Decr 31st 1860.

Hon Abe. Lincoln.
Dear Sir,

I am a member of the *Republican* Party and reside in Boston Mass. I am now on a visit to Balto. and have made extensive inquiries in regard to the feelings of the People of Balto. on the Subject of *Slavery* and I unhesitatingly say that it will be madness, for you to attempt to reach Washington at any time I have had my head shaved twice merely for making the remark that I consider you a gentleman. Were I to say one word against *Secession* I should be instantly strung up by the Citizens—who are all most excited to madness. I have been ordered to leave this city, by tomorrow noon, and I reckon I will do it. Take this warning for your own sake, and that of your firm friend, Thos. Cadwallerder

P.S. You are at Liberty to make any use of this note you may see proper.

Respectifully
Thos. Cadwallerder

P.S. #2. Address A.B.C. Balto Md as my friends will forward it to me.

Thos. Cadwallerder

MILITARY DEPARTMENT MICHIGAN
ADJUTANT GENERAL'S OFFICE,
Kalamazoo, Dec 31st 1860

Hon Abraham Lincoln (President Elect)
Sir

Serious apprehensions exist in the minds of many of your friends, with regard to your personal safety, either at your inauguration or immediately following it. Entertaining similar views, I do accordingly tender to your Excellency a Regiment of well equipped—well organized and well officered citizens soldiers at present attached to the Military force of Michigan—

Very Respectfully
Yours &c
P. W. Curtenius
Adjt. Genl. M. M.

ANSWERED

Dec. 31 1860

Hon Abraham Lincoln,
Dear Sir:

In writing to you to solicit the favour of your coming to New York City, and addressing our people on the subject of the present and prospective state of national affairs—I feel sensible that my application may be regarded as intrusive, if not impertinent.

But the friends at whose request it is made, (ladies strongly interested in the cause of Republicanism, to further which they have made every effort in their power) urge that the speeches made by you in times past, and shortly before your election, which clearly set forth your views, are not to be obtained for reference in many places where it is most desirable that they should be read by the masses. At the South they cannot be procured at all, and people who are eager to know your real opinions, are compelled to be content with portions actually distorted by being quoted without their context, from Northern papers. Were you to speak now, your words would be given verbatim in the N. Y. Herald and other papers circulating in the South. It is further urged, that many Republicans and friends of the party would greatly prefer hearing your sentiments without the intervention of newspaper correspondents, who are notoriously unreliable. (From one of these we have learned—what we *wish* to believe—that since the election you have openly professed your faith in us—your countrywomen)— Again—it is said, with too much truth, that the Republican Editorials emanating from this City, and circulated throughout the country, are here well known to represent *individual* opinion and feeling, rather than that of influential men belonging to the party. In proof of this, you will hardly need the assurance that the tone of indifference and levity, and the disposition to taunt and irritate the South, is not shared by men of much reflection. And as none of your friends are able to express their sentiments except through the medium of an interested class of writers, the desire to hear your views *repeated*, without mediation, distortion, abridgment, or transposition, is hourly gaining strength, and becoming universal. Clamors and complaints would be hushed to listen to words from your lips—and all believe that those words would help the people to a right understanding, restore public confidence, and do much to allay the storm. In old countries Emperors and Kings have not disdained to speak to the people when a great convulsion seemed at hand. May I beseech you to remember that the people of the United States—comprising all parties—look to you in this hour of peril for succor, and for the inspiration of a new hope. It will be a condescension for you to come to New York, and speak through the Press to those whom you have been invited to preside over, but the condescension would not be inconsistent with the dignity of the Chief Magistrate-elect of a great nation like ours. It would show to the whole world, that the feelings of the man and the patriot, may cause the politician to be held in abeyance. For, as one great cause of the present disturbance is the general feeling of instability and suspense—to which even a painful certainty would be preferable—this would be exchanged for the confidence and reliance, which a *personal* declaration would produce.

We are aware that you have received many requests of this kind, and we hope that you will express to some of your friends here, your willingness to relieve public anxiety by compliance— In proffering this earnest entreaty on the part of a class who must rejoice or suffer with the rest of the community— I must beg pardon for my temerity. As far as I am concerned, my interest in the state of affairs is enhanced by the fact that I have resided many years in South Carolina, my husband having been a professor in the State College at Columbia. And in excuse for my undertaking to appear for my lady-friends, I beg to refer to Mr Horace Greeley, Mr. Dudley Field —Wm Cullen Bryant, and others—to whom I am personally well known.

Respectfully Yours,
Elizabeth. F. Ellet

No 61. West Twenty-sixth Street.
New York City.
Monday. 31st Dec. 1860.

CONFIDENTIAL

Washington Dec 31, 1860

A Lincoln

Dr Sir

My apology for so frequently writing to you is, that we are in a *revolution,* and I am a volunteer sentinal on the walls. It is the plan of the disunionists to have an army in this city within five weeks, to drive out the Republican members and to prevent your inauguration by force. It is expected that in 30 days Maryland will pronounce for the disunionists. Who can say that she will not?

Let me suggest an idea that has occurred to me:—Would it not be a *coup d etat,* were you to quietly, with only a carpet sack, get on the cars, and drop down in this city some day next week or very soon. Would it not knock over and disarrange all the plans of the traitors, and show them they had a second Jackson to deal with. Thousands of our friends would then flock here from all parts, and Maryland would remain loyal. You could either put up at a private house or at a Hotel, as might be deemed most advisable. Our friends would then have a *head* here with whom to advise. The free State Governments would promptly respond to any call made upon them in defense of the Union.

It is all important, that you take the oath of office here on the 4th of March on the steps of the Capital. The moral effect will be worth an army of 10,000 men. If this suggestion is worth anything turn it over in your mind. Perhaps you have already resolved to do so. Secrecy and dis-patch, Napoleon the great, said, were the talsmen of success.

Yours in haste

J Medill

Washington Dec 31. 1860

Dear Lincoln

I have had two interviews with Gov Seward Thinking his views of the condition of the country and the policy to be adopted, may be of interest I will repeat so much as pertains to general politics. He thinks the Southern plan now is, to draw Maryland and Virginia into the revolution before the 4″ of March so as to get possession of the RR from Baltimore to this place, and the telegraph wires With these advantages and these two states swept by the same mania, that is now sweeping the South they hope to prevent your inauguration

This revolution has startled the north, but it has frightened the whole South, to utter desperation The consider secession & a collision inevitable, so instincts of self preservation stimulates them to save the Capital and get the prestige and power this would give them. As visionary as this seems, all men here, have serious fears of it. The most sagacious & calm talk little but are in great doubt and alarm. The southern men have taken exclusive possession, or nearly so, of the Pres. They constantly walk about the grounds of the mansion and although they despise Mr Buchannan, they seem to have him completely in their power. It is Mr S's belief, although all these things look so dark, the effort at violence on the 4″ will break itself down before that time. It seems to me so too, from all I can learn here One thing however seems plainer than any other thing, that is from the rapid change of events following in quick succession, one upon another, no human being *can* tell what the future has in store. It is full of of danger and of hope

Now you are not here. No one assumes to act for you, or plan for the future. There is no head or method to any opposition to treason. Gov S. thinks you ought to select so many of your Cabinet advisers as will come from the north & have them come here & organize & plan something to counteract these dangers

He also told me his theory of the selection of a Cabinet & something of names

His theory would be to select the ablest men in the country whatever of party relations or combinations may have been on your mind, all very well for fair-weather times, ought he thinks now, to succumb to this [*times*] crisis. The one idea, of men of strength, will, prudence & ability ought to control you: for the pinch is, not to advance a party but to save a country from anarchy & destruction. The theory of selecting the leaders of little factions in our party, with a view to consolidate & fairly represent all the elements of our party he repudiated. [*That will*] A complete union of all patriotic men will be made in the fiery crucible [*to*] in which we will be tried. It is strength character and ability he wants.

His favorite man in N. E. is C F Adams, next to him Wells He oppiones the selection of Cameron,—Bates, & recommends Caleb R Smith of Ind The ballance he thinks ought to be from the South except Freemont, who he thinks should be Sec of War.

He has not fully made up his mind about these Southern men yet There is no especial haste about them, for as to how far you can go out of the time of the party depends [*on*] some what on future events.

I will write you again soon

The Gov [*says*] said after my asking permission to write these things to you, that while he does not desire to obtrude his views upon you I might state them as he gave them to me—

Yours Truly
L Swett

Head Quarters
"Springfield Zouave Greys"

Hon. A. Lincoln
President Elect
Dear Sir.

The undersigned commissioned of the "Springfield Zouave Greys" on behalf of the Company and at their unanimous request hereby tender you the services of said Company as a special Escort on the occasion of your journey from this city to your Inauguration as President of the United States at Washington D. C. on the 4th day of

March next. Hoping to receive an early acceptance of our services in order that we may at once commence the necessary preparations.

We remain very truly yours
John Cook *Comdr*

Andrew J. Babcock 1st Lieut
Jno. G. Nicolay 2d Lieut.

Uniontown
Fayette Co. Pa
Decr. 186

Hon A. Lincoln
Dear Sir

I send by the same mail with this letter, a package containing, "Solitary and alone" a veritable *eagle quill.*

The King of birds, from the wing of which this quill was plucked, was shot in this County by a young nephew of mine (now of Du Buque Iowa) in the year 1844.

It was given to me by him, accompanied with the suggestion, that I should present it to the then living and distinguished Statesman Henry Clay, for the purpose of writing with it his inaugural address. As Mr. Clay was not elected President, it has been carefully preserved by me until this time.

I now Sir have the honor of presenting it to you in your character of President elect, to be used for the purpose it was originally designed.

What a pleasing, and majestic thought! The inaugural address of the President, of the United States to be delivered on the 4th of March next, "Deo volente", written with a pen made from a quill taken from the proud and soaring emblem of our liberties.

If it be devoted in whole or in part, to the purpose indicated would not the fact, and the incident be sufficiently potent to "Save the the Union"

Sir, I do verily believe that your name will be honored, in the pages of history if you pursue the course above suggested, while on the other hand, it will go down to generations that shall come after, stigmatized as ambitious, fanatical, and the destroyer of this glorious confedercy— Allow me to say, that I am free from all prejudice and excitement, having never voted for any Candidate for the Presidency but Mr Polk I know no section, but love my whole country, and would not vote for my own father, if he were a sectional candidate, and I esteemed him the greatest and best man in the land— Allow me to say that I am a Northern man, and desire to see our whole country united and living in peace and brotherly love— I write with the most entire respect, desiring to bring the above suggestions before your mind, believing it to be the only course that will produce harmony—

[In pencil:] 1860

President Elect—

Accept the congratulations of a Maine country girl, who has received the glad tidings with great joy, of your election. Allow me to make one suggestion. I have often heard it stated by Physicians, that it was an undoubted fact, that our two last Whig Presidents, Gen's Harrison & Taylor, came to their sudden and lamentable ends, by subtle *poisons,* administered in their food at the White House. Remembering my childish tears and disappointments over the doom of my favorite hero's, I beg you not to slight the appeal of a kind *womans* heart, that you will carefully avoid a like fate, by securing the services of *servants* whom you *know* and can *trust,* (servants for the *kitchen,* as well as for the State) and taking with you to Wash—your *own family Physician.*

May God preserve and keep you, to save a wicked nation, from its many sins!

Hennibeek Hives
Somerset Co.
Maine

[No date; in pencil:] 1860

150–5th Avenue N Y.
Jany 1st 1861

My dear sir.

I find here a great change in popular sentiment. When I left concession & compromize were the order of the day. Now however, all our weak kneed friends & a very Large portion of those who voted against us have joined the party that stands up boldly for the supremacy of law, for the maintenance of civil order, for firm adherence to the Constitution and resolute defence of the Union against all its enemies who are rallying under the flag of treason rebellion perfidy & revolution.

The universal cry is "let the strength of the government be tested, whether our fair fabric is really so weak that it can be toppled to the ground & crumbled to atoms by the first touch of a traitor's fingers against one of its thirty three pillars."

Some alarm has been felt here this morning by a report from *Harrisburgh* that Mr Corruption Cameron has been tendered the Treasury Dept. I do not share such fears, for I know full well that no man with such a record will be asked or permitted a place in your Cabinet.

Please present my respects to Mrs Lincoln with the compliments of the season & believe me to be with high regard your friend

and obdt servt,
James H Van Alen

to Hon Abraham Lincoln

New York January 3d 1861.

My dear Sir,

I have this moment received your note. Nothing could be more fair or more satisfactory than the principle you lay down in regard to the formation of your council of official advisers. I shall always be convinced that whatever selection you make it will be made conscientiously.

The community here has been somewhat startled this morning by the positiveness with which a report had been circulated, reaching this city from Washington that Mr. Simon Cameron was to be placed in the Treasury Department. Forgive me if I state to you how we all should regard such an appointment—I believe I may speak for all parties, except perhaps some of the most corrupt in our own—The objection to Mr. Cameron would not be that he does not [*opinion*] hold such opinions as we approve, but that there is among all who have observed the course of our public men an utter, ancient and deep seated distrust of his integrity—whether financial or political. The announcement of his appointment, if made on any authority deserving of credit would diffuse a feeling almost like despair. I have no prejudice against Mr Cameron except such as arise from observing in what transactions he has been engaged as I have reason to suppose that whatever opinion has been formed respecting him in this part of the country has been formed on perfectly impartial and disinterested grounds. I pray you, again, to excuse [*this*] my giving you this trouble. Do not reply to this letter— Only let us have honest rigidly upright men in the departments—whatever may be their notions of public policy. I am, dear Sir,

Very truly &c &c
W C Bryant

Hon A. Lincoln

Janr 3, 1860 [*i.e. 1861*]

My dear Sir

I have seen Gel. Scott, who bids me say, he will be glad to act under your orders, in all ways to preserve the Union. He says Mr

Buchanan, at last, has called on him to see that order shall be preserved at the inauguration, in this District. That, for this purpose, he has ordered here 2 companies of flying artillery; and that he will organize the militia—and have himself *sworn in as a constable.* The old warrior is roused, and he will be equal to the occasion.

The feeling here is better but there is much excitement and still great anxiety as to the course Maryland may take. The Secretary of State called on me this morning to say that Gov Hicks will remain firm. If he does so, the rest can be cared for.

Mr Gilmore is here, but has not yet been seen

Very truly yrs
Simon Cameron

Hon. A. Lincoln

PRIVATE

Raleigh N. C.
Jan: 3d 1861.

My Dear Sir: I have just read your admirable letter in the Standard of today— I perused it with much pleasure and instruction— Your views are indeed conservative & patriotic and sustained by strong reasoning, & I hope the circulation of the letter may do great good— The charge of being *submissionists* so often preferred against those who are desirous to exhaust every constitutional means for the redress of our wrongs, before resorting to the dire necessity of revolution, is as vile a slander as ever was propagated— When the hour of trial comes, these men, who are now denounced & vilified, because they are not ready to precipitate their country into revolution & bloodshed, will prove as true to their section and as firm in the maintenance of their rights, as the most rabid of their traducers.

I have not yet despaired of the Republic. Your letter has been read with much gratification by the conservative men in this place— In haste

Yours truly &
Resptly
H. W. Miller

Senate Chamber, Jany 3–1861

Hon. A. Lincoln,

My Dear Sir,

Baker is making a very fine speech & as I think getting the advantage of Benjamin—

I have now very little apprehensions of an outbreak here, or of any attempt to prevent your inauguration— The administration has determined to enforce the laws & protect the public property—. Gen. Scott has as I understand full powers vested in him, not only to preserve the peace here, but to protect the public property everywhere— Holt is a true Union man, & for enforcing the laws— This I *know*— I also know the determination the President has arrived at, but I do not know that he will not be backed down from his position as has been often done— If Scott is allowed to pursue his own course he will soon check the spread of secession— Our friends have free intercourse with Gen. Scott, & you may be sure he means [*wants*] to do his duty. The administration has been caught in its own trap— After encouraging secession by an agreement to do nothing to prevent its spread, & to leave the public property in a position that the disunionists could at any moment take possession after the 4th of March, the plot has burst over the heads of the parties to the conspiracy, & they have been forced to take steps to [*put down their*] strangle their own boutting.

The tender of the office of Sec. of Treasury is regarded as a matter accomplished here & I will say no more about it; but I shall not be surprised if a very strong protest against it reaches you from Pa. Quite a number of members from Pa. came rushing to me in regard to it greatly excited & declaring openly that it would be the ruin of the party in the State, & take away all the benefit which the party expected to gain by purifying the government—

Yours truly

Lyman Trumbull

New York January 4th 1861.

My dear Sir,

I wrote to you yesterday concerning the rumored intention to give Mr. Simon Cameron of Pennsylvania a place in the Cabinet which you are to form. I had then scarcely spoken to any body on the subject, but since that time I have heard the matter much discussed and I assure you that the general feeling is one of consternation.

Mr. Cameron has the reputation of being concerned in some of the worst intrigues of the democratic party a few years back. His name suggests to every honest Republican in this State no other than disgusting associations, and they will expect nothing from him when in office but a repetition of such transactions. At present those who favor his appointment, in this State, are the men who last winter seduced our legislature into that shamefully corrupt course by which it was disgraced. If he is to form one of the Cabinet, the Treasury Department, which rumor assigns him, is the very last of the public interests which ought to be committed to his charge.

In the late election, the Republican party, throughout the Union, struggled not only to overthrow the party that sought the extension of slavery, but also to secure a pure and virtuous administration of the government. The first of these objects we have fully attained, but if such men as Mr. Cameron are to compose the Cabinet, however pure and upright the Chief Magistrate may himself be,—and it is our pride and rejoicing that in the present instance we know him to be so,—we shall not have succeeded in the second.

There is no scarcity of able and upright men who would preside over the Treasury department with honor. I believe Mr. Gideon Welles of Hartford has been spoken of. There is no more truly honest man, and he is equally wise and enlightened. We have a man here in New York whom I should rejoice to see at the head of that department, Mr Opdyke, the late Republican candidate for Mayor of this city a man who has made finance the subject of long and profound study, and whom no possible temptation could move from his integrity. If a man from Pennsylvania is wanted, that State has sons whose probity has never been questioned—so that there will be no need to take up with a man hackneyed in those practices which make politics, a sordid game played for the promotion of personal interests.

I must again ask you to pardon this freedom for the sake of its motive. It has cost me some effort to break through my usual reserve on such matters, but I feel a greater interest in the success and honor of your administration than in those of any which have preceded it.

I am, dear Sir, truly yours
W C Bryant

to
Hon A. Lincoln

Office Register of Wills, Etc.,
No. 6 County Buildings,
Philadelphia, Jan. 4 1861

Hon. Abraham Lincoln
President Elect,

Sir, We are informed by telegraph from Harrisburg that Hon. Alex. K. McClure the Chairman of our State Committee has gone to Springfield to resist the Appointment of General Cameron as a member of your Cabinet. If this report is true Mr McClure certainly misrepresents the wishes and feelings of the People's party of this State. General C. contributed far more of means and pesonal effort to the accomplishment of our triumph in this State than any other man in it, and the people of this city are unanimously desirous that Pennsylvania interests may be represented in your counsils by him; no man in the State is more familiar with her wants or more faithful to her interests and his appointment would be regarded as an asurance that the long delayed protection to them is at last to be conceded. Whatever may be your determination in this matter, it will be heartily acquiesed in by your supporters here because we have unbounded confidence that your course will be controlled by a patriotic desire to conserve the best interests of the whole country— But if your choice should fall upon a Pennsylvanian be assured that the appointment of no one can be received with more heartfelt gratification by your friends than that of General Cameron

Very Respectfully

Saml Lloyd

Washington Jan 4 1860 [*i.e. 1861*]

Dear Lincoln

Things look much better than when I wrote before Mr Seward and Gen Cameron, since his return, have set on foot many things which will do good. Genl Cameron has been to Genl Scott & got him to get from Buchannan full authority to do as he pleased until of 4" of March I mean in reference to the Inauguration. He has ordered two companies of Light Artillery & will shortly order two more to come & remain here Scott says he will order enough to insure quiet

The announcement of the appointment of Cameron makes considerable stir. I think the announcement of the next man whoever he may be will do the same thing When it is known about Seward there will be the same fuss.

If you should select Chase or Schenck there will be a howl Probably it will be the same in Indiana I dont know so well about this. The Mass. men called on me to-day & seemed anxious about Adams. I told them nothing except that the appointment, I did not think had been made

They then wanted me to telegraph you to hold off a day or two until they could be heard. As the statement I made of Seward's feelings might hasten your action, I thought I would do so.

It seems to me you dont need any more Cabinet officers here on the ground. What I said about no one taking responsibility to do any thing was not true, for Seward has since said to me, that he was doing every thing he could same as if he was really Sec of State.

Now that Seward & Cameron are on the ground it seems to me enough

Nothing is known here in reference to the tender to Seward.

It strikes me to send new men here, when it is necessary to keep every thing profoundly still would not be so well as to let two old stagers go alone. I will see Seward & I think now that Cameron is here he will agree with me. I'll write you again tomorrow

Yours truly
Leonard Swett

Gen'l Scott told Mr Cameron this morning that Buchannan was acting "*nobly*" now Nobly was the word he used

150—5th Avenue
Jany 4th 1861.

My dear sir,

I have the authority of a Cabinet Minister for the statement that there is a well founded apprehension that an attempt will be made by the rebels to seize Washn. It is the opinion of some of our coolest & sagest friends that your *immediate* presence at Washn. in view of this imminent peril, is most important. The announcment that the President-elect was on the ground to share our perils & responsibilities would send an electric thrill throughout the land and in its effect on our friends and foes would do much to lessen the danger.

Besides, so great is the imbecility of Mr Buchanan, that it may become necessary for Genl Scott to issue orders for the concentration of troops at the Capital, on his own responsibility and in this step he should be sustained by him who in a few days will be the Commander-in-Chief.

I will not trespass further on your time, for I know all I could say, will readily suggest itself to you.

I apprehend the secession of Virginia, even though her convention may have a majority of nominal unionists.

In great haste
I have the honor to be
Your friend & servant
James H Van Alen

To
Hon Abraham Lincoln
&c &c &c

[Endorsed:]
Plot to Seize Washington
J. H. Van Alen
Jan. 5, 1861

Washington City Jany. 4, 1861

My Dear Sir:

Yours with the message to Genl. Scott came back from Massachusetts this morning. I have just seen the General and delivered to him your message at which he seemed much gratified. By appointment I am again to see him in the morning, when he will confer fully with me in regard to matters proper for you to know. The General is in vastly better spirits than when I last saw him. He and the new Secretary of War (Holt) of whom he speaks in the very highest terms, act in the *most perfect harmony,* and the President is *now* in accord with them. It appears to be well understood that there now exists a formidable conspiracy to seize the Capitol. In it are men of high public position. The President and the War Dept. understand it and measures are already taken to protect the city. Two companies of horse artillery have been ordered from Fort Leavenworth, and one from West Point to be here as soon as possible. One company from Plattsburgh and one from Boston are also ordered here. There are now here about 200 marines. The militia of the district are also about to be organized. Every possible means will be taken to protect the city.— Measures are also being taken to hold as many forts as possible, that are not now taken. On the 8th of this month a force leaves Charleston to capture one of the most important forts on the Coast of Florida, and a U. S. sloop of war is on the way now to protect it. "The little band at Fort Sumpter is in fine spirits," and Scott says that is all he can say now about matters in Charleston harbor. These things he authorized me to say to you, although he will keep you officially advised, of many of these matters.

We are in a way to find out the thread of the conspiracy— We (that is Seward, Gov Grimes of Iowa, Tappan of N. H. and myself) have procured the services of two of the most accomplished detectives from N. Y. City, who are now pursuing the trail. Certain it is, there are traitors everywhere. Even the [indecipherable] fraternizes with the treason going on. Douglas's speech yesterday was utterly infamous and damnable—the crowning atrocity of his life. Baker did well.

Shall write to-morrow in regard to my interview with Scott.

Our State must be put on a war footing by the Legislature.

Truly &c. Yours,
E. B. Washburne

Hon. A. Lincoln

New York, Jan 4, 1861

Dear Sir,

The ship begins to feel the Helm a little! The President is slightly braced

Mr S. is in communication with the reliable Members of the Cabinet.

Gen. Scott is looking after the safety of the Capitol.

I came here with reference to important Treasury interests, and to assist in *secretly* getting a Steamer off to Fort Sumpter.

If the President can be kept up to his duty much evil can be arrested.

We shall have a *United* North—a condition about which I have been filled with solicitude.

The knowledge that a conspiracy to *Usurp* the Government exists. Will probably defeat it.

Very truly Yours
Thurlow Weed

Hon. A. Lincoln.

PRIVATE

Boston, Jany 5, 1861

Sir,

Observing that the name of John C. Fremont has been mentioned as a candidate for a place in your Cabinet—you will please excuse a fellow-citizen for stating the following facts:

1st He has been and still is,—a defaulter to the Government—

2d When in command, in Mexico, during the War,—he approved claims to an amount nearly a million of dollars—where but about *one tenth,* only of the sum was due,—& only one tenth was allowed by the Committees of Congress & by the War Department & paid—The balance was not demanded—

3d He was tried by a Court Martial,—and found guilty on every specification enumerated (33) and dismissed by the President—tho' restored on account of other services—

4th—He waylaid a U. S. Senator & offered violence for *supposed* reference to himself—in debate— He challenged a Superior Officer—to a duel

5th—He has not the confidence of those of know him the best—and *does not* command the respect of any respectable Army Officer—

These things are upon official record, at Washington—& therefore do not require any announcement of names to confirm them—

A friend

Chambersburg Pa Jan 5/60 [*i.e. 1861*]

To Hon A Lincoln

Dr Sir

I saw a dispatch in Forney's press from A K McClure stating that he had been to see you. I as a citizen of the same town & a strong supporter of the Republican party would ask you, to inquire into A K McClure's Character as a man & a politician before you would place any confidence in him or believe him one word he says. I would ask you to examine the issue of the Valley Spirit published on the 22d or 27th of August 1859 whilst he was running for the State Senate. The eiditor of the paper brought 27 charges of corruption of the blackest kind & how did he meet them. Why sir, He prosecuted the eiditor before the election & after it was over & he discovered that the truth could be given in evidence in a libel suit & saw the depositions & knew what witnesse's they had, He was afraid to try the suit & left his character stained as a villain & scoundrel, Sir I dont only ask you to look at that paper, as it may be troublesome to obtain or perhaps you may get one before long, but to inquire of Daniel O Gehr or I H McCauley or B. Chambers or any man of high respectability in the community, (of course men of the Republican party) Why sir, He was beaten in his own ward & I think in the town, but by spending his money, very freely he was successful. This county gave you 1000 or over of a majority The Col is a very good talker, but a more treacherous man never lived. I dont ask you to believe this from an unknowen friend but I refer you to the issue of that paper or to any citizen you may choose to ask, (not to A N Rankin who is a tool of his) Perhaps Hon S. Cameron has the paper I have reference too. He has deceived all his friends & never can be elected again as long as he lives to fill any office in this district. Sir, it may be improper for me to write in this manner, But I do it with good motive to place you on your guard so that you may know what kind of man he is, I state nothing but the facts & the truth must be told though the Heavens should fall. Hon Simon Cameron is the most popular man we have in the State of Pennsylvania I see that he is talked of as cabinet officer. A more Honorable man could not be found in our state. Hoping this letter will be confidential

I remain Yours Respectfully

R V Johnson

N.C

Perhaps I may mistaken in the number of the paper but it was during the Campaign of 59

R V J

Washington Jan 5 1860 [*i.e. 1861*]

Mr Lincoln

Dear Sir,

Since the Mass delegation wrote you, I have heard the New England appointment considerably talked of. Not quite *all* the Mass delegation are for Mr Adams although they have unitedly recommended him This I know A prominent Rep Editor in that State also proposed Mr Wells I have heard no one find fault with Mr Wells Every body seems to think it would be a very good appointment Pitt Fessenden said although he did not know him personally he thought well of him. Of course if you appoint Wells Adams' friends will howl & vica versa. There is not a Congressman here who dont think you ought to consult *him* & take him or *his* friend in the Cabinet. From all I can learn of the Town I think by the time you had been here a week you would either be bored to death or in a condition in which you never could sensibly determine [*every*] any thing,

From all I can learn I do think Wells is the best that can be done in New E. although I did not before I came Every body thinks Colfax is a clever fellow but a gun of [*two*] too small bore. Smith of Ind is very well spoken of The only man I have heard object is Baker Trumbull is for Judd I suppose he has told you so I guess Farnsworth is although he says he is not Kellogg Washburn & Lovejoy are opposed to Judd There is a good deal of diversity about Southern men I think the Seward people are for Gilmor, but from all I can learn I think there is a great question about the propriety of it They all say he is a timid man, changeable, no opinion of his own I think Etheridge or Davis stand better Etheridge is a talented but a rattling man, much like Gridley. Henry Winter Davis, it seems to me has more ability than any of them,

Things are looking better, Scott has complete control He has today reinforced fort Washington 12 miles below I think the danger has passed Tomorrow Old B sends in a Jackson message Cormency of Albany & others of his stamp are here bearing up the democracy to stand by the Union

Seward's appointment is just getting out & believed It is received like Cameron's—is warmly advocated & opposed

Yours

L Swett

Washington Monday

Dear Lincoln

I dropt a remark in my letter last night which might be misunderstood I said if I remember, that I regarded the danger as passed I mean by this that sufficient military strength was being concentrated here to insure [*in*] your Inauguration That I have regarded as the overshadowing danger to such a degree that I for a moment forgot general question of secession

I regard the general question as unchanged except so far as I can see, the South are making steady progress

Yours Truly
L Swett

[In pencil:] Jan'y 6, '61

Suffolk, Virginia
Jan 11th. 1861

Abraham Lincoln Esq.
Dear Sir:

I love my Country, as well, I believe, as I love my life; and I love every man who is willing to risk his life to save his country.

The Union is sick unto Death, if not dead already;— You are the only man who lives, who can restore it to life—

Mr. Lincoln, do not regard this proposition as an idle one.

Will it be too great a humiliation to you, to go in your closet, & on your bended knees, read the proposition over once— Remember, it is to Him you humble yourself—not to man—if there is any good in it, He will show it to you;—if there is no good, He will show it to you.

The action proposed may cost you your life—but what of that? It will save your Country from civil war, and it places you as a moral hero in the estimation of the whole world, next to Washington, if not by his side—

No moral spectacle, in the whole history of man, would be so grand as yours, and I humbly believe, that it would enshrine you with unparalleled love, as the chosen President, in the hearts, of the whole American People— But, if you were struck down, the next minute after you did it, by the fury of madmen, North or South, it would win for you an imortality of the purest fame, worth a hundred Presidencies.

Will you go to Charleston,—you must go in disguise—not from fear, but no one must know what you intend to do—and there, throwing off your disguise, upon the chasm of the Earthquake of terror, which trembles beneath the Nation, *Resign, Fully,* to the will of the *Nation.*

God designs to humble this people, and you, its head, must bow first.

He will then still the raging of the People, as He stilled the raging of the Sea, and closed the mouths of the lions for Daniel.

I am, Dear Sir, an humble young lawyer & citizen of Virginia, a pupil of Colonel Francis H Smith, of the Military School of Virginia,—was an elector for Bell & Everett,—am an admirer of patriotism unto death, whether called by the name of Republican, Whig, or Democratic. And if you will treat this appeal, made in humility & prayer, with that respectful consideration which is due to the spirit & purpose with which it is penned—

I am Dear Sir,

Your Obedient, humble
Servant:

R. O. Whitehead,
Suffolk,
Virginia

No One, but God & yourself, knows what I have written—

Rockford Jan 7th 61

To Honorable Abraham Lincoln
Dear Sir

As you are soon to ocupy the Presidents house at Washington I would inquire if you would want to employ a gardner I am an ornamental gardner by profession. and understand all the branches of gardning from the vegetable department up the flower garden, taking care of fruit trees shrubery &c I have been trained up to this business from a boy and think I could give perfect satisfaction Also am handy in keeping things in order about buildings I am a New-hampshire man and have always been a Republican I have a wife who is an experienced nurse in sickness and can do needle work Also have an educated daughter who can work at nice needle work, also a smart active boy who could wait upon your family My family are all pious, and members of the Presbeterian church. We can furnish the best of Testimonials as to character and industry We would like a situation in your family Any thing trusted to our care could be depended upon I have lived in in Rockford five years and have followed the business of Landscap and ornamental gardning

Should you wish for information I will refer you to the Rev L H Johnson of Rockton Ill our former pastor and minister Should you wish for our services we will be in readness at your call. Will you please to have the gooness to give an answer

Your Obt servant
Samuel S Dimond

Hon Abraham Lincoln

P S Please to refer to Dr A. M. Catlin of this city. Also to Rev L H Johnson of Rockton Ill

To His Excellency
A. Lincoln,
Dear Sir—

The tender of a seat in your Cabinet to Hon. Simon Cameron, of this State, it is believed has been made and accepted.

Though unknown to you, there can be no impropriety in my congratulating you upon the selection of Mr. Cameron as one of your Cabinet advisers— The appointment will meet the hearty approbation of nineteen-twentieths of the tax-payers of Pennsylvania, without reference to party predilections— It will meet their warmest approval because he has always been unwavering in his support of a protective tariff— In this respect he is more closely identified with the interests of the people of this State than any public man we have—

But independent of this, it is an appointment "fit to be made" He has been an active, ardent, & leading Republican since the organization of the party— He has probably done more to give the party strength in the Old Keystone than any single man in our ranks. The positive character of the man, together with his ability & great executive capacity, made him at once the leader and backbone with us— We are, on this account, exceedingly gratified that you have rewarded him & placed him where he will not only be able to serve the people of this State but the country at large—

As to the disappointed politicians who murmur of his appointment, I will venture the remark that most of them stultify themselves by such a course, after their unanimous recommendation for the Presidency, which they gave him in the State Convention—

With great respect, I am

Yours
Chas. M. Hall
Lewisburg, Pa. 7 Jan 61

Living Age Office
Boston 7 Jan. 1861

To the Hon. Abraham Lincoln
Springfield Illinois

Dear Sir I am so rooted in the habit of thinking affectionately about you—that prehaps I intrude upon you with too little ceremony. But I have just written a letter to the President—& will now fill up the measure of presumption by saying a few words to you.

I wrote to the President, in deference to Mr. Forney's exhortation in his paper;—that all persons, public or private, who could say a word to encourage perseverance in a patriotic course shd. do so. I had formerly a short correspondence with him, when the Negro question had been peacefully settled.

Having been born in N. J. before the close of Washington's administration; & having been in the habit of looking at public affairs, on all sides, for nearly 45 years, I have sometimes before ventured to give unsought opinions. At the time of Calhoun's nullification I visited Washington to propose to Prest. Jackson a plan for settling the controversy—obtained his approbation & that of Mr McLane, Sec. of the Treasury; & published it in Charleston & Richmond papers. Congress met soon after, & Mr Clay proposed the plan, which Mr Calhoun eagerly accepted—both of them with the knowledge given of the President's approval already secured.

Pardon me for introducing myself.

What I wished to say to you related to the Cabinet Officer to be chosen from Penna. or New Jersey. This is perhaps a difficult problem. Penna. tho' giving so great a majority, did not go into the contest on Republican principles *merely*. And there has been a great endeavour there to make capital for a gentleman who seems to me more of a politician than a Statesman.

When the papers said that you had offered a post to Wm. L. Dayton of New Jersey, I thought it had been wisely done. I have never seen him; but wrote to him during or after his Senatorship, on the Fremont canvass, because I greatly liked his moderation and sagacity. By the way most of the *Taylor* men deserved the same praise, tho' I think not in the same degree.

If you must have a Penna. man, how would Mr. Grow do? I know nothing of his character, public or private, but from his course in Congress. He perhaps represents the Homestead principle, which is practically an excellent barrier against Slave extension.

About 20 years ago I prepared as Amendments to the Constitution, that the President shd be elected for 7 years; not be eligible again; but be for life a member of the Senate. This was approved by the Albany Argus, Mr Van Buren's paper.

I tried to impress upon Mr Clay (President Jackson having

seemed favourable to it)—a plan for a National Currency. It is very simple & would work itself:—Let the payments of the U. S. be made by drafts upon the Mint in Philad.—& upon the Treasuries in N. Y. & New Orleans. These drafts to be engraved, & of various amounts —from $1000. down to $10.— One of the objects being to displace Bank Notes.

I would not have drafts upon any place without having the money lying in that place to [*meet*] pay it with.— But the effect wd. be that many millions of this paper would never be carried in for payment. Regular monthly returns would shew the operation of the system—& perhaps after years of trial, Congress might permit the investment of a safe part of the idle specie, in U. S. Stocks.— In the meantime the [*only*] advantages would be two fold: 1. A safe currency. 2. A check upon the dilatation of Bank Currency, which is a continual provocation of "speculation"—& is entirely opposed to the Constitution.

I have no room to speak of the immense strength which the P. O. Department might give the Union; a matter familiar to my mind since John McLean's time. We see somewhat of it, even as it is, in S. Carolina

May God guide & bless you, is the prayer of

E. Littell

Nevada City Jany 7th /61

your excellency
Abraham Lincoln
Dear Sir

Happy indeed to find that our cause at this time has not met with a defeat, I was once afraid that Illinois would hardly come out on the side of truth, but for the last five years I have been receiving a paper from my friend Mr Edwards of Shawnetown from the vacinity where I formerly resided which removed all doubt some time previous to the election, knowing you so long from caracter when I lived in Illinois accept as a slight indication of friendship a California cane the wood might have been Manzinneta a native of these hills but it is a native of Mexico called Cazaba in this I consulted my own taste not knowing yours, wishing you wisdom when clothed with authority to govern this growing republic with Judicious prudence at this critical period is the prayer of your

Obt. Servt.
S. M. Orr

House of Repr.
Jany. 7, 1861

STRICTLY CONFIDENTIAL

My Dear Sir:

Great commotion and excitement exist to-day in our ranks in regard to a *compromise* that is supposed to be hatching by the Weed-Seward dynasty. Weed is here and one great object now is to obtain your acquiescence in the scheme to sell out and degrade the republicans. Leonard Swett is the agent to be employed to get you into it. He is acting under the direction of Weed, and it is said writes a letter to you dictated by Weed.

No word of caution from me to you can be necessary. If you waver, *our party has gone.*

Truly Yrs.
E B Washburne

Hon. A Lincoln.

The enclosed is a correct copy of a letter taken from the person of Mrs Thomas, sister of Jackson who shot col Ellsworth at Alexandria Va in 1861. Mrs Thomas' husband is in the 3d Auditors office Rich-

TROOPS ON THE SOUTH GROUNDS OF THE WHITE HOUSE
Contemporary drawing by Waud
Reproduced from the original in the Library of Congress

mond Va she has made several trips to Richmond, came from there lately with her daughter a young lady. have procured their outfits & were on their way back yesterday May 13th/63 when arrested on acqueduct bridge,

Respectfully, forwarded to his exellncy the President of the United States for his information

Henry B Todd
Capt & Pro Mar.

Capitol Hill
Jany. 8th 1861

My dear Mrs T.

I waded over to Geo Town the other day in the mud, cold, slush, snow & Geo Town nastiness generally, to try & hear some account of you & your politic, You may believe I was some what "rampant" when Mrs Stewart told me that you had been to W.City & was actually living in Alexandria yes living in town—and I all the time thinking of you as the innocent charming spirit of the woods and Mistress of the darling romantic cottage but it was provoking in you not to say a word or send me a line as to the moving crisis—& of you Secession from *dear* Fairfax to woe begone Alexandria. How to you know but that I might have gotten up some Military display for upon my word your perseverence & energy in carrying the point of "going to town to live" in spite of all obsticles equals Major Andersons removal to Fort Sumpter— I suppose tho' that you no longer care for us unhappy doomed Washingtonians, & that already you look upon our beautiful city as the future Pigstye of Black republicanism— My Dear is'nt it awful to think what we are coming to— no wonder respectable Virginians feel a contempt for a people who say Lincoln must be peaceably inaugerated in our midst to live in the "White House" surrounded by his black faced & hearted followers that he is to dictate, usurp & ride rough shod generally over Southern blood— I declare it is frightful—if Virginia dont rally to the rescue—there is no knowing what will become of us—if she dont—& in the future you see us all leaning on the arms & acknowledging great fat niggers for our "Lords & Masters"—dont blame us or think it is our own taste or judgement but remember one has to succomb to circumstances— When I think over the times & fall into a train of thought I exclaim to myself is it possible, I have lived an old maid up to this time to end in becoming a niggers wife— Would to heaven I had married old Pete Cash years ago—but patience & a hope & trust in Virginias aid—maybe we can "keep 'em" out 4th March— I heard of your brothers company—& I said all hail & honor be to your good & patriotic son of your county—if we had a few such as you no fear of the great spindle shank flat footed villians of the "Linkum" order, casting on anchor this ground— I go my death for Jims company, & have a mind to give them a Flag—with the inscription, Lincoln the elect of traitors to the South—away with him, we own him not & never shall his presence pollute the roof that once sheltered the immortal Washington— "Ain't that splendid sister Milly" I was surprised to find Mrs Stewart & your brother Charles Union & compromise, & calling Jim cracked on the subject— I felt chocked full of fight—& would have pitched into them—but for fear of raising the convent alarm bells—of course you think as I do everlasting ruin & confusion to Lincoln & company. If it was'nt for Lue, I don the pantaloons & musket join Gov. Wise & be one of the first to put the halter on old Abe's neck— I expect you will be worried to death reading this letter for I am not half done yet but my dear friend politic is my existance now I eat politic—drink politic (Tea is no wheres with me) only think of that— I sleep on politic, dress up in politic, & when I say my prayers say I Believe in God, the South & Governor Wise, unconditional secession the utter destruction, hanging up and shooting down of Abe Linkums party & followers, the resurrection of the South with Virginia as its head leader & Washington City its Capitol I tell you I feel equal to becoming a second Joan d'Arc— Now I want Mr Thomas to come out— now is his time—*now he has the oppertunity* to bring out the elements of success in his character that have hitherto slept now is the time for a man to leave his name to fame, when his ashes shall have mingled with earth & consecrated the soil upon which they repose—now is Mr Thomas for himself & his country—now if he leaves the quibbing talking scarey distrustful of the future party, and onward in faith with a voice that shall ring forth over the country. Virginia foremost in freeing herself from English despotism, is also ready to repel the vile traitorous Republican invaders of her fireside & of her sister states. Great & stirring times bring forth the contingent points in mens character & how often a decided action, turns the wheel of fortune when all seems against us & places us upon a stand of immortality. For a man of talent to belong to a party—that preaches up "let us wait a while" in such times as these, it is a moral suicide—and he undeserving of christian burial— You see I am on the "rampage" about Mr. Thomas. Dont you think I had better write him & may be he would show the letter to "Lundy" & so I'd have the consolation of rescuing two standerd bearers to my countrys glory— If you want to become a great mans wife, now is your time— If Virginia takes her stand, & does the fair thing all will come out glorious & prosperous in end—if she dont why we are the meanest dirtiest set on earth we are no better than Easau who sold his birth right for mess of potage & a great deal worse than Peter Schlemil, who sold his shadow to the devil— When I look over at the Capitol, & down our broad Avenue—then at the clear blue sky resting as it were up the unfinished top of Washingtons Monument in an embrace of love & protection, at the bright waters of the old Potomac worshiping at is base—I think is this all to pass into the hands of traitors—who are trying to pull down the institutions he built up with his blood, & that men whose wifes breakfast at candle light—scour tins & mop up the floors of their houses—are to ride rampant over us, I say Good Lord! Shade of Washington! & Mrs Martha's velvet Kirtle preserve us from such a vulgar calamity— As soon as you can come up—it is only ten cents now, between us, and who would'nt pay ten cents to hear me on Politic. How are you & the children— If I can I will run down & see you but my dear for the truth you know outside politic I have a deal of writing to do—& have to be punctual but I will run over if I can—but for heaven sake keep Mr Thomas on the right side—& dont you notice any one, that dont preach everlasting smash, fire & sword to a union under Lincoln— Love to all the children & as ever Your friend

Julia Matie

P. S. my best respects & three cheers for Jim & his soldiers

[Endorsement below, from back of last page]

Miss Julia Matie Washington
to
Mrs A. M. Thomas—
Copy of Rebel letter
Jany 8. 61

Philadelphia Jan 8th 1861

Hon. Abraham Lincoln

Respected sir it is with feelings of no little gratification that I write to you at the solicitation of a great many warm and hard working republicans; congratulating you upon the wise and judicious selection of a Cabinet Officer from Pennsylvania in the person of Simon Cameron. Rest assured that you have made the best choice for the Keystone, you well know the tarif was the leading question in the canvass here, and it was that issue alone which enabled us to elect Col. Curtin and afterwards to carry the state for you and Mr. Hamlin— we told the people here that the republican party were committed to the measure of protection, and (in the iron districts especially) there was a regular stampede from the ranks of our opponents. Genl. Cameron is regarded all through the state as the champion of Henry Clay's great system of "protection to American labor" and all feel that the interests of Pennsylvania will be in safe hands, with the Gen'l. in the Cabinet.

Gen'l. Cameron's knowledge of monetary matters eminently qualifies him to be Secretary of the Treasury, and Pennsylvania Republicans well know that the organization of the party is permanant with so prominent a man in the leading councils of the Federal Administration, Trusting that success may attend your official acts

I am your obedient Servant

Lemuel. C. Reeves

corrg. Sec. "Continentals".

1708 Brown St Philada.

(PRIVATE)

Washington

Jany 10 1861

Hon A. Lincoln.

Dear Sir;

My position here among all our friends is such that I hear on all sides. Having no wish but for the good of the country and as the best means of attaining it, the success of your administration I write you now to inform you of the state of feeling among our friends here.

While some object to Mr Seward, the great majority will acquiesce and look with favor upon his being Secretary of State But the rumor that Mr Cameron was to go into the Cabinet also, from Mr Weed's relations to Gov Seward and his financial relations with Mr Cameron gave great and painful apprehensions lest a certain class of jobbers & speculators might come too near the Treasury, lest Albany & Harrisburg corruptions would be transferred to Washington We have overcome our political adversaries by showing up their corruptions. We must not be suspected. The name of Mr Chase in connexion with the Treasury gives much better satisfaction.

Mr Bates is well received Let me suggest two names Major Anderson for the War Department Commodore Hiram Paulding for the Navy.

These men are made of the right stuff and will be received with universal enthusiasm Anderson you know well, Paulding a son of

Paulding who captured Andre, the glorious old Commodore who *performed* his duty so well in seizing the Fillibusters, that this administration has thrust him aside. We want men of deeds, in these times. These appointments in these times would rouse the enthusiasm of the country. It is not in old politicians that you must seek all your advisers in such [*these*] revolutionary times.

Pardon me for this frank, unasked suggestion. It comes from my heart and is expressed entirely in confidence.

Your southern members might then be Anderson, Bates, and Blair for the Interior, say,

Seward	State
Chase	Treasury
Anderson	War
Paulding	Navy
M. Blair	Interior
Bates	Atty Genl.
&c	&c &c

I do not doubt that the names of these two men I have suggested would give a power and a popularity which no other names would give (at this time.)

But it may be best that you do not fully determine at present, The Cotton States are in a revolution, The Contagion is spreading through all the Slave States like an epidemic.

If Virginia joins I think Maryland will join also, They will in that event with their organized forces unite to drive us from the Capital before the 4th of March. Treason & Embicility have long presided at the White House; it stalks openly in the Senate, every day; the men who lead treason against the government, remain in high places, as long as they can, to negotiate the surrender to traitors; the disease is so deep seated that it must run its course.

No compromise would stay it. An offer to do so would be treated with contempt as runing from our fears.

If under the threat of secession, we now yield, we are slaves, from slaves.

For one I will not consent, though the grave should open this very hour. If God so wills it, that we must drink of the cup of civil war be it so.

I will fight for the Constitution, & its supremacy—for liberty—and equality—under it to the letter and, and, I will never consent that it shall be made a slavery extending constitution come what may.

If Mr. Seward as we now anticipate or rather as we now fear shall go for a compromise to surrender the free territories acquired or to be acquired from Mexico to Slavery, it will force upon you another question whether your whole Cabinet shall not be reconstructed from top to bottom He speaks on Saturday We shall see

Respectfully
Yours
J. R. Doolittle

Sheffield Bureau Co
Jan the 10 1861

Lincoln I got my old horse Shod yesterday, I thought I would come to Springfield to see you, but after Sleeping all knight the Cogetations of my head was troubled, and I awoke and low. If I was to travel through the cold to Springfield I could have no Satisfaction with you, for you are sorounded continually by A class of minds that cares for nothing but office, and would sacrifice you or Jesus or any body else, and what few honest men there is left in the land has to stand back I would be mighty glad to see you you may have forgotten what I told you the 30 day of last January, A standing on your Stair Steps, or at least my answer to your [*my*] question. if you have forgot I have not, and here is the question, you asked me in your friendly good manner, Tom tell me whether your Spirits says I will be Nominated for President or not, I told you in my bold independent manner that as certain as you lived, you would be Anominated and Elected President, but you never would take the Chair in peace,

Now O Lincoln it is all fulfilled to the letter of the law, and now I ask you as an honest man, to write to me and tell me what you think of my prophecy, if I will come to Springfield whether I can get to see you alone one hour,

O Lincoln I still hope our country will not be distroyed, but I see awful danger of weeping and wailing and nashing of teeth, this is from your true friend that wants no Office from the Presidents Chair to the fourth Corporal, nor never will hold

Thomas, S, Edwards, Sen

N B Please tell me whether Baker will be to Springfield till the first of Feb

Please tell me how Stewert Stands in Politics now,

Please tell me how Old Arch Heringdon Stands in Politics,

Washington City Jany 10 1861

STRICTLY CONFIDENTIAL

My Dear Sir:

To my observation things look more threatening to-day than ever. I believe Va. and Maryland are both rotten to the core. We have had one of our friends from N. Y. (the kind I wrote about) in Baltimore, sounding matters there, and he gives most unfavorable reports. *Great danger is to be apprehended from that quarter.* The very worst secessionists and traitors at heart, are *pretended* Union men, and we have found out that one of these very men, has been in consultation with Corwin as to how to *protect this city! ! !*

You can have no idea how much relief your friends here feel at the latest report that Cameron will not go into the Cabinet. Cameron has acted the fool completely—showing round your letter offering the place to him to any body and every body as a child would show a toy.

And now for the Treasury as Seward is understood to go into the State. All the best and most reliable and most unselfish men say *Chase.* It seems to be regarded as a necessity now that he should go in. The report is here that he can go into that dept. if he desire it. Immediate steps will be taken here to get him to accept. If it were understood to-day that Chase would take the Treasury, the country would draw a long and easy breath.

Truly, &c
E B Washburne

Hon. A. Lincoln

Albany, Jan. 10, '61

Dear Sir,

During my brief visit south (in Washington) I heard several Members speak in favor of your going early to Washington. I saw, also your Letter to Gov. Seward, and entirely concur in the views you entertain.

One of my reasons for endeavoring to hold the Border States by conciliation, looked to the presence of their Members to make a quorum while the Votes are being canvassed.

The other danger (though seriously contemplated by Wise, Floyd &c &c) is over. *That* conspiracy collapsed.

Washington councils would confuse and complicate rather "aid and comfort."

Secretaries Stanton and Holt are doing their duty nobly. The former is in constant communication with Gov. Seward.

In this present aspect of Rebellion I cannot but regard the Firing into the "Star of the West," as a favorable omen. It will, while arousing the whole North, bring some Southerners to their senses.

Very truly Yours,
Thurlow Weed

Hon. A. Lincoln

Columbus, Jany 11, 1861

CONFIDENTIAL

My dear Sir,

Remembering your regret that your friends had not informed you more frankly & fully in relation to one gentleman, and desiring exceedingly the success of your administration, I have made up my mind, with a good deal of reluctance to say a word to you in regard to another

The name of Mr. Smith, of Indiana, is quite frequently mentioned as one of those from among whom you may select your administrative advisers. Mr. Smith is an excellent public Speaker and a zealous Republican & would fill, as he has filled, very creditably a seat in Congress. I have no other feelings toward him personally, than that of kindness and good will. But it is due to you to say that his reputation has been so seriously affected by his railroad & other transactions that his appointment to a place in your Cabinet would impair the credit & endanger the success of your administration.

Your nomination over Mr. Seward was due in great part as you are well aware, to the belief that you would give the country a pure financial administration, whereas serious apprehension was felt of a different result from the influences supposed to surround him. It is as absolutely indispensable that this belief be realized as it is that the expectation of substantial advantage to the cause of freedom from your election be not disappointed.

Permit me to suggest the expediency of confidential consultation in respect to gentlemen whom you may think of inviting into your administration with such of your friends as you most rely on, through whom, either from their own knowledge or by their confidential correspondence or personal experiences, you can easily obtain the full information essential to safe conclusions.

You know my feelings for I expressed them forcibly when with you. God grant that we may see the old integrity & wisdom of Washington & Jefferson restored & that you may be the honored instrument of the blessed restoration.

With unfeigned respect & esteem

Yours most truly

Hon. A. Lincoln — *S. P. Chase*

P. S. I noticed yesterday in the correspondence from this city of the Cincinnati Commercial a statement that you had tendered me the post of Secry. of the Treasy.; and thought it best, since what actually transpired cannot properly be made public, to say to the correspondent, whom I happen to know, that his informant was mistaken, and requested him to correct his statement as "from the best authority." Having touched this subject I ought perhaps also to say that, on reflection, after leaving you, I concluded to wave my objection to communicating with our mutual friends in New York until after your final decision, and availed myself of your permission to consult with them. My letter was, of course, in strictest confidence & communicated nothing you would not have more freely communicated, if conversing with them. I have not yet recd. an answer.

Washington, D. C.
Jany. 13. 1861.

My Dear Sir:

The great event of yesterday was Seward's speech. I did not hear it, but there is a divided opinion in regard to it among our friends. Some say it was letting down, and others say it was a wise, judicious and *timely* speech, and on the whole, I think so. It gives great satisfaction to the border State men who are with us. Reverdy Johnson says it will save Maryland. It undoubtedly gave great satisfaction to the subterranean influence here, as we learn by our N. Y. friends, and last night the current in this city ran strongly with us.

The thread of the conspiracy to seize this city will be broken by the preparations of Genl. Scott and the going away of the members from the seceding States. The retiracy of Tombs, Jeff. Davis, Clay, Brown and others weakens secession here very much. It seems now these men wanted to be permitted by their States to remain here till 4th March, but their States would not agree to it, and have called them home.—

It looks to me *now* more favorable for quiet *here* than it has done for sometime.

The report that Chase takes the Treasury gives unbounded satisfaction to our friends here of all shades,

Yrs,
E B Washburne

Hon. A Lincoln

The South, Jan 14th 1861

Mr Lincoln
Dear Sir

In addressing you, I am prompted by the kindest motives. I wish to warn you of the peril you will be in, if you attempt to be Inaugurated on the fourth of March next, for the South, having two strong, motives for desiring your death or resignation, have resolved to take your life, in the event of your not relinquishing the office awarded you by the obnoxious party. One is, that your removal will restore them to the Union for it is the man, representing the abhorred political party, and not the Federal Union they dislike, and the other is, that the slave population have the impression that your Inauguration will be the signal for their liberation from bondage, and that, from that moment, they will be no longer under the control of their masters, some indeed already treat their owners with marked disrespect, supposing the hour of their release from servitude near. Consequently the whites here, cannot without endangering their own lives allow you to take the Presidential seat, as the blacks in their disappointment at discovering that you did possess the supposed power, and that they were still claimed as property, would, it is apprehended, rise en masse and commence a *servile war*. Even now many are living in constant fear of insurrection on the part of the negros. Trusting that God will guide and counsel you, and also Mr Hamblin for he is equally doomed should he attempt to fill the office of Vice President,

I remain yours very respectfully.

J—a. J—s

Lebanon Tenn.
Jan. 14, 1861

Mr. Abraham Lincoln
Hon. Sir,

You have the honor of being the President elect, & you can now immortalize you name by resigning your claims to the Presidency, at least if the masses could but know that you had acted from a patriotic motive.

The Constitution abiding citizens of the U. S. would all be loth to acquiesce in such a sacrifice of constitutional right; yet if there is no other means for the malady of our country, & your resignation would prove effectual, then all the conservative element of the country would try to be reconciled, & even the Secessionists could never doubt your patriotism.— I have been South in the Gulf States & discussed these points & I believe, in connection with guaranty of the execution of the Fugitive Slave laws, even in a chain of the Free., along the border Slave States; it would bring reconciliation.

Excuse my impertinence & let my love of country plead for it. I write because Ive not heard from the North on this point.

Your friend truely
J. H. Woods

BANK OF NORTH AMERICA

New York Jany 15. 1861

Hon. A. Lincoln.
Dear Sir.

I enclose for your perusal, and reenclosure in the accompanying envelope, a letter from Capt. Doubleday to his wife. A previous letter to me dated Jany 3d stated that men, arms and munitions of war were constantly passing Ft Sumter, to supply the battery erecting on Morris Island. That he had constantly urged Major Anderson to forbid all such supplies as were evidently intended for warlike purposes to be sent to that post, or any other occupied by the enemy, for the purpose of cutting off the communication of the garrison with the sea, considering the keeping open of communications as one of the most vital principles of warfare. Maj. A. refused. This letter will show you that he has still further refused to do his plain duty. The phrase in the conclusion of the letter [*ref*] "Southerners here" refers to Maj. A. Lts. Talbot & Davis, the latter though an Indianian being a strong pro slavery man. I send you this letter without my brother's knowledge, that you may see who is, and who is not true. The condition of the garrison is this. They number 60 (men) soldiers and 11 musicians. They have only hard bread, pork and beans enough to last with economy four months They have no coal, nor any other fuel, except parts of some old buildings, enough to last about forty days. The men and officers are worn out with watching and work. The enemy are rapidly strengthening their batteries on Morris & Sullivans Islands, and have sunk vessels, loaded with stones, in the channel, so as to prevent large ships approaching Ft. S. Every day the situation of the garrison grows more critical, thanks to the vacillation and incompetency of Mr. Buchanan and Maj. Anderson. I write warmly because I see so plainly that all this could have been prevented. Depend upon it Maj. A.s heart is not with his duty.

Yours Respy
U. Doubleday

The enclosed slip from the Evening Post shows that my view is also entertained in Charleston.

[Endorsed:]
Capt Doubleday
(Jany 15) 1861
On Ft Sumpter

Philad. January 16, 1861

Abraham Lincoln Esq
Springfield Ill
Dr Sir

On the 31 December last Major Robt Anderson at Fort Sumter was writing a private letter to a friend here and I give you a quotation of the closing part of it

"thus far had I written when your letter of the 28. was brought in, and I thank you from the bottom of my heart for your whole souled commendation of my course— the newspapers State, that a Telegram from Washington mentions that a messinger, was to be dispatched this morning with orders for me to return to Fort Moultrie— Great God can that be true! I pray *him* to direct me what to do in the Strait in which such instructions, will place me— I have not the heart to write another word— I must reflect, and try to get some light from on high, to guide me."

Yrs. truly Rob. Anderson

Now I observe by the newspapers that Mr Chase of Ohio is to have a place in your Cabinet and I cannot but exclaim with Major Anderson—"Great God can that be true! No I will not believe it— It would be such an *outrage* on the whole country—the appointment *at any time* of such an Ultra Abolitionist would everywhere be so considered and justly too—or are we to be ruled by the Wendell Phillips" Garrisons! Sumners &c for of these is Mr. Chase— The people of Pennsylvania that voted for Abraham Lincoln did not suppose they were voting for an *Abolitionist*

With great consideration

Your Ob Servt.
[*Anonymous*]

W City 18th Jany 1861

Dear Sir,

Mr Sweet a resident of Ill. has asked me to write you a line touching our present condition. I promised him to do so. I can give you no news, these you have. I have been for 30 days, in a Com. of 33, If the States are no more harmonious in thier feelings & opinions than these 33 representative men then appaling as the idea is, we must dissolve & a long & bloody civil war *must* follow, I cannot comprehend the madness of the times Southern men are theoretically crazy. Extreme Northern men are practical fools, The latter are really quite as mad as the former, Treason is in the air around us *every* where. It goes by the name of Patriotism. Men in Congress boldly avow it, & the public offices are full of acknowledged secessionists— God alone I fear can help us,— Four or five States are gone others are [*drifting*] driving before the gale, I have looked on this horrid picture till I have been able to gaze on it with perfect calmness, I think if you live, you may take the oath, And now a word as to yr. Cabinet. I hear of Seward, Bates, & C B Smith, These I think are good selections, They are intelligent, & men of firm purpose, I know Smith better than the others, He is very industrious & capable of hard & long continued labor, & well informed, It has been objected that he was one of the Mexican Commission, In all the storm of calumny that was placed on me, I never heard that he was charged with any thing wrong. I *know* he acted in all that business with perfect integrity But if he should not be preferred & Ohio is looked to, then I am well satisfied Schenck should be taken, He is in all our principles & policy exactly right, & possesses in an eminent degree, administrative talent—

If you go to N. England Simmons of R Island is better fitted for the treasy. than any man I know in America, His Character is without a blemish, His knowledge of our Commercial & financial system is more accurate & extensive than [*any*] that of any man now in public life, He is, was, & always will be, a sound Whig

When [*you*] will you come here, I hope soon

Yr friend
Thos. Corwin

Hon A. Lincoln

Senate Chamber, Jany. 16/61

My Dear Sir,

I would have answered yours of the 7th before, had I been able to communicate anything satisfactory in relation to Gen. C. but as that matter is in other hands, I presume you are better posted about it than I. The Gen. was sore at first, but I think is now feeling better, & I doubt not can be reconciled. Gov. Seward approached me in regard to the matter, & I gave him a memorandum of that part of your letter relating to Gen. C. I have had several conversations with Gen. C. but did not tell him of the letter from you. Gov. S. this moment tells me he has not communicated the matter I gave him to Gen. C. & he seems to think there may be more trouble in quieting Gen. C. than I anticipate. I have understood that Mr. Swett had had free intercourse with Gen. C. & he will probably be able to post you fully—

A very prudent Friend, who is better posted in regard to matters here in the District than any other man, & knows more of the designs of the conspirators than anybody else, has suggested that you ought not to have it given out here, on when you were coming here but to let some of us here know the time & the route—

Truly Yours
Lyman Trumbull

ROOMS OF THE YOUNG MEN'S REPN. UNION

Newyork January 17th 1861

At a meeting of the *Board of Control* of the *Newyork Young Men's Republican Union,* held on Thursday January 17th 1861, the following *Preamble* and *Resolutions* were unanimously adopted.

WHEREAS. The existing crisis in our National History seems destined to be decided only by a firm, courageous and conservative course of action on the part of all who love the *Union* and who respect the *Constitution,* and *Whereas,* The vacillating, cowardly and treasonable policy of *James Buchanan* has, thus far, served only to foment *discord,* encourage *Rebellion,* and precipitate *Revolution,* without casting a ray of hope upon the future peaceable settlement of the question at issue, and *Whereas,* The election of *Abraham Lincoln* and the inauguration of an *honest, conservative,* and *unsectional administration* is calculated rather to cement and unite in one fraternal bond the various interests of the country and presents no just pretext for dissatisfaction—much less for *Disunion,* therefore

Resolved, That the *Republican Young Men* of *Newyork* utterly disown and repudiate the idea that peaceable *Secession* is possible, and that the permanency of this *Union* is dependent upon the whims or wish of any single *city, state,* or *section.*

Resolved, That we disclaim, for ourselves and for the *Republicans of Newyork,* all thoughts of *Compromise* in the face of existing dangers and angry threats—beleiving that a *Government* sustained temporarily by such means must be degraded in the estimation of the World and remain during its further uncertain term of continuance a scorn and a byword among men.

Resolved, That we endorse, in advance, any action proposed by the *incoming administration* which shall present a *firm unyielding front of opposition to traitors* and which shall indicate a policy devoted solely to the *enforcement of the Laws, the up-holding of the Constitution* and *the perpetuity of the Union.*

Resolved, That—the preservation of the *Union* being the pressing exigency of the hour, we earnestly recommend, with that view, the appointment, as *Secretary of War,* under the President-elect, of *Hon. Cassius M. Clay of Kentucky,* whose character and past career give abundant warrant that, by his wise counsels and his well-tested energy, the new administration will be strengthened in the discharge of duty, the *Union preserved, Rebellion checked and Treason punished.*

Resolved, That a copy of these Resolutions duly authenticated by the President and Secretary of the *Young Men's Republican Union,* be transmitted to *Hon Abraham Lincoln.*

Charles T. Rodgers
President

Erasmus Sterling
Secretary.

SOC. HISTORIC: CHICAGO:

Historical Rooms.
Jan. 18. 1861.

To the
Hon. Abraham Lincoln
Dear Sir,

I have the honor to inform you, that, at a Statute meeting of this Society, held the 15th instant, you were elected one of its *Honorary* members.

Will you please oblige the Society, by informing the Secretary in writing, if it is agreeable to you to accept this appointment.

I have the honor to be,
with the highest respect,
Dear Sir,
Your obedient servant,
William Barry,
Secy. &c.

Lynchburg Va Jan 18th 1861

Hon Abaham Lincolmn
Springfield Ill. *Dear Sir*

I have heard several persons in this place say that if you ever did take the President Chair that they would go to washington City expressly to kill you. for your wife and Children sake dont take the Chair if you do you will be murdered by some cowardly scoundel have you had any application for this post if not I wish you would let me have it– if you take the Chair as the president of the United States but dont you take it. resign. if you dont you will be murdered I write you this as a friend I am a friend of yours please answer this letter so I can know whether I must go to washington City and raise a body of men to guard you

Yours truly &c
R. A. Hunt

Harrisburg Jan. 19th 1861

To His Ex. A Lincoln
President Elect of the United States
Sir

I am the pastor of the first Presbyterian Church Harrisburg Pa. and have been since 1818, now 43 years. When I was first settled in this place the Hon. Simon Cameron was a youth. I have known him somewhat intimately ever since, especially in his relations as a [*father*] son, a husband father, friend and neighbour, and can testify that in all these respects his character has been not only [*exemplary*] unexceptional but highly exemplary

Yours most respectfully
Wm R DeWitt

STATE OF NEW YORK
EXECUTIVE DEPARTMENT

Albany, Jan 19, 1861

His Excellency
Abraham Lincoln
Prest-Elect of the U States
My Dear Sir

The period is near at hand when you will decide as to the route you will take in your journey to the Seat of Govt to enter upon the discharge of the high duties for which you have been most honorably chosen by the people of the United States.

Believing as I do that there will be at this Season of the year, *less* fatigue in travelling by the way of Buffalo Albany & New York than by any other route, I accordingly recommend it I most cordially invite you to the Capital, and tender to you the hospitalities of the State, and of my house and respectfully urge you to arrange to spend at least one day in Albany. You are aware that our Legislature will be in session at that time as it is now; but you cannot realize the great satisfaction it will afford the members of the Legislature, if this invitation shall be accepted. But not to them more than to your numerous friends in Albany & vicinity, and yet to none more than to your friend & obedient svt

E. D. Morgan

Washington Jany 19, 1861.

Hon. E. B. Washburne

Sir In answer to your inquiry I will make a plain statement of facts. Some ten days ago it was rumored that Genl. Cameron had declined a seat in Mr. Lincoln's Cabinet. One of my colleagues suggested my name for the place. I objected untill it was ascertained from Mr. Cameron himself if it were true as I would have no contest on my account. A short time afterwards General Cameron called on me as he said to inform me that he had absolutely declined going into the Cabinet, and wished me to allow my name to be used as most likely to unite all factions—I asked him, as a question of honor, whether he might not yet be induced to reconsider his determination and accept. He answered that there was no earthly contingency which would induce him to go into Mr. Lincoln's Cabinet; and again urged me to allow my name to be presented. I consented. His friends in the House who had signed his recommendation joined on mine under his advice—

If it be possible (as I fear) that he has so far forgotten his honor as to consent to be again considered a candidate, you may well understand how I should view it personally. I do not say *what I know* of the Generals antecedents— But his character may be well infered from this Act—I must ever look upon him as a man destitute of honor and honesty

With Great Respect
Thaddeus Stevens

Marion Alabama January 20th 1861

Dr Sir

Being Desirous of Embarking in the farming & timber trade, and hearing of your Eminence as a Rail Splitter is my Reason for writing to you being a Speculator in Southern lands and having an Interest in Every State South and wishing to improve that Interest and hearing of your Profound Judgement of the Fence question. I will with Due Deferance ask your advice as to fencing in my South Carolina Georgia Alabama Mississippi Louisiana and Florida Lands. there is a variety of timber which rails can be made of for Instance John Brown Rails Horace Greely do Fred Dougelass do Black Republican do States Rights do and Constitutional Rails now I would Like to Know which in your honest Opinion and Judgement is the Best timber to fence in this valuable Land with give me your views as to timber lasting Longest in Sections or Solid. and as to the courtesy and Respect to be Exercised as to their Rights and priviledges Betwen Farmers with Sentiments of Equal Rights to all the States and Exclusive priviledges to none I remain Respectfly your Friend if you Stand by the Constitution to the Letter and Intent

A. Jackson Democrat

Beware the Ides of March

As an honest man I tell you the Southron people will not Stand your administration unless the Personel Liberty Bills are Repealed and the Fugitive Slave Law is carried out you may think this is written to Intimidate you But it is for no such purpose what I have stated are facts and you will find it So in Less than Six months

the Southron States will not be Coerced mark that in your Book you are in a hard place But come up to the constitution like a man and the country will move on in prosperity we will not Stand Abolition in any Shape Whatever

Let Northern men Stay at home and attend to their own Buisness and Lett Slavery Alone and they will Live longer and be more prosperous charity begins at Home and they had better take care of the poor and unfortunate at Home than to be meddling with Others peoples property. we want nothing but our Rights in the Union and will protect them out of it

Logan Co Ky
Jan 20nd 1861

Hon Abe Lincol
Dear Sir

The negros have taken up the notion, or rather it has been taught them by beggars and Gipsies, that as soon as you were elected they would all be free, They have commenced their work of poisoning and Incendiaryism. Now all I want to know *is,* if you do not intend such a thing, is, for you to *make* them know it; *so that they may go to work and wait until the next* presidential Election to cut up again. I wish you would ask your Estimable Lady how she would Like, Just as she *gets* a good cook for some stragling begger, peddler, or *fortuneteller* to come along and pursuade her that some one would give her higher wages on the other side of town, *For God sake* Dear Sir give us women some assurance that *you* will protect *us,* for we are the greatest *Slaves* in in the South

Respectfully
Sue H Burbridge

PRIVATE

LEGACION MEJICANA
EN LOS
E. UNIDOS DE AMERICA.

Springfield, Ills, January 21st, 1861.

Dear Sir:

I have the honor to inclose you "the New York times" of which I spoke to you this afternoon and the "Herald" of the 18th instant which has something on Mexico.

It was my intention as well as my desire to see you once more before I leave here, but seeing you so busy and so much engaged and not wishing to distract you at all, I am compell to beg you to take this note, as my bidding adieu and to accept the assurances of great esteem and respect with which

I am, Sir, your obedient servant,

M Romero

Hon. A. Lincoln,
&c &c &c

Washington City Jany 22. 1860 [*i.e. 1861*]

Honord. Sir

In the name of all that is past, all that now is, or is to be, May I approach you, not that I may be rewarded, not that I may secure the Pelf which thousands hope through you, but that I may say but one word for my *integrity* and in that, *evry thing for my Country.* At Chicago, under the Pressure which Sought an acceptable representative for the *"Pivotal States"*, Ultraism was Seward, Conservatism was Lincoln,—the first was *abstract,* the last was *Practical Whiggery,* No one could object that the *abstract* and the *Practical* might be combined, *Seward* therefore appropriately stands with Lincoln in the Combination, but in the name of God Can it be that with this is to be intermingled, Such incongruous and repulsive elements as *Chase,* Cameron and Judd.— In more than a hundred speeches after your nomination I placed you before the people as a *Clay* Whig. I am an Ohio *Whig* and Lincoln man, and Can it be that Ohio Whiggery is forever to be weighted with a Chase, while a *Corwin* and a Ewing survive, In the name of our great *leader* who is dead, Spare us this for Heavens Sake— I am to you nobody, yet for 16 years I have been a voter, and these men of Ohio represent the idea of 9/10 of 231,000 voters. Soundly Whig, alias Republican, with a few democratic Dissenters— Do not wed us where we cant be won.

Secession is anti Whig, it is sound Loco-foco State rights, Let us have men who will not be called upon to eat their own record, if unhapily, American Citizenship, *must* be Saved by the Stuborn will of *Federalism,* alias *Whig.* If the Union is lost, *all is lost,* if it is saved *as it must be* let us do it in the name of that Patriotism which won us in 1844–American Citizenship & American glory as it was with our idol of that day, Not as now *feigned* by those who Calumniated *him* as long as *he* lived, & now feign to worship *him* dead– One thing as a youthful, but an ardent Soldier of 1844 I pray you, if you visit our Clay State for a Constitutional adviser, do not designate an anti Clay man, Give us our first love, Whig, Whig, Whig, and anti Slave, as it is, *was,* & ever will be,–

Intending to see you inaugurated *as I live, I do know* that the *Crisis* "will have been reached and passed" What then, Whig-Whig-Whig– As I love the name of the slandered Clay, as I love my Country, I would pray that *you* may vindicate both–

Your Servant
Clifford Arick

P.S. However this may be approved by you, or otherwise, in charity for one who doubts much, *but loves intensely where you loved,* forgive & conceal this–

C A

New York January 22, 1861.

My dear sir,

At the risk of being deemed somewhat troublesome, yet with the greatest respect and deference, I take the liberty of addressing you once more on the subject of your cabinet appointments.

I believe you do not differ with me in regard to the importance of giving Mr. Chase a place in the Cabinet, as one whose wisdom, rigid integrity and force of character would make him a most safe counseller and efficient coadjutor of the Chief Magistrate, not to speak of the need of his presence as a counterpoise to another member, who, to commanding talents, joins a flexible and inulgent temper, and unsafe associations. The appointment of Mr. Chase would give a feeling of security and confidence to the public mind which the rascalities of Mr. Buchanan's cabinet have made exceedingly sensitive and jealous, and would, it seems to me, settle the point in advance that the new administration will be both honored and beloved. For some time to come, the federal government must depend largely upon its credit for its resources, and how potent is the effect of placing an honest and economical man at the head of the Treasury Department, is shown by an example now before our eyes. General Dix, with all his mistakes, is a man of unquestioned integrity, and his appointment as Secretary of the Treasury has already greatly raised the credit of the government brought so low by the misconduct of Cobb.

Now, according to what I learn from Mr. Opdyke, who has just returned from Ohio, it is nearly certain that Mr. Chase would not take a place in the Cabinet, unless it were offered him early. He is not inclined to do it at all, preferring a seat in the Senate, but this preference he would forego; yet there are, I am told, some personal reasons, as well as others connected with the choice of his successor in the Senate, that will, if the offer be delayed, induce him to remain where he is. I am not a judge of the force of these reasons; it is enough that they exist.

The only motive for delay is the hope of pacifying Mr. Cameron and his friends. It is thought here, by some who know him to be very tenacious of his purposes, that there is no probability of doing this effectually, whether the offer to Mr. Chase be postponed or not. If, however, it be possible to satisfy him, it is to be considered, whether it will not be as easily done after Mr. Chase shall have been fixed upon as now, and whether the hope of obtaining better terms may not lead Mr Cameron to affect to spurn any reconciliation, as long as the appointment which he expected is kept open. One thing, however, is perfectly clear, that by failing to secure the services of Mr. Chase in the Treasury Department, both the country and the Republican party will lose infinitely more than the incoming administration can possibly suffer from the enmity of Mr. Cameron and his adherents.

I leave the subject here, that I may say a single word on another.

From Mr Opdyke, I learn, that, in a letter written to you several weeks since, on the subject of "protection", I did not make myself fully understood. It seemed to me that I had clearly expressed my meaning when I said, that those who thought with me were "willing that this should be an open question." I wish merely to express a hope that the administration would not throw its entire influence on the side of protection. The Republican party not being agreed among themselves on that point, the Cabinet policy as it seemed to me, should be so moderate as not to disaffect the friends of free trade.

I am, dear Sir, truly yours,
W. C. Bryant.

Hon A. Lincoln

Hon. Abm Lincoln
Dear Sir.

I write to say that the assertions made at my house and reported in my note to Mrs Lincoln respecting a plan for preventing by force your Inauguration, are fully contradicted from the most reliable sources. The "Maryland Guard" and Militia of Washington are I believe fully prepared to *prevent* any attempts of such a nature; but to bring into this region an armed force for protection, would most certainly result disasterously for the peace of the Country.

Maryland and Virginia though slow to act will never yield what they regard as their rights. They only wait to see what is to be done before taking their stand.

The friends of Union here, look to the magnanimity (or we may say the policy) of the republican party to offer the olive branch of compromise and reconciliation—unless this, in *good faith* shall be done, we are a *doomed people,*

I remain with much respect (hoping and praying for our unhappy Country), your Obt St

Almira Lincoln Phelps

Eaton Place
Baltimore, Md
Jan 23, 1861.

Louisville, Jan. 24th 1861.

My dear Sir,

In a letter which you wrote to me a few months ago, you spoke of my having opposed you strongly as a candidate for the Presidency. Yes, dear Sir, I did oppose you, and I did so because I foresaw most distinctly then, as we all have since known, that your election would cause a dissolution of the Union. Personally I liked you better, far better, than either of the other three candidates, but I could not help knowing, or at least believing, that your election would inaugurate a fearful strife among us.

In all the Presidential canvass, Mr. Lincoln, I bore warm and strong testimony to your personal and political integrity. I brought some odium upon myself by this course, but I was most certainly conscientious.

We now have most terrible political troubles ahead. I am confident that you will do your duty according to your understanding of it. I do not know whether you and I are to be in one confederacy or in separate confederacies, but most certainly, I shall, however situated, endeavor to do you the fullest justice. And perhaps my situation will be an important one.

And now, Mr. Lincoln, I have a favor to ask of you, which, I think, you will take especial pleasure in granting. The dearest friend I have in the world is Mr. John J. Piatt, a cousin of Donn Piatt, whom I am sure you know, and as ardent a friend of yours as there is in the country. He has been with me for several months in Kentucky, but has never faltered for one moment in his devotion to the

Republican Party. I want you to give him a fine office, and I will tell you why. In the first place I think him the finest, the most glorious literary genius in the whole country, and, in the second place, he is engaged to the most brilliant poetess in all our land, who cannot marry him until he shall have obtained a position in which he can support himself and her. Mr. Lincoln, they are both poets, great poets, and I shall be infinitely rejoiced if you will say that Mr. P. shall have a position under your administration. I ask it of you as a personal favor—ardently, earnestly. I think I can safely promise you, that, if you shall enable the two poets to marry, they will name their first boy either after you or me!

Very truly yours,
Geo. D. Prentice

Geo. D. Prentice Ky
for John J. Piatt

Pittsburgh
Jan 24 1861

Dear Lincoln

I am here, sick on my back, & likely to remain so for several days, may be, a week

I took a severe cold just before leaving Washington which by the exposure incident to travel since has thrown me into a fever, I think I have it broken now,

Gen'l Scott sent word to me the evening before I left through T. Corwin & Col Stone that he wanted you to send a *messenger* to W before you went informing him all about your route, time of departure &c &c He dont want this by letter for fear the mail will be robed He wants quietly to station such force about Baltimore, I suppose as will protect you, in any event

I shall come to Springfield as soon as I am able

Yours Truly
L Swett

St Louis Jany 25th 1861

Hon Abram Lincoln

Dear Sir,

Permit me to solicit from you the employment of Chief Cook at the White House. It would not be modest on my part to speak of my qualities and knowledge concerning the culinary business—still you will permit me to state that I learned my profession in Paris, New York, New Orleans and was for several years Chief Cook at the Planter's house and at Barnum's hotel here—for the present I am Keeping the Hotel de L'Europe— Should you desire to have an interview with me, I shall immediately come to see you and will endeavor to satisfy you in all respects.

I take the liberty to refer To Hon Ed. Bates. Hon. Frank P. Blair Jr. Hon. O. D. Filley Mayor of St Louis, Seymour Voullaire Esq. State's Atty. of Mo. Mess Barnum & Fogg of Barnum's hotel, and Mr. Stickney of the Planter's house

Resply Yours
Chas. Pfefferling

P.S. Should you deem proper to answer this, please send the letter to the Care of Seymour Voullaire Esq—

C.P.

New York, January 25th 1861.

Dear Sir,

Some years ago a number of citizens of New York caused dies to be struck, in which to strike a medal, commemorative of the life and public services of the great Clay;—in order that they might thereby transmit to remote posterity, in the most enduring and classic form, a correct resemblance of his lineaments.

A medal was accordingly struck in gold, and presented to him. One hundred and fifty were also struck in bronze. After which the dies were broken.

Many of the medals were presented to various States of the Union, and to leading public Institutions, at home and abroad.

I reserved, at the time, one of them, with the intention, if ever such a result should occur in my day, of presenting it to the citizen of the school of Henry Clay, who should first be elected to the Presidency of the United States.

I rejoice that that event has, at last, occurred, and, recognising in you, a true disciple of our illustrious friend, I take great pleasure in carrying out my purpose, by hereby transmitting the medal to you, and begging your kind acceptance of it.

With profound respect,
I am, Sir, your Fellowcitizen,
Daniel Ullmann

His Excellency,
Abraham Lincoln
President Elect of the
United States.

Washington January 27, 1861.

My dear Sir

Mr Cameron showed me the letter you had sent to him and seems entirely satisfied with it.

I saw Mr Robert E. Scott of Virginia to day pursuant to appointment. He is a splendid man and he would be a fit and creditable representative of the Southern Union party. Whether he is not too exacting for his section to make a practical minister for you is quite doubtful in my mind—I will think more.

Recent events in Virginia have opened access to me for Union men in Virginia and other Southern states. Among others Mr James Barbour of the Senate of Virginia has visited me. He is a Democrat but the master spirit of the Union party, and he left upon my mind a most favorable impression as an man of talent spirit loyalty and practicability— We will talk of him when you come here—

The appeals from the Union men in the Border states for something of concession or compromise are very painful since they say that without it those states must all go with the tide, and your administration must begin with the free states, meeting all the Southern states in a hostile confederacy. Chance might render the separation perpetual. Disunion has been contemplated and discussed so long there that they have become frightfully familiar with it, and even such men as Mr Scott and William C. Rives are so far disunionists as to think that they would have the right and believe—in going if we will not execute new guarantees which would be abhorent in the North,

It is almost in vain that I tell them to wait, let us have a truce on slavery, put our issue on Disunion and seek remedies for ultimate griefs in a constitutional question.

This is the dark side of the picture. Now for the brighter one. Beyond a peradventure disunion is falling and Union rising in the popular mind— Our friends say we are safe in Maryland— And Mr Scott and others tell me that Union is gaining rapidly as an element in Virginia—

In any case—you are to meet a hostile armed Confederacy when you commence— You must reduce it by force or conciliation. The resort to force would very soon be denounced by the North, although so many are anxious for a fray, The North will not consent to a long Civil War— A large portion, much the largest portion of the Republican party are reckless now of the crisis before us—and compromise or concession though as a means of averting dissolution is intolerable to them. They believe that either it will not come at all, or be less disastrous than I think it will be— For my own part I think that we must collect the revenues—regain the ports in the gulf, and, if need be maintain ourselves here— But that every thought that we think ought to be conciliatory forbearing and patient, and so open the way for the rising of a Union Party in the seceding states which will bring them back into the Union—

It will be very important that your Inaugural Address be wise and winning.

I am glad that you have suspended making Cabinet appointments The temper of your administration whether generous and hopeful of

Union, or taut and reckless will probably determine the fate of our country.

May God give you wisdom for the great trial & responsibility—

Very respectfully & truly yours

William H Seward

The Honorable
Abraham Lincoln

You will need to let us know when you are coming here, to take lodgings at one of the hotels, and maintain a freedom of access towards every body I would ask you and your family to stay with me, but that I know it would be wiser for you to endure the annoyances of a hotel for the short time before the inauguration.

Some shrewd men still say that the danger of force assembled here remains— I think otherwise—but my temper is always hopeful.

[Endorsed:]

Hon. Wm. H. Seward
Washington
Jany 1861

On Condition of Country
and prospects &c &c

COPY

Springfield Ill Jany 28th 1861.

Hon. Edward Bates

Dear Sir:

Hon. A. Lincoln desires me to write to you that he has determined on starting from here for Washington City on the 11th of February. He will go through Indianapolis, Columbus, Pittsburg, Albany, New York, Philadelphia, Harrisburg and Baltimore.

Albany, New York and Philadelphia are not finally decided upon, though it is probable that he will also take them in his route. The journey will occupy twelve or fifteen days.

Yours Truly
Jno. G. Nicolay

Columbus, Jany 28, 1861.

My dear Sir,

My letters from Washington alarm me, though not easily alarmed. The defence of the city is said by one who certainly knows if anybody knows to be inadequate and the President is represented as incredulous and apathetic. My hope is that the investigations authorized by Congress will expose the danger, and secure a remedy if really considerable.

Another danger is greater still and more imminent—and that is the disruption of the Republican Party through Congressional attempts at Compromises. Our only safety from this danger lies in the adoption & maintenance of the simple watchword—Inauguration first—adjustment afterwards— Let the word pass *from the head* of the column before the Republicans move. I know the temper of the people, and I know that the Republican Party will be defeated in Ohio next fall if the pledge given at Chicago is violated by the passing of an enabling act for the admission of New Mexico as a Slave State or by the proposal by Congress of the Amendment to the Constitution recommended by the Committee of 33. The people are vigilant and jealous. They have been often deceived in their hopes, and fear being again deceived. The friends of Compromise, so prominent Representatives write me, pretend to have your sanction to these measures. I know it cannot be so, but the persistent representations to this effect are doing much damage. Let me beg you to say if you have not already said to some trusted Senator & some trusted Representative that you desire the adoption of no compromise measure [*till after*] before the Republicans become charged with the responsibility of administration through your inauguration. Inauguration first—adjustment afterwards.

I see that your route to Washington is announced through Buffalo & Albany. Will not this roundbout way involve too much fatigue & exhaustion? Indianapolis, Cincinnati, Columbus, Pittsburgh, Harrisburgh, Baltimore would be the natural, direct & least fatiguing route. Pardon this suggestion. I am glad that you have relinquished your idea of proceeding to Washington in a private way. It is important to allow full scope to the enthusiasm of the people just now. But a circuitous journey may not have so useful effects as one more direct—besides being more fatiguing to yourself.

With the highest respect,

Yours truly

S. P. Chase

Hon. A. Lincoln.

Albany, Jan. 28

Dear Sir,

Mr Wood called this evening to show me a Programe of Arrangements for your Journey to Washington, adding that you would probably leave Home on the 7th or 10th February.

Presuming that this information is reliable, I shall advise Gov. Morgan, and be in readiness to welcome you to Albany.

Though in some aspects matters look brighter at Washington, yet the danger of collision is imminent. I am intensely anxious that you get on Board and take the Ships Helm before there is general mutiny among the Crew.

Virginia can be held awhile if the Free States send Commissions to Washington.

A member of our Legislature (Mr Camp) who recently went to Springfield, comes back misusing your name abominably. He says that you desire the Election of Greeley to the Senate, and that if chosen he will have the disposal of Offices. This is an absurd falsehood, we know, but it fools some who are sharp for Office and credulous.

I shall look for a clearer atmosphere and brighter skies if Virginia and Maryland hold on till the 4th of March.

Very truly yours,
Thurlow Weed

Hon. A. Lincoln

Great Western Railway,
Hamilton, Canada West,
29 Jan[y] 1861

The Hon[ble] A. Lincoln
etc etc etc
Springfield
Dear Sir

Permit me to express the hope that in making arrangements for your progress to Washington, you will select the Great Western route

In the event of your doing so allow me on behalf of this Company, to assure you, that every effort shall be made to ensure your comfort & that of your friends accompanying you.

It will afford me much pleasure to appropriate to your exclusive use one of our most commodious passenger cars, and in every way in my power to contribute to the comfort of your journey from Detroit to Suspension Bridge, our Eastern Terminus.

I am Dear Sir
Your most ob[t] Ser[t].
Thos Reynolds
Financial Director

[Endorsed in Mr. Lincoln's hand:] Answer this respectfully

House of Reps.
Jany. 30. 1861.

My dear Sir:

There is a great deal said in the newspapers and a great deal said outside the newspapers about an attempt to seize this city, and a great many people are very much alarmed. I do not suppose you will be alarmed by all the talk. I think I am in a position to *know* as much as anybody about this whole matter. I am in consultation with Genl. Scott and with Col. Stone, who is organizing the militia of the district. Our *friends* from N. Y. three of the best and most skilful men ever in that service, are still here, and I am posted every day in regard to their information. *I am satisfied there does not* NOW *exist any organization to amount to anything, anywhere,* the object of which is either to prevent the counting of the votes, or to prevent your inauguration. I say *now*—what may take place I will not say, but I do not believe any attempt at all will be made *at any time.* I have just left Scott—he is very vigilant and active and will make every preparation he can to meet *any emergency.* I am sorry to say, however, old Buck is hanging back, though the Secretary of War is up to "high water mark" (to use Scott's own language) at the time. Scott has this day sent a paper to the President saying unless he is permitted to bring more troops here, he will not hold himself responsible for the peace of the District. I presume the President will now permit the troops to be brought here. The N.Y. friends are entirely certain there is no nucleus of a conspiracy in this city. The Mayor, although suspected of being a secessionist, was up before the special committee to-day and *swore* there was nothing of the kind going on.

When in Scott's room, Genl. Dix the new Sec'y of the Treasury came in to consult about certain matters. He is clear up to the handle for the enforcement of the laws and the protection of the public property. The old General was hugely pleased at his firmness and the high ground he took. The only trouble now in the cabinet is Yancey, who is believed to sympathize with the traitors.

If Mrs. Lincoln entertain any fears, tell her my opinion is that there is to be no trouble and no danger. I may be mistaken, but do not think I am.

Truly Yrs.
E. B. Washburne

Hon. A. Lincoln

STATE OF PENNSYLVANIA
ADJUTANT GENERAL'S OFFICE.

Erie, January 30, 1861.

Hon. Ab^{m} Lincoln

Dear Sir—I acknowledge the receipt of a note from John G. Nicolay esq. in answer to my communication of the 31st ult.

The State of Pennsylvania being the nearest free state to the National Capital I deemed it my duty to be ready for any emergency, in case of difficulty. From knowledge I have gained by a recent visit to Washington city, I entertain great fears of trouble in that vicinity, and I am mortified to know that the government at Washington rest so securely, while standing in so great danger. If at all proper I would like to confer with you before you start for Washington City, in relation to this matter, and then take the advice of my commander- in- chief Hon. A. G. Curtin, our present worthy Governor, in whom I have an abiding confidence in this crisis.

In all that I do, or have done, I have & will do quietly and without show or ostentation, always keeping my own counsel.

I sincerely hope that the strong arm of the military will not be necessary in sustaining your patriotic administration of the government, but I am proud to say that Pennsylvania, the Keystone of the Federal arch is as devoted now to the union, as she was, when battling with Washington in the defense of that declaration of our rights which was first promulgated from our beautiful metropolis of Philadelphia.

In conclusion, allow me to assure you again, of the devotion of myself, and the militia under my command, to the cause of the union, and the National Flag.

I have the honor to subscribe myself

Your friend & servant

Edwin C. Wilson, Adj. Genl of Penns[ia]

P. S. Ireside at Erie, Pa. There a letter will reach me—

Hon. Ab[m]Lincoln
Pres't Elect,
Springfield,
Illinois

[Endorsement:] Adjt Genl of Penn
Jan 30 1861
On military matters

McLemoresville Ten Jany 31 1861[11]

Dear Sir

It may seem strange to you that I an humble Citizen, without any Previous acquaintance with you, unauthorized By Committee or appointment, would presume to write to the President Elect of the United States, Be this all so. But as a lover of H Clay and this glorious old union

I feel at liberty to have a little talk with you on the subject of our Country. I was Born in the South raised in the South *I love the South* It is *my home* I love the union too I hope and trust in God that It may be preserved You go into the presidential Chair with Tenfold more Difficulties to contend with than *any* other man who has been promoted to that high position,

Destruction is on Its rappid march to precipitate our Country in one common ruin O, the work of Sectional prejudice how baneful thou art to human happiness, In this our hour of extremity is there no hope many true patriots South are looking to you for some expressions that in this dark hour some ray of hope may come, I among many other believe that you will do all within your Power so as to render our the whole Country Peacefull & happy may the God of heaven guide you, I *am no office Hunter*

H F old Line Whig

To Hon Abraham Lincoln
President elect of the United States
Dear Sir

I desire to present to you, through the Hon John Satterlee, a gentleman long identified with the material interests of California, an Union grey shawl, made of California wool and the first manufactured in this State, together with a pair of family blankets of our manufacture, at the Chrysopolis Mills, Mission Dolores San Francisco and beg you to accept the same, not only as a sample of what we can do in this Pacific State, but also in token of our best wishes for yourself & your administration. Respectfully yr obt servt

Donald McClennan
Proprietor

San Francisco
Jan 31st 1861.

Your Excellency.

I hope the interest I feel in your personal safety and in the success of your administration will be a sufficient excuse for my addressing you this unsolicited communication. I have the very highest respect for the integrity and abilities of your master of transportation, Mr. Wood, and did I not feel that *a residence of several years* in the city of Baltimore and four trips up and down the Potomac from its mouth to Washington City had given me some personal knowledge of the citizens and the geography of Maryland that Mr. Wood does not possess, I would not utter one word by way of advice or suggestion. If after reading this communication you and your advisers shall think proper to go *openly* through Baltimore I shall feel fully satisfield that *all* the information in your possession justifies such a course and I will follow you to the last.

From some casual remarks of different members of your suite I have ascertained that the opinion is universally (and I think justly) entertained that the greatest risk your excellency will have to encounter on your way to the national capitol will be in the city of Baltimore and on the road from that point to Washington. I have for many years known Col. George P. Kane, the Chief of the Baltimore police, He was the collector of that port under Presidents Taylor and Fillmore, but in the subsequent dissolution and reconstruction of political parties he turned up a violent democrat. One year ago the legislature of Maryland passed a metropolitan police law for Balt. and Col. Kane was placed at the head of the force. Under his rule the *old* clubs have been generally suppressed, but the equally violent element, to which they were antagonistic, has become almost as obnoxious. I am constrained to state that I have but little confidence in Col. Kane's abilities and less in the integrity of his character. Independent of this there are men in that city who, I candidly believe, would glory in being hanged for having stabbed a "black republican president." In support of this opinion I would respectfully recall your attention to the violent assaults made, in the presence of the whole police force commanded by Marshal Kane *in person,* on the republican procession in that city last summer, I also would cite the murder of one policeman by a rowdy, for attempting to arrest another rowdy for an assault—and the shooting of a second policeman by a couple of assassins while standing at his own fireside for swearing to the identity of the individual who had killed the first policeman.

The Balt. Sun is the vilest secession sheet in the U. S. and nearly all the wealthy and influential citizens are disunionists viz: Thomas Winans, Augustus Albert, Thomas C. Jenkins, William Kennedy, Hon. R. M. McLane, Honl Joshua Vansant, T. Parker Scott, S. Teackle Wallis, Judge Legrand, Judge Presstman etc.

Before arriving at Baltimore you can decide on any one of three courses of conduct each of which can be executed in a variety of ways and I beg to submit my thoughts on the advantages or disadvantages of each separately.

1st You may travel openly and boldly through in the manner you have passed through others; or 2dly You may avoid the city—and 3d. You may pass through incognito and without the knowledge of any one, except such as you choose to confide in.

1st. Going publicly through the city, I have heard it suggested that *regular troops* should be employed as an escort,

To this I would reply that it would take an army of 50.000 men and a weeks preparation. to make a perfectly safe passage through a hostile city as large as Baltimore. Thousands of marksmen could fire from windows and housetops without the slightest danger to themselves. When Gen. Lefebvre Desnouettes attempted to penetrate and seize the city of Saragossa' with an army of 12.000 men he was repulsed and the first Napoleon admonished him that "a city of 80.000 [*men*] inhabitants cannot be taken by the collar." Balt. contains three times 80.000. The emperor himself when he marched upon Madrid instead of seeking to enter that city, planted his batteries so as to command it and a few shells soon brought the inhabitants to terms. Gen. Taylor's assault on Monterey was repulsed and when Gen. Scotts army entered the city of Mexico several of our soldiers were shot from the housetops.

From the foregoing I think it is incontestable that if your excellency visits the city *publicly* you must yield yourself unreservedly to the protection of the local civil and militia authorities

2d. Avoiding the City of Baltimore
This can be done

1st By taking the Cumberland Valley R. Road from Harrisburg Pa to Hagerstown Md and then tapping the Balt & Ohio R.Road in

Virginia a few miles west of Harpers Ferry. This plan would be tedious and the crossing of the Potomac more difficult at this season.

2d By taking a steamer (preferably a war steamer) from Philadelphia to Washington City. The navigation of the Potomac is rather difficult; it is over 100 miles from its mouth to Washington; in many places the scene is narrow and commanded by eminences from which an enemy could seriously annoy if not disable a single ship as the Mississipians have done at Vicksburg. In case you were compelled to land, the inhabitants would be very likely to detain you till after the 4th of March.

3d. Passing through Baltimore incognito
This could be accomplished

1st By leaving Philadelphia privately and unannounced with a very few friends (not more than five) at 10 oclock 50 minutes at night and taking the sleeping car all the way through to Washington, by which means you would avoid the exposure at the crossing of the Susquehanna and the transhipment at Baltimore. You would arrive in Washington at 5 o'clock 48 minutes in the morning. A false mustache, an old slouched hat and a long cloak or overcoat for concealment could be provided, by a friend, while in N. Y. City, No trunks or other articles having marks should be taken. Leaving the hotel at Philada would be the greatest difficulty.

2d. By leaving Harrisburg secretly at 3 o'clock any morning except Sunday, disguised and accompanied as above, getting off the cars at the outer (Bolton) depot at Baltimore and then making your way *on foot* through obscure streets to the Washington cars, approaching them from the South East so as to encounter no crowd and avoid all observation. Two guards should go ahead eight or ten paces and two other persons in rear. You would arrive in Balt at 8.07 A. M. and leave at 8.35 A. M. getting to Washington at 10.20 A. M.

A horse and buggy could be obtained in Balt. that would take you and a companion to Washington in 5 hours.

Respectfully yours. *Capt Hazzard*

No answer is expected

Phil[ia]. *Feb. 2*[nd] *1861*

To the Hon. Abraham Lincoln;
Esteemed Sir,

At the earnest request of our little son Willie, *aged, five, years,* I address you a few lines expressing his warm attachment for you. From the moment of your name being announced for the Presidency, until the present-time, he has been untiring in his efforts in your behalf, evincing a patriotism and zeal, almost unaccountable (for one so young) *Our* preferences were for Mr. Bell, but his eloquent, yet childish pleading has won us over, and we now hail with joy the new administration, feeling assured that your wisdom will be sufficient for the day.

Trusting that your wise counsels may guide and direct this people, and that our kind, Heavenly Father will support and strengthen you, is the sincere wish of your little friend and admirer.

With much regard, I am,
Very Respectfully, *Little Willie Hahn*

No. 2009 Poplar St.
Phil[ia]

Washington, D. C.
Feby. 3. 1861

My Dear Sir:

In my last I wrote you encouragingly in regard to the prospect of a peaceable inauguration, which in my judgment, existed at *that time.* Indeed, I have never participated in the fever of violence here, entertained by many of our most reliable men. In an interview which I had last night with Col. Keyes, the Military Secretary of Genl. Scott, and one of his staff, a man of high character, and of course, an officer of distinguished reputation, I was startled to learn his views in relation to the dangers which threaten the capital. By his position he is particularly charged with finding out everything appertaining to that matter, sifting, weighing, comparing all the testimony in the military department. He is the only man that reads and examines all there is on the subject. Of course Genl. Scott has not the time. He says the evidences in his possession of *a wide spread and powerful conspiracy to seize the capitol are overwhelming, and he has no doubt whatever on the subject.* That the only thing to prevent the attempt will be the presence here of a sufficient force to hold the city against all comers, *which he does not expect will be had.* He says that in addition to the 600 or 700 regulars now here, there should be at least 10.000 volunteers.— *He has the gravest apprehensions that this capitol will be taken.* All the Departments are now filled with traitorous clerks, who would do all in their power to surrender up the building to a hostile force.

As I wrote you so differently from this, I have felt it my duty to give you the opposite views of a distinguished military man in a *position to know all that can be known to anybody.* I will not undertake to say whether he is correct, or not. You can judge for yourself what credit is due to his statement. Col. Keyes is a northern (Massachusetts) man, a true republican, and devoted to his flag and his country.

I have been slow to believe, as you know, but I am satisfied that we must soon begin *to prepare for the worst.* This is of course private.

Truly yours
E. B. Washburne

Hon. A. Lincoln

P. S. If our Legislature does not immediately put our State on a war footing, it will be guilty of criminal neglect. Not a moment is to be lost. I think you ought to advise with some of the members on this subject, and have action taken without delay. The time has come when bold and decicive action must be taken, or all will be lost, as everything is lost in revolutions by timidity and temporising.

EBW

[Endorsement on envelope:] Washburn.
"The Conspiracy to seize the Capitol."

Mr. Lincoln left Springfield, on his circuitous journey to Washington, on the morning of February 11, 1861. Mrs. Lincoln joined him the following day (his birthday) at Indianapolis.

OFFICE OF SUP'T OF CITY SCHOOLS.

Springfield, Ill., Feb. 11th 1861.

Hon. A. Lincoln:

Dear sir,

I cannot repress my desire to say to you, *Good-bye!* I did not call in person, for this purpose, because I know you were pressed enough with company.

When the train bearing you passed my residence this morning, my heart said, God bless Lincoln, & make him second to none but Washington!

Be assured, (I speak what I know)—that thousands of earnest prayers daily ascend to Heaven for you & our beloved country.

Yours with very great respect,

Francis Springer.

Hon. A. Lincoln,
Washington City
D. C.

By kindness of Mrs. Lincoln

STATE OF NEW YORK.

EXECUTIVE DEPARTMENT.

Albany, Feb 14, 1861

My Dear Sir,

The telegraph this morning informs us Mrs Lincoln is with you. Permit Mrs Morgan and myself to tender to Mrs Lincoln, as I have previously to you, the hospitalities of our house, and to urge upon you both the acceptance of this invitation My Carriage will be at the station & convey Mrs Lincoln direct to our house I write in great hast as the train is about leaving

Faithfully & humbly
Yours

E. D. Morgan

His Excellency
A. Lincoln
Buffalo,

Prescott House
New York
Feby 15th 61

To the Honble
Abraham Lincoln
Lady & suite

Permit me to say that I am giving English Opera at Niblos Garden in this City.

Should it be agreable to you to attend during your stay in the Metropolis nothing could afford me greater pleasure or confer on me more compliments than the honour of your presence

With respect I beg to remain

Yours truly
Anna Bishop

Baltimore
15th Feby '61

Dear Sir—

On consultation with some of our leading Republican friends, it has been deemed unadvisable, in the present state of things, to attempt any organized public display on our part, as Republicans, on the occasion of your approach to and passage through Baltimore, on your way to the Capitol, however gratifying it would be to our feelings to do so. But it has been proposed, that, as many of the gallant little band who voted for you in this City, as may choose to do so, shall meet you, as your political friends, in their individual capacity, either at Philadelphia or Harrisburg, according to the route you may take, and accompany you thence to Baltimore, and on to Washington. We further propose to have at the depot, a sufficient number of open barouches with four horses each, for yourself and suite, to convey you and them to [*your*] the Hotel, should you decide to stop in Baltimore, and thence to the Washington depot, or if not, from one depot to the other.

It is possible, that the Mayor and councils may take action, and give you a formal reception, in which case, they will, of course, provide the necessary conveyances and escort, but as yet, we have had no intimations of the kind. The City authorities are all opposed to us, and some of them are even hostile. On the other hand, the Bell, Breckinridge and Douglas organizations, may take some action, either together or separately, to manifest their loyalty to the President Elect, but we have deemed it best not to mix ourselves up as a party, with their movements, but to leave them free to follow their own inclinations. The Bell organization, called the Minute Men, it is suggested, may do something of the sort, but nothing is known positively.

I am authorized by those of our Republican friends, who have consulted on the subject, to communicate their suggestions to you, for your consideration, and if agreable to you, we should be pleased to be informed, at the earliest practicable moment, when you propose to be in Philadelphia or Harrisburg, and from which point, you will approach our City. If you should decide to stop in Baltimore, we are of opinion, that the masses of our community will gladly avail themselves of the opportunity to testify their appreciation of your presence, and to hear from your own lips, one of those felicitous responses to their salutations, which have gone so far to win the popular heart.

I have taken the liberty of handing this note to you through the hands of Governor Morgan, lest it might reach you in time thro' any other channel. Waiting your early reply.

I am Faithfully yr. Friend
W. G. Snethen
190 Hoffman St.
Baltimore

To the President Elect
Albany
NY.

[Endorsed:]
Reception in Balt!

Springfield Ills.
Feb 17th 1861

Hon A Lincoln
Dear Sir.

It will not be necessary for me in speaking of John Hanks to recount His virtues to you. You know His worth His capacity and His Defects If He has any—I only wish to say this to you that If you can find it within your reach to confer some mark of respect upon Him during your administration I know of no Man who will feel it more keenly than John Hanks Himself. Besides it will be felt and appreciated all over the county In which He Lives as a Just recognition of old personal ties. No atribute of human nature is more beautiful when fitly illustrated—Than the acknowledgement of former relations In life when one may be supposed to have forgotten them by reason of advancement to distinction and power In Earthly honors. The difficulty I plainly see will be to overcome the Misfortune Mr Hanks labors under of not knowing how to write—Should you be able to confer upon Him some position where this requirement may be dispensed with—You will have favored an old friend and pleased everybody Else further than this as the personal friend of Mr Hanks I do not ask or desire you to go

Most Respectfully Yours
R. J. Oglesby

I subscribe to the above

Isaac L Pugh

House of Representatives.
Feby. 19. 1861

My Dear Sir:

I last night received your letter from Cleveland O, of the 15th inst.

After consultation with, and the full approbation of, Judge Trumbull and all my republican colleagues in the House, it has been concluded that a furnished house shall be taken for you and your family from the time you arrive here until the 4th of March. All think that would be much better and much pleasanter than going to a hotel. I shall have engaged none but the most reliable and trustworthy servant (colored) for Steward. I shall take a colored man who kept house for my brothers and myself for two years and the most excellent servant I ever knew. The house is well furnished, with a sufficient number of rooms, and is really admirably adapted to the use you want it for. On the first floor, it has a reception room and a dining room—on the second two large parlors and in the rear a fine private room; and in the third story four good sleeping rooms. I suppose you will want no persons besides your family and your private secretary, but if you should, you will know by this how much room there is and how many you can accommodate. I shall provide an excellent man, also knows everybody, to be about the door, so no improper persons can enter. It is presumed the persons accompanying you as a suite will go to Willard's Hotel. I have agreed to pay ten dollars a day for the house while occupied, and the whole expense will be less than one half of what it would cost at a hotel, and those with whom I have talked agree that the arrangement proposed will be far better than going to any hotel, as it will be a great deal more quiet, more *safe*, and will give you a great deal better command of your time. At the hotel, you would be literally run over, but in your own house these things can be much better controlled.

Please have your secretary drop me a line, informing me the number you propose having in your family in order to guide the servants in preparing the first meal, whether it be dinner or supper.

I will be at the depot on your arrival here, and if agreeable will take charge of Mrs. L. and your children and take them right to the house, leaving you in the hands of the politicians and office seekers.

I shall endeavor to make everything as satisfactory to you as possible. With regards to Mrs. Lincoln and hoping soon to greet you here,

I remain,
Very Truly,
Yours etc.
E. B. Washburne

Hon. A. Lincoln.

[Notation:] E. B. Washburne
1861
Arrangements for receiving the Pres.—
on arrival from Illinois

Mr. Seward's son, Frederick H. Seward, carried the intelligence of the Baltimore plot to Mr. Lincoln in Philadelphia. He had received similar reports from Allan Pinkerton. As a consequence he abandoned his scheduled itinerary, and left his suite in Harrisburg, traveling through

Baltimore incognito. He arrived in Washington at six o'clock on the morning of Saturday, February 23, and went directly to Willard's Hotel instead of the private residence which was to have accommodated him until he took the oath of office.

Washington Feb. 21st.

My dear Sir.

My son goes express to you—He will show you a report made by our detective to General Scott—and by him communicated to me this morning. I deem it so important as to dispatch my son to meet you wherever he may find you—I concur with Genl Scott in thinking it best for you to reconsider your arrangements. No one here but Genl Scott, myself & the bearer is aware of this communication

I should have gone with it myself but for the peculiar sensitiveness about my attendance in the Senate at this crisis

Very truly yours
William H Seward

The Honorable
Abraham Lincoln.
etc etc

My dear Sir:

Please receive my friend, Col. Stone, chief of Genl. Weightman's Staff, & a distinguished young officer with me in Mexico. He has an important communication to make.

Yrs. truly
Winfield Scott.
Feb. 21, 1861.

[The envelope is addressed:]
From Lt. Genl. Scott
Hon. W. H. Seward,
Etc, Etc, Etc.
By Colo. Stone,

Feb. 21st/61

A New York detective officer who has been on duty in Baltimore for three weeks past reports this morning [*to Col. Stone*] that there is serious danger of violence to and the assassination of Mr Lincoln in his passage through that city should the time of that passage be known—He states that there are banded rowdies holding secret meetings, and that he has heard threats of mobbing and violence, and has himself heard men declare that if Mr Lincoln was to be assassinated they would like to be the men—He states further that it is only within the past few days that he has considered there was any danger, but now he deems it imminent—He deems the danger one which the authorities & people in Balt—cannot guard against—All risk might be easily avoided by a change in the travelling arrangements which would bring [*the*] Mr Lincoln & a portion of his party through Baltimore by a night train without previous notice—

[*February 22, 1861*]

Dear Sir

I think it my duty to inform you that I was advised last night by a gentleman that there existed in Baltimore, a league of ten persons, who had sworn that you should never pass through that city alive—This may be but one of the thousand threats against you that have emanated from some paltry Southerners, but you should know it that your friends may be watchful while you are in the place as it was asserted positively to be the fact. God defend and bless you—The prayers of many go with you.

A Lady.

Friday Morning
11 ½ A. M.

[Notation on back of letter:]
Baltimore

PRIVATE

Washington

Mr. Lincoln.

You should know, that the supposed intimacy, with Mr. Lamon is doing you great injury among your best friends. His room has been the head Quarters of Cameron's strikers. His position here is very bad in other respects, and the Republican Senators, show around the notes he wrote in your behalf for a Conference, as proof of ignorance and vulgarity, to your prejudice. Can this not be corrected? It will embarass you greatly, if not done.

A Friend

[Endorsed:]
February 25 (?) 1861

CONFIDENTIAL

27 Park Row, N–Y–
February 25/61

Mrs. Abraham Lincoln–
Washington.
D–C–

Dear Madam.

My object in addressing you, is to make known and expose to you, the Machinations of a certain Lady from Brooklyn. N.Y. who has some noteriety in certain circles at Washington. I am informed this morning, that Mrs. Alfred G. Benson. of Brooklyn, has left for Washington, with the avowed purpose, of circumventing if possible, Mr. Simeon Draper, of this City. It is supposed that Mr. Draper, is a Prominent Candidate for the Collector-ship of this Port. One of Mrs. Benson's Sons has had some difficulty with Mr. Draper, which resulted in Mr. Draper, obtaining a Judgement against Young Benson. I am informed that Mr. & Mrs. Benson, now openly declare that Mr. Draper, shall not be appointed collector, if they can prevent it, and Mrs. Benson, has left for Washington, for the professed purpose of Ingratiating Herself into Your confidence, in order to better accomplish her purpose—Mrs. Benson, was admitted to the Confidence of the "White House", during the Administration of President Tyler. and if her statements are to be relied on; Many removals and appointments were made through her influence—She is a Lady, of much Talk. Refinement and Intelligence—

I believe that the motives which actuate the Parties mentioned are dishonorable and Base—and trust they will receive no countenance from Your Ladyship or the President Elect. I well know all the Parties in question, and well know whereof I affirm—Simeon Draper, is one of the most reliable Republicans in our Country—As chairman of the Republican, State Central Committee in this State; No Mans efforts were more wisely exerted and directed than were his—He stood during the late Campaigm, as the counsellor and Adviser of the Wide-awake Organization of this City—and State. And to whom they owe a debt of Gratitude for his wise Counsels and cheerful contribution of funds—As a humble Republican, I cannot consent to have him unjustly assailed and withhold my Protest—

As I am a stranger to you: Although I have the pleasure of being introduced to you at the Delevan House", in Albany. as well as to President Lincoln: I beg leave to refer you, to Hon. James Humphrey, M. C—and Hon. O. S. Ferry, M. C. from Connecticut.

Hoping the President Elect, May be able to bring order out of Confusion and your Residence at Washington, May be as Felicitous to Yourself as it is Gratifying to your numerous friends—I Remain, Dear Madam—

Yours, Verrry Truly
Iverson W. Knapp
Pres. 15th Ward Wide-Awakes—

[Notations, in different hands, on 4th page of letter:]

I. W. Knapp
1861—New York
Mrs. Benson &
Hon. S. Draper

Knapp
warns $Pres^{t}$ of Wm Benson who is trying to circumvent S. Draper.

New York Feb 25th/61

Respected Sir,

I trust you will not think me either presuming or impertinent in addressing you, for I assure you it is not my wish to be either,

First I must introduce myself, my name is Sarah A Robison, I am an orphan, and am 20 years of age, I am at present residing with my Brother, No 79 East 15th St, He voted for you last fall, and the crisis attendant upon your—election has affected his business so much that I do not think I would be doing him justice to look to him for support in such a time.

I saw in today's paper where numerous persons were making application for various appointments, I wonder if I cannot make application for an appointment too, I will not attempt to—bribe you with apples, as I have seen it stated in the Herald that a man did in Wellsville, However as I do not aspire to a *foreign* mission I should like (with the assent of your worthy lady) the appointment of Governess to your Children, which place I would try to give the utmost satisfaction in, I would ask as a particular favor that the contents of this letter may be kept secret from all except your own family as I am aware that in the present state of things the slightest thing in connexion with your name forms a subject for the public press,

Respected Sir I should be exceedingly happy to receive a reply to my note, and if you think it worthy of a reply I should like to have one at your earliest convenience, as I expect to leave this part of the city soon and in that case might not receive it,

Please present my respects to Mrs Lincoln, and accept my best wishes for your mutual happiness and welfare. Very respectfully yours,

Sarah A Robison, No 79, East, 15th St New York.

New York Febry 25, 61. Sarah Robinson applies for the situation of Governess in the W. House.— Sarah Robinson To be Governess

PEOPLES' EXPRESS,
FOR THE COLLECTION OF NOTES, DRAFTS, BILLS, ETC. PACKAGES AND BAGGAGE FORWARDED TO ALL PARTS OF THE WORLD

J. B. Wass, Proprietor,
63 Broadway, New-York.
307 Pacific Street, Brooklyn.
New York February 25th/61

Hon Abraham Lincoln
President elect of the United States
Dear Sir.

This is to tender you the Services of *One hundred able bodied Men.* No one of them will weigh less than One hundred & fifty pounds. and the Shortest Man. Stands five feet Six inches) Who will be ready on three hours notice, to proceed to Washington or any other point in the United States to defend your person. and the laws of the Country, As a guarentee of my responsibility I will refer you to Hon James Humphrey, Member of Congress from the second district of New York. And I assure you every man of our Club may be relyed on.

I have the honour to be your most Obedient Servant

Jerome B. Wass
63 Broadway
N. Y.

Mr. Abraham Lincoln

[in pencil and a different hand:] Feb 27 1861)

Excellence!

I beg pardon to your Excellence! if I take the liberty to address to you without any introdution: but I hope, that your Noble heart will excuse me.

I have wrot to your Excellence! during your permanency in New, York. Having not received answer! I hav take the determination to write to your Excellence! again. I am Italian married Lady—, with two american Sons. My Father was many years, in the Service of his Majesty George IV King of England. As a "Corriere di Gabinetto" and was Secretary of her Highness Caroline of Brunswick, wife to George IV. In my youth, I was very found of of music. I left my Country, (Milan) in the years (1835) at the age of 15 years, engaged for Mexico, as a "*Prima Donna*" in the Italian Opera troup in that Capital. I have bean in Havana, New.Orleans, and in all the United States. I have many acquaitance in New.York: but, only one, good friend! this is Romaine Dillon Esq.[n] God! father of my younger Son "*Cesare*" this good friend, hold a high position at Ryo Janeiro, Brazil, by the Governement of Washington. In New.Orleans, we have lost all our money in Commertial speculations. With the remaining money, of our last engagement in Mexico, we purchase a Country Residence in Hougtonville, two miles south of Rahway New Jersey, were we reside. Adverces circumstances have trust us in a critical position. Nothing remain to us, but only our Country place, which is in Mortgag for ($1,200). Having no means to take up the Mortgag, and no means, to live in this Country, and not probability, to any Opera engagement: some time go, we advertised in the New.York Times, and Herald, our Country place, for Sale

> For Sale—A Very Handsome Villa in the township of Woodbridge, New-Jersey, two miles south of the City of Rahway, and five minutes' walk from Hougtonville dépôt of the New-Jersey Railroad, and one hour's ride from New-York. The house is new, well arranged, and handsomely built, surrounded with ornamental and all kinds of fruit trees, including 200 Isabella grape vines from Italy—stocked with all kinds of flowers. The villa is situated in the most delightful part of the State on high and healthy land. A new stable, carriage house and out buildings, and about three acres of land all in garden style. Price $6000. Apply to A. Vattellina, on the premises. Letters for Rahway, N. J.

with the intention to take up the Mortgag, and with the remaining money, go to Italy. But, alas! . . we have not succeded. In my despair, make me lay a Petition to the Prince of Wales, hoping he would help me, in name of my Father "Theodoro Majocchi".

The Honorable Daniel E. Sickles, in Washington, he give my petition to the English Ambassador, Lord Lyon. I have received answar from his Grace the Duck of Newcastle, that I have sended to your Excellence! in New York.

I have wrot to the President Mr James Buchanan, upon the same petition. The answer from Mr Buchanan, I deed sended to you, in New.York.

If our good friend Romaine Dillon Esqr could know our present circumstances, we ar sure, he would help us. His Brother Robert james Dillon Esqr in New.York, told me that his brother Romaine intention, was to come bak from the Brazil soon. With this hope we have weated for is coming! but in reeding the New.York Times, I see that Romaine Dillon was to remain in Brazil for long time yet. Now, is to late to address him, because, next month of March, the Mortgag will be foreclos, and our Proprety, will be sacrified for the amount of one thousand and two hundred dollars. ($1,200) and of corts, myself and my childrens, on the Street! without hope to retourn to our Country.

The orrible future of our situation, fright me. I have tryd to find some persons in Rahway, to hold the Mortgag: but hunnaply, in the hard time, is impraticable. The thought com to me, to lay our circonnstances, to your Excellence! I heard spik very favourably of your magnanimity and humanity. Your Excellence! is blessed with Childrens! in name of *God!* and in name of your dear Childrens, I implore your protetion: Save me and my Childrens. Do Sir! take up the Mortgag, and hold yourself our Property, until is sold, for a resonable price. After, I will advertise immediately our Residence for Sale again. My lawyer, is Mr Thomas H Shafer of Rahway New.Jersey. I confess my temerity, but our situation is orrible and frightful, that make me daring, hoping in your Noble heart, a favorable answer.

God! bless you and your family. I will pray *God!* for your prosperity and happines.

I have the Honor to be, Excellence! Your Loyal, Humbly and Respectfully Servant

Amalia Majocchi Valtellina

Rahway New.Jersey
February 27(1861

[Notation on 4th page of letter:] Madame Vattelina asks the President to take up a mortgage on her villa, near Rahway, New Jersey

---

From Mr. Lincoln's Message to Congress in Extraordinary Session, July 4, 1861:

> On the 5th of March (the present incumbent's first full day in office), a letter of Major Anderson, commanding at Fort Sumter, written on the 28th of February and received at the War Department on the 4th of March, was by that Department placed in his hands. This letter expressed the professional opinion of the writer that reinforcements could not be thrown into that fort within the time for his relief, rendered necessary by the limited supply of provisions, and with a view of holding possession of the same, with a force of less than twenty thousand good and well-disciplined men. This opinion was concurred in by all the officers of his command, and their memoranda on the subject were made inclosures of Major Anderson's letter. The whole was immediately laid before Lieutenant-General Scott, who at once concurred with Major Anderson in opinion.

Nº 58.

Fort Sumter, S.C.
Feby 28th, 1861.

Colonel S. Cooper,
Adjutant Genl U. S. Army:
Colonel:

I have the honor to report that they are continuing the work reported in my communication Nº 57 I send, herewith, Memoranda, hastily prepared, by the officers of this command, giving their individual opinions as to the number of men which would be required to re-enforce us. The problem is one of considerable difficulty—as the Southern Confederacy have the advantage of knowing the intentions even, of our Government, and are thus enabled to make suitable preparations—These gentlemen were directed to consider the harbour closed—it is fair to consider that all of the channels would be closed as soon as information is received of the intentions of the Government.

I confess that I would not be willing to risk my reputation on an attempt to throw reenforcements into this harbour, within the time for our relief rendered necessary by the limited supply of our provisions, and with a view of holding possession of the same, with a force of less than seventy thousand good and well disciplined men.

Enclosed is also a sketch of the present appearance of the works on Cummings Point, prepared by Capt Seymour.

I am Colonel,
Very Respectfully,
Your obd^{t} Sv^{t}.
Robert Anderson
Major 1st Artillery.
Commanding.

[Endorsed:]
90 A 1861

Fort Sumter, So. Ca.
Feb. 28, 1861
Robt. Anderson
Major 1st Arty.

Forwarding estimates of number of troops required to reinforce Fort Sumter.

(No. 58)
(10 Enclosures)
Rec^{d} A. G. O. March 4, 1861.

The following message from the German free workingmen of Cincinnati may have been presented to Mr. Lincoln during his stop in that city, February 12–13, 1861.

[*Feb. 1861*]

To Abraham Lincoln,
President elect of the United States.
Sir,—

We, the German free workingmen of Cincinnati avail ourselves of this opportunity to assure you, our chosen chief magistrate, of our sincere and heartfelt regard. You earned our votes as the Champion of free labor and free homesteads. Our vanquished opponents have, in recent times, made frequent use of the terms "Workingmen" and "workingmen's meetings" in order to create an impression, as if the mass of workingmen were in favor of Compromises between the interests of free labor and slave labor, by which the victory just won would be turned into a defeat. This is a despicable device of of dishonest men. We spurn such Compromises. We firmly adhere to the principles, which directed our votes in your favor, We trust, that you, the selfreliant because selfmade man, will uphold the Constitution and the laws against secret treachery and avowed treason. If to this end you should be in need of men, the German free working men, with others, will rise as one man at your Call, ready to risk their lives in the effort to maintain the victory already won by freedom over Slavery.

Fort Sumter S:C
March 2nd 1861

Colonel

I have the honor to acknowledge the receipt of the letter of the Honble. Secty. of War dated February 23rd postmarked 26h.

The work at Cummings Point was prosecuted, yesterday, with a good deal of energy, on the embrasures of the new work this side of the bomb proof battery: Some heavy guns, landed recently, were moved, yesterday, and taken along the beach, passing out of our sight, around the bend of the island leading in the direction of the Light house. The earth has been banked up in front of the covered way, about half way between the bomb proof battery & the three gun battery, presenting the appearance of an intention to form a new battery there. Small parties were, also, engaged at the battery just at the eastward of the three gun battery on Morris island, & also on the Fort Johnson mortar battery. They are also making another battery at Fort Johnson, between the mortar & the gun battery. To-morrow, I will probably, send you a sketch, showing the present appearance of the works on Cummings point.

I am now engaged placing some heavy guns 42 & 32 pan on the parapet, so as to command the space in front of the gorge, where an attempt may be made to plant the iron clad raft. I will endeavor to raise one of the 10 Columbiads in position on the parapet, so as to get one discharge, having the other filled with lead—thus giving as great momentum as possible. Should the Columbiad burst, as I think it will, the effect produced on the raft will well repay for its loss.

I am Co:
Respectfully
Your obt servt
Robert Anderson
Major 1st ArtY
Comdg

P. S. I enclose, herewith, a mem. showing the supply of commissary stores on hand, and the number of days they will last, using the fall ration—as the fishing season will soon open here, we may make the meat ration do for a longer period than the one named

RA

[Endorsed:]
A 92. 1861.
Ft. Sumter, So. Ca.

March 2, 1861.
R. Anderson
Major 1st Artillery

Ackn. receipt of letter of the Sec. of the 23d ultimo; reports progress of work on Cummings Point, etc—and encloses list of Subistence stores on hand, which will subist the whole command 28, days.
One enclosure.
Recd A. G. O. March 6, 1861.

Sparta Tennessee March 3d 1861

Gov— Johnson sir:

I avail myself of the present opportunity of addressing you with a few lines. You would confer a great favor on me by handing Mr Lincoln this letter. And tell him that my father and mother are acquaintance of yours and Mother is a daughter Mordecai Lincoln who you were well acquainted with; and I think from the acquaintance you have with our family that you could recommend me to Mr Lincoln. I am as well qualified to fulfill a clerkship as any person in Tennessee; and as Mr Lincoln has offices to give to the people that he would confer a great favor on me to give me an office. I have writting 2 letters to Mr Lincoln and think the reason that I never have received an answer that he receives so many that he has not any time to read all letters that is sent him I can bring good recommendation from any person in the neighborhood where I live he would want if he so required it. I am a son of Milton Gross who formerly lived in Greenville and Clara Gross Yours truly

Jesse Lincoln Gross

P. S.

Dear relation I am a going to ask a favor that I never have ask the public. I have three sons that I have educated and spent most of my means in so doing. I am a widow and have no means to put my sons in to business with, and no relations to assist me in Tennessee And you would confer a great favor on me if you would put than in to business Your niece

Clara P Gross

Engraving after photograph by Wood reproduced from the *Illustrated Times*, London, 1861

The unfinished dome of the Capitol of the United States as it appeared in 1861. Contemporary drawing by Waud reproduced from the original in the Library of Congress

NO 61

Fort Sumter, S C.
March 3. 1861

Col. S. Cooper
Adj^t Genl USA
Col.

I have the honor to report that they continued the work, mentioned in No 60, through the day, and are, to day, (Sunday), prosecuting their work at the battery at the end of Cummings Point & at the mortar battery at Ft. Johnson.

The atmosphere is so hazy, that Cap. Seymour cannot make the sketch, I designed forwarding to day—

I received yesterday a private note from His Excellency Govr Pickens exhibiting sentiments of the highest sentiments and the most kindly feeling

I am Colonel,
Very respectfully,
yr obt ser^t
Robert Anderson
Major 1st Arty
Comdg

[Endorsed:]
A 93. *1861*

Fort Sumter, So, Ca, March 3 1861,

R. Anderson Major 1st Artillery

Reports they continued the work mentioned in No. 60. through the day and to day (Sunday) are at work at the end of Cummings point, and at the mortar battery at Fort Johnson.—
Rec^d A. G. O. March 6, 1861.

Washington March 3. 1861.

Dear Sir.

Hoping that, in a day or two, the new President will have, happily, passed through all personal dangers, & find himself installed an honored successor of the great Washington—with you as chief of his cabinet—I beg leave to repeat, in writing, what I have before said to you, orally, *this* supplement to my printed "Views," (dated October last) on the highly disordered condition of our (so late) happy & glorious union. To meet the extraordinary exigencies of the times, it seems to me that I am guilty of no arrogance in limiting the President's field of selection to one of the four plans of procedure, subjoined:—

I. Throw off the *old,* & assume a *new* designation—the *Union party;*—adopt the conciliatory measures proposed by Mr. Crittenden, or the Peace convention, & my life upon it, we shall have no new case of secession, but, on the contrary, an early return of many, if not all the states which have already broken off from the Union. Without some equally benign measure, the remaining slave holding states will, probably, join the Montgomery confederacy in less than sixty days, when this city—being included in a foreign country—would require permanent Garrison of at least 35,000 troops to protect the Government within it.

II. Collect the duties on foreign goods outside the ports of which this Government has lost the command, or close such ports by acts of congress, & blockade them.

III. Conquer the seceded States by invading armies. No doubt this might be done in two or three years by a young and able General—a Wolfe, a Desaix or a Hoche, with 300,000 disciplined men—estimating a third for Garrisons, & the loss of a yet greater number by skirmishes, sieges, battles & southern fevers. The destruction of life and property, on the other side, would be frightful—however perfect the moral discipline of the invaders.

The conquest completed at that enormous waste of human life, to the north and north west—with at least $250—000,000, added thereto, and *cui bono?*—Fifteen devastated *provinces*—not to be brought into harmony with their conquerors; but to be held, for generations, by heavy garrisons—at an expense quadruple the net duties or taxes which it would be possible to extract from them—followed by a Protector or an Emperor.

IV. Say to the seceded [*sisters*]—States—*wayward sisters, depart in peace!*

In haste, I remain,
Very truly yours
Winfield Scott.

Hon. Wm H. Seward
etc etc etc

On Monday, March 4, 1861, Abraham Lincoln was inaugurated as sixteenth President of the United States, and responsibility for the restoration of the Union became inescapably his, but that high duty was easily forgotten by those to whom a change in administration was principally important because of opportunities for place and preferment.

Washington,
March 4th 1861.

PRIVATE & CONFIDENTIAL

Dear Sir: I beg that you, yourself, will give this note your candid consideration. The office of Brigadier General has become vacant by the treason of Gen. Twiggs. Col. Sumner is an applicant for the post. I too having been educated at West Point, and having served faithfully for thirty three years, presume to apply to you for this vacancy. I am as old if not a better soldier than Col. Sumner. We were both appointed Captains on the same day, the 4th of March 1833. just twenty eight years ago to day. He has been advanced by subserviency to Democratic rulers, while I have been kept down. He was a Douglass democrat, up to the day of your election, while I was persecuted on account of my love of Freedom and the Whig and Republican parties.

Two of my juniors have been advanced over me, to the situations of Generals, merely because they were good Democrats, and I am now anxious, even if I should fail, that a good Republican should be appointed. Col. Sumner is a good soldier, but the Democracy have had enough of Army favors, and if we look into the treachery of some of our Army leaders, you will say more than enough.

I am anxious to command in this City, under Gen. Scott, to preserve it, if possible, from being desecrated by traitors,

I have the honor to be,
Very Respectfully,
Your mo. ob. serv.
David Hunter
U. S. Army.

To His Excellency,
A. Lincoln,
President of the United States.

[On envelope:] David Hunter Mch 4, 61 (in pencil) asking promotion

Arabkir, Turkey, March 4th, 1861.

Mr. Abraham Lincoln,
President of the United States of America,
Dear Sir.

On this day, so distinguished in the history of the United States, our thoughts revert frequently to our beloved native land and we endeavor to picture to ourselves the scenes, which are there being enacted and especially in the city of Washington. As thousands of our native country men will have the privilege of seeing you and congratulating you upon the honor of being elected to the office of chief magistrate of a mighty nation, we should be most happy to avail ourselves of the same privelge, did circumstances permit; were it not, that we are separated by many thousands of miles by land or by sea from our native shores. But—such being the case, we trust we may be permitted the privilege of doing with pen & ink, what we should be so happy to do by word of mouth, And we hope, that we may not be considered as intruding upon your precious time by this brief note of congratulation. And allow us to express here the pleasure, which we felt upon being informed of your election. Though not permitted ourselves to cast any vote, we shared in the joy of those hundreds of thousands of freemen, who so nobly and so successfully fought in the cause of righteousness and freedom. —And we at this station (Arabkir) have no reason to regret the result of the election, especially, as My associate here, Rev. Sanfred Richardson is from *Illinois* (Peoria), and myself from Maine—(Hallowell). You may perhaps not be uninterested to be informed, that this place "*Arabkir*" is situated near the heart of *Asia Minor,* about 300 miles South of Samsoun on the *Black Sea.* It is about five years since we came here to reside with our two families, ourselves being direct from America; & Mr. R.s family from Erzroom, where they had resided several years, being there at the time of the late Russian war. From having lived so long in this land and learned something of its manners & customs, form of government etc, we are enable the better to appreciate the blessings, which are enjoyed by the people of [*the*] our beloved native land; the blessings of civil & religious freedom, of education and civilization, and especially of the Christian religion. And by as much as we feel attached to our native country, by so much are we saddened to hear of the difficulties, which have recently arisen in the Southern States, & especially in South Carolina to disturb the harmony and peace of the whole country. But our trust is in Almighty God, that he may bring good out of this apparently stupendous evil, and cause all these things to work together for the advancement of the cause of truth, righteousness & freedom, and especially we pray, that He may grant unto you & others associated with you in the government, strength & wisdom, equal to your day in these trying times.

Very truly and respectfully yours

Geo. A. Pollard

Missionary of the American Board of Commissioners for Foreign Missions.

[Endorsed:]
H. D. Faulkner 1861 New York Political

16 Wall St. New York
March 5th 1861

His Excellency
Abraham Lincoln
My Dear Sir,

I read your Inaugural approving every arguement it contains, and my heart responded "Amen" to every patriotic sentiment therein expressed– I took it home and read it to my wife, and she seemed delighted with it– This morning I called on a Breckinridge Democrat and put the question "How do you like the Inaugural?" "First rate, It is short and full of pith, was the reply"–

I then called on a "Silver Gray" friend and asked him. "How do you like the Inaugural"? "Splendid It could not be bettered" he answered

I then steped into the office of a staunch Douglass man and inquired "How do you like the Inaugural?" "All right & if Mr Lincoln will stand firm to his position I am with him heart and hand" was his answer–

It being about lunch time I droped into the restaurant of the black man across the street and says. "Well Mr Ray how do you like the Inaugural "I think he has hit the nail on the head, our folks will all stand by him" said he–

Lastly I called on a stock broker and asked the same question, and added "how does the Inaugural effect the stock market" "We are afraid there is too much fight in it, the market is feverish" was his answer–

From these indications I think the honest portion of the American people are with you and will hold themselves subject to your direction whether it be storm or sunshine that may follow

I am very Respectfully
Your Obedient & Humble Servant,
H. D. Faulkner

Washington March 4th 1861

My dear Sir,

The high respect I entertain for General Scott induces me to ask your perusal of the enclosed letter which I have received from him.

Very respectfully
Your friend & obedient servant
William H. Seward.

The Honorable
Abraham Lincoln
President Elect

War Department,
March 5th., 1861.

Sir:

I have the honor to submit for your consideration several letters, with inclosures, received on yesterday, from Major Anderson of the Artillery, and Captain Foster of the Corps of Engineers which are of a most important and unexpected character. Why they were unexpected, will appear from the following brief statement.

After transferring his force to Fort Sumter, he addressed a letter to this Department, under date of the 31st. of December, 1860, in which he says "Thank God, we are now where the Government may send us additional troops at *its liesure*. To be sure, the uncivil and uncourteous action of the Governor in preventing us from purchasing anything in the City will annoy and inconvenience us somewhat, *still we are safe*". And, after referring to some deficiency in his stores in the articles of soap and candles, he adds, "still we can cheerfully put up with the inconvenience of doing without them for the satisfaction we feel in the knowledge that we can command this Harbor as long *as our government wishes to keep it.*" And again, on the 6th. of January, he wrote "My position will, should there be no treachery among the workmen whom we are compelled to retain for the present, enable me to hold this post against any force which can be brought against me, and it would enable me in the event of a war, to annoy the South Carolinians by preventing the from throwing in supplies into their new posts except by the aid of the wash channel through stone river."

Before the receipt of this communication, the government, being without information as to his condition, had despatched the Star of the West, with troops and supplies for Fort Sumter, but the vessel, having been fired on from a battery at the entrance to the Harbor, returned without having reached her destination. On the 16th. of January, 1861, in replying to Major Anderson's letter of the 31st. of December, and of the 6th. of January, I said "Your late despatches, as well as the very intelligent statements of Lieutenant Talbot, have relieved the Government of the apprehensions previously entertained for your safety. In consequence, it is not its purpose, at present, to reenforce you. The attempt to do so would no doubt be attended by a collision of arms, and the effusion of blood—a national calamity which the President is most anxious to avoid. You will therefore report frequently your condition, and the character and activity of the preparations, if any, which may be being made for an attack upon the Fort, or for obstructing the government in any endeavors it may make to strengthen your command. Should your despatches be of a nature too important to be entrusted to the mails, you will convey them by special messengers. Whenever, in your judgement, additional supplies or reinforcements are necessary for your safety, or for a successful defence of the Fort, you will at once communicate the fact to this Department, and a prompt and vigorous effort will be made to forward them."

Since the date of this letter, Major Anderson has regularly and frequently reported the progress of the batteries being constructed around him, and which looked either to the defence of the Harbor, or to an attack upon his own position, but he has not suggested that their works compromised his safety, nor has he made any request that additional supplies or reinforcements should be sent to him. On the contrary, on the 30th. of January, 1861, in a letter to this Department he uses this emphatic language: "I do hope that no attempt will be made by our friends to throw supplies in—their doing so would do more harm than good." On the 5th. February, when referring to the batteries etc. constructed in his vicinity, he said "even in their present condition they will make it impossible for any hostile force, other than a large and well appointed one, to enter this Harbor and the chances are that it will then be at a great sacrifice of life:" And, in a postscript, he adds "Of course, in speaking of forcing an entrance, I do not refer to the little strategem of a small party shipping in." This suggestion of the "strategem" was well considered in connection with all the information that could be obtained bearing upon it and in consequence of the vigilance and number of the guard boats in and outside of the Harbor, it was rejected as impracticable.

In view of these very distinct declarations, and of the earnest desire to avoid a collision as long as possible, it was deemed entirely safe to adhere to the line of policy indicated in my letter of the 16th. of January, which has been already quoted. In that, Major Anderson had been requested to report "at once" whenever, "in his judgement additional supplies or reënforcements were necessary for his safety or for a successful defence of the Fort." So long, therefore, as he remained silent upon this point, the government felt that there was no ground for apprehension. Still, as the necessity of action might arise at any moment, an expedition has been quietly prepared, and is ready to sail from New York on a few hours notice, for transporting troops and supplies to Fort Sumter. This step was taken under the supervision of General Scott, who arranged its details, and who regarded the reinforcements thus provided for as sufficient for the occasion. The expedition, however, is not upon a scale approaching the seemingly extravagant estimates of Major Anderson and Captain Foster, now offered for the first time, and for the disclosures of which the government was wholly unprepared.

The declaration now made by the Major that he would not be willing to risk his reputation on an attempt to throw reinforcements into Charleston Harbor and with a view of holding possession of the same, with a force of less than twenty thousand good and well disciplined men, takes the Department by surprise as his previous correspondence contains no such intimation.

I have the honor to be, Very Respectfully, Your Obt. Servant,

J. Holt

To The President.

[Endorsed:]
Mr. Secretary Holt To the President. March 5, 1861.
With a letter of Major Anderson to the former, inclosing papers from No. 1 to No. 10

Remarks Of Lieut. Genl. Scott on the within.—

When Major Anderson first threw himself into Fort Sumter it would have been easy to reinforce him. Fort Moultrie has since been re-armed & greatly strenthened, & many powerful new land batteries (besides rafts) have been constructed;—hulks sunk in the principal channel, etc etc. The difficulty of reinforcing has now been increased 10 or 15 fold. First the President would allow no attempt to be made, because he was holding negociations with the So. Carolina commissioners; then we (Secretary Holt & myself) [*we*] could not [*obtain from*] prevail upon him & the Secretary of the Navy, to let us have a ship of War, which forced us to employ the *Star of the West,* [*but*] & she, but for the imbecility of her commander, might have landed men & subsistence. Before the Cabinet, I next submitted (orally) either [*that*] succor [*must*] be sent [*given*] by means of ships of war, fighting their way to the fort, or 2. that the Major should ameliorate his condition by the muzzles of his guns—that is, enforcing supplies by bombardment; bringing to merchant vessels & helping himself (giving orders for payment) etc etc or surrender. But before any resolution was taken—Mr. Secretary Toucey, making difficulculties about his vessels—another commissioner arrived, from So. Carolina, causing a farther delay. Next, after considering many plans of relief, the President, two Secretaries, Capt. Ward & myself settled upon the employment, under the captain (who was eager for the expedition—) of the four, or more, small steamers, belonging to the *Coast Survey.*—Three, or four weeks ago I have no doubt the captain would have succeeded; but he was kept back by some thing like a truce established between the President & a number of principal seceders—here, in S° Carolina, Florida etc—which truce or informal understanding, included Ft Pickens. [Hence a company, intended for the latter, is still in the sloop of war, the Brooklyn, lying off the fort, at Sea, with orders not to land till an attack shall be made by the Secessionists.]

Whether Capt. Ward, notwithstanding the great increase of Carolina batteries & the opinions of Major Anderson, Capt. Foster etc, would *still* be willing, or deem himself able to [*attempt the*] succor [*of*] Fort Sumter (even for a few weeks) I cannot say; [He ought to be called for:) but it is evident that the officers of the fort have changed their opinions, with the great change of circumstances, & now see no alternative but a surrender, in some weeks, more or less, as they well know that we cannot send the tthird of the men (regulars) in several months, [*weeks*] months, necessary to give them relief beyond a few weeks, if for a day. Evacuation seems almost inevitable, & in this view, our distinguished Chief Engineer (Brigadier Totten) concurs—if, indeed, the worn out garrison be not assaulted & carried in the present week.

Respectfully submitted to the President, thro' the Secretary of State.

Winfield Scott
March 5, 1861.

Note. The foregoing remarks are written in the night far from my papers.

W. S.

STATE OF NEW YORK
EXECUTIVE DEPARTMENT.

Albany, March 5. 1861

His Excellency
Abraham Lincoln
My Dear President

I cannot let one day pass without expressing to you the satisfaction I have felt in reading and in considering the Inaugural address,

None can say, truthfully, they do not understand its meaning. Kind in spirit. firm in purpose, national in the highest degree, the points are all well made, and the call is fairly stated and most honorably met. It cannot fail to command the confidence of the North, and the respect of the South.
I write in haste, but desired to say thus much to day. In common with numerous friends, I have been trying for several years to bring this Government back to the principles of the Fathers. I now believe the last effort is a success.

Faithfully yours
E. D. Morgan

Washington, Mar. 6, 1861

My dear Sir,

I accept the post which you have tendered me.

My distrust of my own judgment in this decision, and of my ability to perform adequately the duties about to devolve on me, is very great; but trusting to your indulgence and humbly invoking Divine favor and guidance, I will give my best endeavor to your service and our country's.

With the highest respect,
Yours most truly
S: P: Chase

President Lincoln.

[Notation on envelope:] S P Chase
Accepting appt as Secretary of the Treasury

Henry Winter Davis, who wrote the following letter, was formerly a prominent member of the House of Representatives and a cousin of David Davis.

To The President of the United States
Sir

Though not entitled to intrude on you any suggestion touching your appointments, I beg to be allowed to express to you the interest I feel in the filling of the vacancy on the Supreme Court Bench: & I venture to press on you the peculiar fitness both in experience, learning, judicial habits & judicial cast of mind, of the Hon David Davis. I know that you are better acquainted with his capacity than even I am. The vacancy must not be filled by a gentleman from a Slave State: for the *Court* distribute the Districts among themselves: & Judge Daniel though resident in Virginia held his court in the extreme South. The slave states have now their full share on that Court: that consideration is therefore out of the way: & Judge Davis is himself at any rate a Marylander by birth & a large landholder in that State. He is in the full maturity of his age & capacity & would give promise of a long term so essential to the stability of the administration of justice.

No appointment would better grace your administration

Very resply
yr obt. Servt
H. Winter Davis
6 March 1861.

[Endorsed:]
H Winter Davis Recs David Davis for Judge of the Supreme Court.

Samuel Cooper, to whom the following letter was addressed, went to Montgomery, Alabama, on March 7, 1861, to offer his services to the Confederacy. He was made adjutant and inspector general of the Confederate Army and was its senior officer throughout the war.

NO. 65

Fort Sumter S. C. March 7th 1861.

To
Colonel S. Cooper
Adjt. General U. S. A.
Colonel.

I have the honor to report that the South Carolinaians continue working at the points noted in yesterday's communication—I am gratified at being enabled to report that we succeeded, yesterday, in raising one of the 10in Columbiads to the parapet—I hope to place it in position, without their knowledge. An unexpected fire from so heavy a piece of ordnance will, in all probability, produce excellent results.

I still trust in God that I may not have to use any of the preparations I am making here.

Two of our men, recently discharged from one of our companies, left this post yesterday, for New York *via* Charleston.

The Officers and men continue, thank God, well and in good spirits.

I am Colonel very respectfully
Your Obedt Servt.
Robert Anderson,
Major 1st Artillery,
Commanding

[Endorsed:]
105A 1861
Ft. Sumter, So, Ca, March 7. 1861.
R. Anderson Major 1st Artillery
Reports the So. Carolinians continue working at the points noted in yesterday's communication. Has succeeded in raising one of the 10in Columbiads to the parapet; two discharged men have left this post: command in good spirits.

Rec.d (A. G O) March 11. 1861.

New Haven, Conn.
March 7. 1861

Mrs. Lincoln
Dear Madam

It is with much sorrow that I have noticed the name of R. C. S——, as being occasionally in the society of yourself & family, & apparently intimate with the President.

Mr. S—— is a corruptor & destroyer of domestic virtue. I speak from bitter experience, when I tell you that a dear sister-in-law has been ruined by him, & the peace of her family forever destroyed. Two other families, I am assured on the best authority, have been similarly ruined by him. I have no doubt others have also suffered.

It would give great pain to many persons of the highest respectability, to hear that Mr. S. had been appointed to any office by the President,—not merely because of a moral unfitness, (for a man who has broken down this greatest barrier of virtue, can be restrained by no moral forces) but because it would afford a vile man facilities for his demoralizing practices, which he does not now possess.

Sincerely do I beg your pardon for this intrusion. I feel constrained to withhold my real name—but from no unworthy motive,—but may say that I am a clergyman, & could refer you to mutual acquaintances in Illinois

Thousands of prayers, dear Madam, are poured into the ear of God for you & your honored husband.—that in all the high duties to which he is called, he may have wisdom from on high to guide him.

May he be surrounded by good counsellors, & fill the offices of the land with good men,—is the prayer of yours very sincerely

P.P. Johns

Fort Sumter S.C.
March 8th 1861.

To
Col. S. Cooper
Adjt. Gen'l USArmy

I have the honor to report that parties are still at work at the points, alluded to, in yesterday's letter. Last night, the numbers of guard boats was doubled four were out all night. This morning, a shot was fired in the direction of this work. The accompanying letters will explain the matter. As my flag was about leaving to bear my letter to the commanding officer of Morris' Island Maj. Stevens, Commanding the battery, from which the shot was fired, arrived, and gave me the fullest explanation, and the most satisfactory assurance that the shot was accidental. He thanked me for my forbearance, etc.

The letter to His excellency, the Governor, I thought proper to write, in justice to Maj. Stevens.

Lieut. Snyder, to whose energy and skill, I am greatly indebted for getting up the 10^{in} Columbiad, will try to raise another—they will be a very valuable acquisition to my parapet battery.

I am, Colonel, with the highest regard
Your obed't Servant
Robert Anderson
Major 1st Artillery
Commanding,

[Endorsed:]
106A *1861*
Ft. Sumter, So, Ca. March 8th 1861.
R. Anderson Major 1st Artillery

Parties continue working at the points alluded to in yesterdays letter; the number of guard boats have been doubled; also, that a shot was fired, this norning, in the direction of this work; encloses copy of correspondence with reference thereto, etc,

(2 enclosures)
Rec^{d} (A G O) March 11. 1861.

COPY.

Fort Sumter, S. C.
10½ A. M. Fri: Mar: 8. 1861.

To
Officer Commanding
Morris' Island,
Sir:

At ½ past 8 o'clock, this morning, a shot, fired from one of your batteries, struck very near this work.

Two hours have passed, without the arrival of a messenger from you, with an explanation, or an apology, for what, I have considered an accident. I now, have the honor to send this note, respectfully desiring information from you in reference to this matter.

I would also urge upon you the propriety of issuing such instructions, as will, certainly, prevent the repetition of a similar occurrence.

I have the honor to remain,

Respectfully,
Your Obdt. Serv.t
Robert Anderson
Major. U.S.Army
Comd.g

N The original was taken to Col. Gregg Comdg. Morris' Island by Major Stevens, to show Col. G— the view I had taken of the matter alluded to *RA*

COPY

Fort Sumter, S. C.
March 8th. 1861.

His Excellency,
F. W. Pickens,
Governor S.C.
Sir:

Fearing that you may infer, from the report received in reference to the shot fired, this morning, from the now plated battery, at Cummings' Point, towards my Fort, that blame is attachable to the Officer in command of that battery, I hasten to state that Major Stevens has just called, and I am glad to be enabled to say that his explanation was entirely and perfectly satisfactory.

It was an accident which, I am satisfied, will not be permitted to happen again.

I have the honor to remain

With high regard,
Your Obd.t Serv.t
Robert Anderson
Major USA
Comdg

RECEIVED MARCH 11TH 1861

Fort Sumter S.C.
March 8th. 1861

Genl Jos. G. Totten
Chief Engineers, U. S. A.
Washington D. C.
General:

The general activity in the surrounding batteries still continues. The practice with their heavy guns continues daily and they appear to have attained to a pretty accurate estimate of ranges.

This morning early five guns were fired in practice from Fort Moultrie. Soom after, about 8 oclock, three guns were fired in practice from the iron plated battery on Cummings Pt. The two first appeared to be blank shots, but the third containing a shell or ball, struck the face of the wall of the Esplanade of this fort, about 2′ below the edge, penetrating to the depth of 10″. It was in direct line for the main Gate. The shot or shell fell out into the water, but will be sought for at low water to ascertain the calibre.

The shot was probably put in the gun by some mischievous persons, but the facts of the case will undoubtedly soon be brought to light.

We yesterday finished mounting our ten inch columbiad on the right gorge angle, to bear on Cummings Pt. & Ft Moultrie,—also the flats opposite the gorge.

We shall try to get up another on the left gorge angle. Two more 42 pounds have been mounted en barbette,—one of them at the left gorge angle, to be ready for the "Raft" when it comes down.

Other preparations are in progress.

Very Respectfully Your Obt Servt

J. G. Foster

Capt. Eng[rs]

Devoted to DRESS REFORM, Woman's Rights. and to the Physical, Mental and Moral Elevation of Humanity.

Office of THE SIBYL,
Middletown, N. Y.
March 8th 1861

President Lincoln

May I a wife, mother tax payer and hard working woman of America be heard, when I ask from you, a man in power a juster recognition of woman's individuality than has hitherto been shown her in the distribution of such offices as she is well fitted to fill?

It is useless for me to remind an inteligent citizen of our progressive west of the growing spirit of discontent among the hard working, *unrepresented tax paying* women of America in relation to the manner in which men arrogate to themselves all power offices etc etc

The power is now yours to heal to some extent this growing spirit of discontent and wounded selfhood by giving to the working intelligent tax paying women who have indirectly helped to raise you to power, a small share in the many offices at your disposal; It will be only an act of simple *justice* which thousands of women trust you will honor your administration by performing Thousands of Post and other offices might be filled in this way by worthy women in lieu of making them pass for able bodied men to suck who are too lazy to split rails or plow,

I have consulted none of your political friends here save my husband as to the propriety of offering myself as an applicant for the P.M department here— I know I have acted unusual but did not care to imitate the dozen or more corner lounging politicians circulating papers for the place—my claims are full as good as theirs while I would refer you to Hon Wm H. Seward & Hon C. H. Van Wyck as to my probible abilities for the [*place*] duties—though I trust you will alone consult President Lincoln the choice of the people as to the propriety of giving women at least one recognition of selfhood in old Orange, though I hope thousands of women will thus be recognised through the land, not merely in the byway and unprofitable offices which men refuse to accept but in the places of trust and good pay—

I will not enlarge on woman's "rights" and "wrongs" but will trust to you to right some of the injustice meted out to her at present.

Resp^t

Hon A Lincoln Pres^t U. S. A

From Mrs Lydia Sayer Hasbrouck M. Q.

Jackson Miss
March 8. 1861.

Dear Sir,

I understand you are in for *Coercion* and that old Uncle Sam is short of funds. I am somewhat disposed to help you, and hereby freely contribute for that purpose according to my limited means, and herein enclose you fifty dollars. Be pleased to receive for your self my warmest wishes for your speedy overthrow and the total dismemberment of the Dark Repub. party. Hoping that the Rifles stationed on the "House Tops" during your Inauguration did not suffer for the want of *Whiskey*—I remain yours etc,

Wm. L. Phelps

My kindest regards to Senator Wade of Ohio.

My Dear Sir.

This is the day for regular meeting of the Cabinet. But I will notify the members specially

W. H. S.

Friday morning.

WAR DEPARTMENT

March 9th. 1861

Sir.

In reference to the Telegraphic Despatch just submitted for my consideration, I have the honor to state that under existing laws, this Department has no power,—nor has the government any—to prevent the shipment of munitions of war to the seceding states. The matter was pressed upon the attention of the military committee during the late session of Congress but resulted in no action, I believe, on its part.

Very respectfully
Your obt servt
J Holt

To The President.
[Endorsed:]
Cabinet
March 9th 1861
Holt, Sec War

Head Qrs. of the Army
Washington, March 11, 1861.

Sir:

The time having been allowed to pass by when it was practicable to fit out an expedition adequate to the succor of your garrison, before the exhaustion of its means of subsistence—you will, after communicating your purpose to His Excellency, the Governor of So Carolina,—engage suitable water transportation, & peacefully evacuate Fort Sumter- so long gallantly held—& with your entire command embark for New York;—your officers & men taking with them their small arms, accoutrements & private effects.

Very respectfully yrs.
Winfield Scott.

Major R. Anderson,
U. S. Army
Comg Fort Sumter.
[Endorsed:]
Lieut. Genl Scott,
to
Major R. Anderson.

Project of a letter that I wish to send to Major A.

Respectfully submitted to the Secretary of War.
Winfield Scott.
Mar. 11, 1861.

FORT SUMTER.

The President has done me the honor to address to me certain professional questions, to which he desires answers. I proceed with them categorically.

"1. To what point of time can Major Anderson maintain his position, at Fort Sumter, without fresh supplies or reinforcement?"

Answer. In respect to subsistence, for the garrison, he has hard bread, flour & rice for about 26 days, & salt meat (pork) for about 48 days; but how long he could hold out against the whole means of attack which the South Carolinians have in, & about the city of Charleston & its Harbour, is a question that cannot be answered with absolute accuracy. Reckoning the [*batteries*] troops at 3,500 (now somewhat disciplined) the batteries at 4 powerfull *land*, & at least one *floating*—all mounting guns & mortars of large calibre, & of the best patterns;—& supposing those means to be skilfully & vigorously employed—Fort Sumter with its less than 100 men—including common laborers & musicians—ought to be taken by a single assault, & easily, if harassed perseveringly for several previous days & nights by threats & false attacks, with the ability, from the force of overwhelming numbers, of converting one out of every three or four of those, into a real attack.

"2. Can you with all the means now in your control, supply or reinforce Fort Sumter within that time?"

Answer. No: Not within many months. See answer to Nº 3.

"3. If not, what amount of means, & of what description, in addition to that already at your control, would enable you to supply & reinforce that fortress within the time?"

Answer: A fleet of war vessels & transports, 5,000 additional regular troops & 20,000 volunteers, in order to take all the batteries in the Harbor of Charleston (including Ft Moultrie) after the capture of all the batteries in the approach or outer Bay. And to raise, organize

& discipline such an army, would require new acts of Congress & from six to eight months.

Respectfully submitted,
Winfield Scott.

Head Qu. of the Army,
Washington, Mar. 11, 1861.

DEPARTMENT OF STATE.

March 11.

My dear Sir,

I received last night what seemed to be authoritative as an announcement that Mr Fessenden withdraws his claim upon a chief or any mission. This is a relief.

I like Clay for Spain—And am prepared to dispose of the question at once.

I like equally Corwin to Mexico—and am also ready—

As to Fremont and France—the prestige is good—But I *think* that is all. If as I have heard, he is to be engaged in raising money there for his estates, it would be a serious complication—Besides this he is by birth and education a South Carolinian and I am not certain of his being so very decided in the defence of the Union as a minister at Paris ought to be—I would rather send Dayton there—For England I am sure Mr Adams far above all others adapted to British Court & Society and infinitely more watchful capable, efficient, reliable every thing—New England is an important point. What better can we do for her. N. Jersey gives us little, and that grudgingly—I think Daytons appointment would be as much too large for her as any thing else we are likely to do for New England would be too small for her.

After considering these things you will please decide. I can wait on you this morning on this subject if you wish, or I shall be ready to acquiesce at once in your decision without further conference.

Please hold in reserve Secretaryships of these legations They are almost as good as missions and hardly less important.

Very respectfully
Your obedient servant
William H Seward

The President

PRIVATE

NORTH ATLANTIC TELEGRAPH.
TEMPORARY OFFICES
62, Moorgate Street, London, E. C.
March 11th 1861

To
President Lincoln

My dear Sir, Since my letter of Friday last, I have learned that the question of the recognition of the Southern Confederacy has not been before the Cabinet of St James. That Lord Palmerston and Lord John Russell said on the evening of the 9th Inst. that they hoped our affairs would be peaceably settled. They regretted the course of the north in Congress on the tariff. The recognition of the southern Confederacy, will not be done in haste. This is the substance of the conversation. The editor of the Times, Mr. Delane is savage on the tariff and will urge a recognition at once and will be decided against the north, provided the tariff passes, which we hope will not be the case.

It has been the worst policy in the world for the north to pass the tariff the moment it got power, by the absence of the south and it will do *all for the south* that they could wish, so far as England is concerned. The south can command millions, if the tariff bill passes. You have no idea of the effect it has had.

Mr. Dallas hopes for the Union and is expecting a successor. Great will be responsibility upon your Minister here. You need a common place honest union man, not too much of a politician, nor lawyer, nor anti-slavery. He ought to be conservative in all things, except as to the Union and on that be firm, but not offensive.

There are my opinions and of course you will not care for them or for me, but I do not charge you a cent for them—I do not want office, never did want office, nor never will, (I hope) I have no favors to ask of any one, except I have a wish that you will stand by the Union.

I think Colfax was wrong to withdraw the mail service from the south. Never cease to give them mail service. As the forts are for the protection of the people, if the Governors of the respective states think they will not need the aid of the U S soldiers there, I would move them all away and hire some old women to keep them clean You do not need to occupy the forts but collect your revenues outside. Kill them with defensive actions and abstain from offensive.

Yours vy Respectfully
Tal. P. Shaffner

N. B You can depend upon the sayings I have given you as coming from Lord Palmerston and Lord J. Russell. The moment application is made here for recognition I will let you know.

Mr. Abraham Lincoln.
Sir:

Having not received answer, of my three letters, that I have sended to you, one in New.York, and two in Washington, including a letter from Ex President Mr Buchanan, and one from the Duke of New Castle.

I have taked the determination, to inform you, with franchise, upon my astonishment! . . . How a Great Personnage! like your Excellency! surrounded of glory and ornamented of fine education, learned, and great talent! Not answer, a Lady letters? (Realy, is not good prelude). If *God!* put your Excellence! in the position to govern the American Nation! *God!* expect from you wisdom, equitablety, impartiality, humanity and kindnes. Before *God!* all creatures to be equals. Pride: is"Vanitas, Vanitatis, et Homina Vanitas! If a unhappy Creature, that for total overthrow of her fortune, ask protection for her relieve! is duty of the reigning to protect her, and answer at her letters.

Your high Position, and your tittle of President, not absolve you, and give you not privilege to miss the urbanity, politeness and amability, to answer a Lady letters.

If all personns, would not answer to the letters! the World will be fall in anarchy. If the First Magistrate will not answer at Lady letters! What will do the people?

If you whant do nothing for a unnhappy Lady! is your duty—Excellency—send to me bak the letters of Mr Buchanan and the Duke of New Castle.

Your Respectfully
Amalia Majocchi Valtellina

Rahway New.Jersey
March 11 1861

Richmond
March 11th 1861

My dear Sir

I feel assured that the motives which prompt me to do so justify me in trespassing on your time. Mr Lincoln's inaugural which in my opinion has been greatly distorted, from its true intention, by our people, has had a most unhappy influence upon some of the members of our Convention. We have a noble band of conservitives who are bravely withstanding the powerful outside pressure that is being brought to bear upon them but our ranks are being sadly thinned by desertions and we cannot say how long we will possess a majority of the Convention unless something is done to aid us.

The inaugural is being used in the country to induce constituencies to instruct their representatives and those who are weak fall before them. Here we have no press to sustain us. Our opponents throughout the State are of those who belong to the most active class of politicians and availing themselves of all the arts of the demigogue are working hard to give an evil turn to the public mind. You see then under what disadvantages we labor. We secured a triumph and victory by promises of peace and adjustment, and now when we find our State on the brink of a crumbling precipice you may conceive what is the wear and tear of soul and body. We have now almost nothing on which to stand. For myself General I care nothing, I would be willing to lay down prospects, life, every thing to save this Union which I love so dearly and whose fame your deeds have so greatly heightened, but unless the Administration does something to relive the tension of the public mind here, the conservative party in Virginia will be swept away like chaff before the wind and with it goes I think every hope for the preservation of the Union—

A collision between the Federal Government and any of the seceded States would leave us powerless. The disunionists know it and gloat over the article in saturdays Herald which points to the probable movement of reenforcements and the attempt to collect the revenue in those States—South Carolina is kept apprised of our position and will seize the slightest pretext for a collision. Could I be permitted to advise I would urge upon the Administration to abstain from any effort to reenforce the forts or to collect the revenue in the seceded States, and I would even go futher and advise the withdrawal of the troops that are now there, as calculated to remove the thorn in the side and depriving them thus of any pretext for complaint; Such a course would reassure the weak and give additional strength to the strong; it would give quiet and rest from excitement to the people in those States, enable them to reflect on the consequences of what they have done in passion and I think tend greatly to bring about, what the conservatives of Virginia are so earnestly laboring for, a restoration of the Union. General, I know how gratingly such views may fall upon your military ear and you must know how earnest I must think the need when I advise the non-enforcement of the law; but here is an emergency where the enforcement of a law may cause the distruction of all law in a vast portion of the country. The opinions I have here expressed are entertained by a large proportion of the conservatives of the Convention, for many of whom I am authorized to speak. We wish for an authorisation, unambiguous indication of a conciliatory policy on the part of the Administration; if we get it soon we can sweep the State in the spring elections and will send to Congress gentlemen and statemen an not such men as misrepresented us in the last Congress; if we do not get it we cannot carry a district in eastern Virginia. I only speak of this matter as bearing on the legislation likely to save the country

I have written this because I thought it right that you should know how your friends stand and because I thought you would like to be informed on the subject.

Did I know any member of the cabinet I would have communicated the same facts to him

Very truly yours
Wm C. Wickham

Leut. Gen: Scott
Washington

[Endorsed:]
W. C. Wickham
Richmond Va—
Mch 1861—
To Genl Scott on the
state of affairs in Va—

Portland
March 13. 1861

To the President.

Sir—It may be a pleasure to you to know that the evacuation of Fort Sumpter will be fully approved by the entire body of Republicans in this State—and I doubt not in all the country.

It is undoubtedly a Military necessity, and admits of no question as to its expediency. At first, the suggestion struck us unpleasantly, but when we learned the actual position of affairs, we saw that the measure is inevitable, and is a legacy of humiliation from the last administration, which cannot be declined. We hope no such necessity exists in the case of Fort Pickens.

A thousand thanks for the noble words of your inaugural—they inspire the country with confidence, and fill the hearts of your friends with joy.

With great respect
Truly yours
Neal Dow.

Neal Dow
Portland. Mch. 13. 1861
On evacuation of Ft. Sumter

AGENCY OF THE ILLINOIS MUTUAL FIRE INSURANCE CO.

Springfield March 14th 1861

"Dear Old Abe"

We hear with pain and regret that you are debating about Evacuating Sumter lowering our Glorious old Flag that Washington through so many trials and Privations unfurled and sustained to be trampled on by traitors and to be made the hiss and scoff of the World. Do you know that Genl Washington or Jackson never said "*I cant*" and do you know that your old crippled friend that has always stood by you for the last 20 years has fought by your side for & with you, has never yet uttered that word, except in derision. Say the word By the Eternal, Fort Sumter *shall* be reinforced and that glorious old Flag sustained and my word for it 100,000 good and true men with Jim Hill amongst them will at once respond to the call. The democracy are going to have a jollification on the Evacuation. You are now the head of this nation and of course know more and better than we the reasons that are leading to this result but for Gods sake for Humanity and for your own honor dont let that word *Cant* form any part of the reasons

Yours Truly
James L Hill

EXECUTIVE MANSION

March 18. 1861

Will the Attorney General please give his opinion in writing whether the Executive has any lawful authority to make such an order as the foregoing, and return this paper, with the answer, to me?

A.Lincoln

[Endorsed:] Rec[d] Mar: 19–61. Proposed Order for
Military Bureau, in the
War Dep[t]

Executive Mansion March 18th 1861.

To the Secretary of War:

Sir: You will favor me by issuing an order detailing Lieut. Ephraim E Ellsworth, of the First Dragoons, for special duty as Adjutant and Inspector General of Militia for the United States, and in so far as existing laws will admit, charge him with the transaction, under your direction, of all business pertaining to the Militia, to be conducted as a separate bureau, of which Lieut. Ellsworth will be chief, with instructions to take measures for promoting a uniform system of organization, drill, equipment, etc. etc. of the U. S. Militia, and to prepare a system of drill for Light troops, adapted for self-instruction, for distribution to the Militia of the several States. You will please assign him suitable office rooms, furniture etc. and provide him with a clerk and messenger, and furnish him such facilities in the way of printing, stationary, access to public records, etc. as he may desire for the successful prosecution of his duties; and also provide in such manner as may be most convenient and proper, for a monthly payment to Lieut Ellsworth, for this extra duty sufficient to make his pay equal that of a Major of Cavalry.

Your obt Servt

WILLARDS HOTEL

Washington, Friday March 22
1861

Dear Sir.

I desire to have the appointment of Minister to Turkey, as the office suggested in the application already made by me has been given to another person.

My claims are:—

Five years devoted service in the republican cause, during which time, *I have been as prominent as a public speaker & in the cause as any other man in New—York.*

No person has been oftener honored with the duty of delivering "elaborate" addresses & speeches on great critical occasions. No one has done more indispensable ward organization business

I have given my time and my strength to the cause, & have but lately left a sick room where I was confined for four months—the illness brought on by excessively hard "campaign" duties.

Every republican in New York would receive my appointment with pleasure and satisfaction

I refer to Seators Harris, King, Sumner, Wilson, Baker, Mr. Dayton, Mr Cavode, Mr E. I. Morris etc etc etc

As I have sacrificed my health for the administration, I have claims which every one acknowledges.

I have written this note to you emphatically, as I find to the infinite surprise of myself and my friends, that my claims have been ignored in the appointments to Europe. I have lived long in Europe, & am familiar with its politics etc.

I remain with great respect
Your obedient Servant
Wm Henry Fry

Will you favor me with an interview?—

To the President.

PRIVATE.

March 23.
"61.

My Dear Mr. Lincoln,

I have asked of the departments the reward of some, dozen or so, men in my state who have rendered especial service: and made great sacrifices in the Cause which brought us into power. It would be a mortification to me for life, if they were now overlooked. I beg you *will not forget them,* when presented to your consideration. Especially will you remember John H. and Jno. Rawlings of Madison County Ky. who have gone *through all the mobs in* my defence! I am sorry to trespass upon you: I know how much your time is needed in greater matters—*how much you need repose for your health cure*—but these obligations sit upon my conscience—and should I prove unfaithful to those poor men who have without me, no advocate, our success instead of being a source of joy and triumph would leave me but a life-time remorse and humiliation!

I expect to be in Washington about the 18: apr: to receive my instructions. Trusting you may *systematize your time:* and be then somewhat relieved of officeseekers, I remain truly,

Your obliged friend,
C. M. Clay.

P. S. I promised D: G. G. Templeton Covington Ky. to name to you him especially for the P. O. at that place: he is on my list to Blair.

C. M. C.

His Ex:y. A. Lincoln
Pres: US:
Wash. D. C.

N. B. I call your attention to the plan of pacification sent by M. C. Johnson Esq. Pres: of the N. Bank of Ky. to the National Intelligencer, and N. Y. Times; I don't know whether published or not. Mr. J. is considered the best lawyer in our state, and a man of most solid judgement. He proposes that an agreement be made that the U. states collect the revenue—the seceding states take a vote of the people for or against the union—if they go out—acknowledge their independence, and give them the revenue *there* collected—and the forts. Thus *peace* would by the *Senate* which *has the whole* and *only power*, *So to treat,* would be restored in 20 days and the soldiers all go to work—! and business revive!

C. M. C.

[Endorsed:] C. M. Clay
March 23.61
Asking that certain appointments be made—

The undersigned members of the Washington Bar, and citizens of the District of Columbia, having learned that Col. Ward H. Lamon has been favorably mentioned in connection with the appointment to the Marshalship of the District of Columbia, and that it has been asserted by some persons that his appointment would give offence to the people of the District, desire to state that in their opinion the assertion is gratuitous and without foundation in fact, and that they conceive that his appointment would receive the cheerful acquiescence of a majority of the people of the City and County, and give general satisfaction. Mr Lamon's antecedents justify this declaration. He is a native of Virginia, where his parents now reside, he married in that State and has numerous connections and kindred there, though for some years he has claimed citizenship in Illinois from which he now hails.

For these reasons, without referring to his qualifications for the position, his gentlemanly deportment since his brief sojourn here, the undersigned cannot perceive the least ground for umbrage to the people at the appointment, should the President incline to confer it upon him.

Washington March 23d 1861. . . .

Green Bay Wis Mar 23, 1861

Hon Abraham Lincoln
Dear Sir

I take the liberty of writing to you & making the following request for my little daughter, now about seven years old, which is, that you will send her your likeness She is a very strong supporter of yours & has been ever since your nomination Although all her little playmates are Democrats & almost every inducement has been used to make her turn she holds firm, Her Grandfather who is an old Henry Clay Whig tried to induce her to go for Bell & Everett by all kinds of offers but it was of no use & one gentleman offered her a pound of Candy if she would only hurra once for Bell & Everett or Douglas, it was a great temptation but it was of no use, It is very surprising what an interest she takes in all that concerns you She reads everything in the papers and knows more of what is going on in politics than I do, & takes every occasion to defend you against all attacks from every source. A good many have tried to make her opposed to you but she sticks to you and tells them it will all be right now you are President. She has always been very anxious to have a Lincoln Medal but as I was unable to get her a good one here I have taken the liberty to make this request of you, which I hope you will grant as I think she really deserves to have a good likeness of you. Enclosed I send you Two Dollars to defray the expense.

Yours Very Respectfully
Joshua Whitney,
of Green Bay
Wisconsin

P. S. The name of my little daughter is Emmeline H Whitney

[Endorsed:] Returned money & photograph May 23, 1864.

RED MARCH 27/61

Fort Sumter S. C.
March 24. 61

Genl Js. G. Totten
Chief Engineer, U. S. A.
Washington D. C.
General:

Everything is quiet around us, being Sunday, and no work is being done except on the Mortar battery on James 2d, where a few men are still at work strengthening the parapet. Yesterday, the mortar practice from Morris Id, disclosed the position of two batteries: one between breaching batteries Nos 1 & 2, and the other between No 2 & 3.

I could not estimate the number from the firing, but information was received ten days ago that four mortars were then in position. Probably the number is now increased, as new mortars have been received from Virginia.

Yesterday by direction of the Governor, a steamer came to the fort to deliver the furniture, instruments and papers, that I left in the house I occupied on Sullivans Id. Almost everything was delivered safely. I have the honor to be

Very Respectfully. Your Obt Servt.

J. G. Foster, Capt. Engrs

[Endorsed:]

1996

Rec Mar 27 F^{t} Sumter Mar 24/61 Capt J. G. Foster
Position of batteries on Morris Island and probable number of mortars
Furniture instruments etc delivered up by S. Cardiman (?)

Rome Mar 25. 1861

To His Excellency, Hon
A. Lincoln President
Dr Sir

I have this day shipped you by Express a very nice pkge of Fall Butter, which please accept from one of your staunchest political friends—

I observe that you are constantly besieged with applications for office & the rumor is you are working too hard, it therefore occurred to me that something nice & palatable in the way of good butter might do you good, & help to preserve your strength to perform your arduous duties. I am a dealer in the article entire in this Town, & can assure you that this is something extra nice, which will suit you & your Family—

I am not asking for any office & only desire good government, & to have honest & true men appointed to office: So far, the President has been fortunate in that respect

I conclusion allow me to beg of you for the sake of our country to use all the means in your power to sustain your health & strength & take time from your severe labors for necessary exercise——

That you may be the means of restoring our country to its former prosperity, is the ardent wish of my heart, & I have great faith, if your life is spared that order & good Government will be surely established under your administration

I am an old citizen of this Co. (Oneida) & formerly one of the strongest supporters of our noble & deeply lamented Henry Clay, the greatest statesman & Patriot that ever lived in these United States—

Knowing too, that you were one of his ardent friends & admirers—is one great reason of the strong & sincere attachment I feel for you, & that you may succeed in your endeavors to bring order out of chaos is my great & earnest desire——

I very Respectfully your Friend & obt Servt.

John B. Bradt

P. S. Keep a goot strong pickle in this butter & in a cool place then it will keep sweet till July

J. B. B.

Please acknowledge rect & oblige

[Endorsed:] John B. Bradt
Rome N. Y.
1861
Tub of Butter

[In pencil:] Mar 25? 1861

Wednesday Noon

My dear Sir,

There are three or four gentlemen from Maryland at my room—Mr. Winter Davis & Mr. Hoffman, with Col. Creswell, who is to be the Unconditional Union Candidate to Congress on the Eastern

Shore & who desire to pay his respects to you. Can you receive them for a moment if I bring them over.

Yours truly,
S. P Chase

The President
etc.

[Endorsed:]
The President is engaged with the Missouri Delegates
I cannot

TELEGRAM

Dated Lexington Ky Mar 27 1861.

To Mr. Blair
Post Master Genl.
For the sake of the cause I accept the Russian mission

C. M. Clay

11/27

Indianapolis Ind.
March 28 1861

Mr. Lincoln,
Dear Cousin,

You will doubtless be surprised, when you glance at the signature of this letter. But when I tell you I don't want office, and am a democrat, you will feel encouraged to read what I may write. I had thought to defer my writing 'till some future day, but then concluded that a disinterested letter among so many office begging ones, would relieve the monotony, and be more acceptable now, than in the future. I called on you when at Indianapolis, but the crowd was so great, I merely said, cousin'Abram', and passed on. You will think, *another* relation because I am *President!!* Well your thoughts will be precisely correct in this case. For had I not thought that it was quite an honor to be even distantly related to the highest Executive Officer in the U. S. I should not have gone to the trouble of writing.

I am not very good at tracing our relationship, but if I read grandfather Shaver's letter correctly, he said his mother and your grandmother were sisters. Their names were Cassner. With the exception of my father's family, all my relatives live in Virginia. Grandfather Shaver is the only cousin by the name of Shaver that you have. He is 77 years of age, Were you to see him you would not be at all ashamed of him as a relative—only his politics. His granddaughter is rather an ordinary personage, but with vanity enough to think Cousin 'Abram' will answer her letter.

I am connected with our Blind Inst. and have been for six years. There is a political jurisdiction exercised over all our benevolent institutions and as I was placed here by democratic directors, I am informed I will be removed by the opposing power.

I spend my Summers in Va. I shall with, or without an invitation call and see you when I pass through Washington.

I hope in answer to this, to receive a letter written by yourself—recollect *by your own self.*

Accept my best wishes for your wisdom in governing the distracted politicians, and believe me

E. Wertha Bowman

P. S. Present my regards to Mrs Lincoln & family

E. W. B

A. L.

PRIVATE

Lexington Ky. March 28th. 61

My Dear Sir,

I yesterday received a telegram, by the Hon. M. Blair, intimating that it would be agreable to you that I should accept the mission to Russia instead of Spain, in order to allow you to send (as I conjecture) Carl Schurz Esq. to Spain; as his mission to Central or Northern Europe, might be offensive to those powers. My family preferred Spain, as well as myself, because of the climate and possible negotiations: but as I had urged the appointment of these German leaders to satisfactory missions for party reasons, I desire to give you assurance of my fidelity to my suggestions, and my personal regard for yourself, by yielding to your wishes and freeing you from your embarrassment. But the Court of St Petersburg is an expensive one—even necessaries being very high: so that my family are in doubt whether it will not be necessary (seven of us!) to separate and a part remain in the U. S. for economy's sake—and this was the the chief source of my disappointment in not having a place in the Cabinet. Many senators promised to raise my salary in Spain to 15,000$, if I would accept that: I beg that you will use your influence to have the Russian Mission put upon an equality with the English and French, 17,500$: as it is an equal power, becoming cosmopolitan full of Americans and other travellers—and the most expensive Court in Europe. Another thing, I must employ a private secretary who speaks French, which will greatly add to my expenses.

Now, Mr. Lincoln, in consideration of my life long sacrifices, and my being again and again put back for the party's sake, (all of which I have done with a good grace) would it be too much for me to ask of you to gratify me at last to some extent by appointing me (*in case of a vacancy*) minister to France or England?

Ever devoted to the principles which brought you into power, and desirous of promoting your personal honor and happiness, I am

truly your friend,

C. M. Clay.

His Ex: A. Lincoln
Pres: U. States:etc.

Washington
D. C.

P. S. I expect to report myself to the state department in Washington about the 17–18 prx. and have engaged a passage to Liverpool on the Persia (Cunard Line) which sails from N York on the 24 prx.

C. M. C.

[Endorsed:] Hon. C. M. Clay
March 28. 61

Desires to go to Spain rather than Russia

Belleville March 28. 1861.

Hon. A. Lincoln.
President U. S.
Dear Sir.

It is asserted in many papers, and has been telegraphed West a number of times that Mr. Seward had declared positively that no citizen of foreign birth should ever receive under Your administration a mission to Europe. I need hardly inform you, that this information, which has not been contradicted, and not been disproved by an appointment of a naturalised citizen to such a mission, has created the most intense sensation amongst the German Republicans all through the country. The democratic organs are fanning the flame, and that the consequences of such a policy would be disastrous there can be no question.

Now as I desire the success of Your administration, the immense difficulties of which no one can better appreciate than myself, I will say in all candor, that the doctrine of Mr. Seward, if he is not misrepresented, can and ought not to be supported by the Cabinet.

The fitness of the appointee ought to be the sole guide. Now while it is entirely proper not to send a person, & particularly at this most unfortunate juncture of affairs, who would be obnoxious to the Government, where he is to be accredited, or even to other important Governments, nothing can be more illiberal, than to exclude such, as are otherwise fit for the Station, and have deserved well of their country, for the reason of their being foreign born. The European Governments never act in such a contracted manner. The French Republic in 1848 sent a German Exile . . . as their minister plenipotentiary to the German Diet. The two greatest ministers Russia ever had in foreign countries were Count Nesselrode a German, and Pozzo de Borgo, an Italian Mr. Reinhard a German was for many years the Representative of France under Louis Philip in Germany.

Albert Gallatin a Swiss was our ambassador in London in former times, and Soulé a Frenchman in Spain. The latter was a fool, but *that* was the objection to him, and not his nativity.

If those amongst the Germans who have rather loudly called for such appointments fail to get them, rest assured, that the Germans will make no complaint, because they are by no means agreed, that they are the proper men for the places they may have desired. It is generally admitted by most of the intelligent amongst them that Mr. Schurtz ought not to have insisted on Sardinia, because it might have embarrassed our Government. The leading French paper in the Union (Courier des Étas Unis) N. Y. while vindicating the rights of naturalised citizens to any office, which they may hold under the constitution, calls the nonappointment of Chs. Schurtz, one of the most prudent acts of the new administration. But he might have been sent to Belgium, or Portugal, or Turkey, if he still persisted in asking for a mission, against his better Judgment and the advise of his friends.—

Now I desire very much that either Mr. Seward should in some manner, if he has been wrongly reported, contradict the assertions made in the press, or that the administration should by its acts disavow such a policy, which is the most insulting to the naturalised citizens, and will drive them in shoals from the Republican party.

The times are gloomy. The strong and enthusiastic Union feeling among the German element, which would have made them draw the sword in a moment for the enforcement of the laws, makes them fret, as it is, under the present peace policy, which but few of the more reflecting consider as being imposed upon You by the most dire necessity. No additional cause for grievance ought to be given. I know that Your heart is perfectly right; that no injustice or illiberality can find a resting place in Your mind. My confidence in you, acquired by an acquaintance of twenty five years is unshaken. My interest in your success compels me to write to you as I do.

And now permit me to make a suggestion. Had You not better call Congress instantly and appeal in Your proclamation to the people! If they want the Union sustained and the laws enforced let them instruct their representatives, to give You the power to do it. If they will not do it, be it so, You have done Your duty, and no sane man can require impossibilities. With my best wishes for yourself and family I remain your sincere friend

Gustavus Koerner

[Endorsed:]
Letter of Hon. G. Koerner, of Ill
About policy towards foreigners March 28 1861.

Sec. of State.

1st. The dispatch of an expedition to supply or reinforce Sumter would provoke an attack and so involve a *war at that point.*
The fact of preparation for such an expedition would inevitably transpire, and would therefore precipitate the war—and probably defeat the object. I do not think it wise to provoke a Civil War begining at Charleston only in [*defence*] rescue of an untenable position.

Therefore I advise against the expedition in every view—

2d. I would call in Capt. M. C. Meigs forthwith. Aided by his counsel I would at once and at every cost prepare for a war at Pensacola and Texas, to be taken however only as a consequence of maintaining the possession and authority of the United States—

3^d I would instruct Maj. Anderson to retire from Sumter, forthwith.

William H Seward.

March 29th.

[Endorsed in Mr. Lincoln's hand:] *In Cabinet*

[In Mr. Lincoln's hand:] *In Cabinet*
Washington 29^h March 1861

Sir

I concur in the proposition to send an armed force off Charleston with supplies of provisions and reinforcements for the garrison at fort Sumter, and of communicating, at the proper time, the intentions of the government to provision the fort, peacably if unmolested. There is little probability that this will be permitted, if the opposing forces can prevent it. An attempt to force in provision, without reinforcing the garrison at the same time, might not be advisable. But armed resistance to a peacable attempt to send provisions to one of our own forts will justify the government in using all the power at its command, to reenforce the garrison and furnish the necessary supplies.

Fort Pickens and other places retained should be strengthened by additional troops, and, if possible made impregnable. The naval force in the gulf and on the southern coast should be increased. Accounts are published that vessels, having on board marketable products for the crews of the Squadron at Pensacola are seized—the inhabitants we know are prohibited from furnishing the ships with provisions or water; and the time has arrived, when it is the duty of the government to assess and maintain its authority.

Very Respectfully
Gideon Welles

His Excellency
Abraham Lincoln
President

105 Blucker St.
New York March 22
[In pencil:] *1860*

Honored Sir

A niece of John Hancock, I take pleasure in presenting to you, an interesting relic of the past, an autograph of my uncle, having the endorsement of your ancestor, Abraham Lincoln, written nearly a century ago: humbly trusting it may prove an happy augury of our countrys future history "The Cradle of Liberty—" "re-built" by John Hancock, and Abraham Lincoln. I remain

With highest respect
Mary Hancock Colyer

To
His Excellency
Abraham Lincoln
President of the United States

[Endorsed:]
Niece of John Hancock enclosing Lottery Ticket for re-building Faneuil Hall
Signed by Jno Hancock endorsed "Abraham Lincoln"

REC MARCH 27 /61

Fort Sumter S. C.
March 23d 1861

Genl Js. G. Totten
Chief Engineer, USA.
Washington D C.
General,

The morning is very warm and plasant and a force is quite actively engaged upon battery No 4 on Cummings Pt. (looking towards the Moultrie House on Sullivans Id,) in enlarging the battery and strengthening the traverse which screens the battery, in rear, from our view. This will make the battery something like a redoubt, like the form given in the margin. (There is a sketch on the right-hand side of the page illustrating the verbal description) I do not know the form or size of the opening at *a*, as the great height of the rear traverse hides everything beyond from view. This height is sufficient to prevent any curvilinear fire, except that from mortars, or shell guns arranged as mortars, from reaching the interior of the battery. Several days ago there were three guns in good firing order in this battery: now, from the work that has been expended on it, and the number of guns seen to be taken in that direction, I have no doubt that six guns are now available, one of which is a columbiad, or an 8″ sea coast Howitzer.

The practice from this battery, almost every day, shows that they have the range, almost perfectly, of the track of a vessel in entering the harbor at the point where the Main ship, the Swash and the North Channels, meet. It appears that much importance is being attached to this, as well as other channel batteries, since Genl Beauregard took command and I am thus particular in reference to it since it will play an important part against any vessel attempting an entrance. I was either mistaken in reference to the point at which the Channel Buoy (*No 3.* see C. S. Chart of 1858) was put down again, or it has been again removed. It is now on *this side of the channel*, that is, on the *side nearest Cummings Pt*, and very nearly in the position given on the chart,—perhaps 20 or 30 yards farther to the south. There is another Channel Buoy, on the same side of the channel, to the south of the above, and nearly abreast of Cummings Pt. This is not on the C. S. Chart of 1858.

Work is still being carried on on the James 2d mortar battery. It is evident that this is being formed into a redoubt, being at the extremity of the left flank of the line of entrenchments covering the rear of Fort Johnson.

At Fort Moultrie, little appears to be doing. This fort, with the very high and well constructed mortars, (as they now are) is well secured from our fire. Twelve guns, in embrasure, bear on the channel; and thirteen guns, in embrasure, bear on this work. Of the Floating Battery, or "Raft," nothing further is known, except that

Capt Hartstein, while here with Mr Fox, from Washington, made the remark that it was "very formidable." He also remarked with reference to the iron clad battery on Cummings Pt, that it was "very strong indeed"; or words to that effect. The above is reported to me: I did not see the Gentlemen.

In this fort I am continuing the construction of the traverse in front of the Hospital, and the filling of the remaining openings on the Gorge, 1st tin, with lead concrete.

I have the honor to be Very Respectfully Your Obt Servt

J. G. Foster
Capt. Engrs

1995 Rec. March 27 Fort Sumter Mar 23/61 Capt. J. G. Foster What is going on at Morris Island with a sketch of the battery—Range of its guns on the track of a vessel entering the harbor Position of channel buoys Mission of James Isl. mortar battery Fort Moultrie: no of its guns bearing on channel & n. on Ft Sumter What is thought of the floating battery & of the iron clad battery on Cummings Point Engs. operations in Fort Sumter

My Dear Sir.

I have read Mr Bates' note—and I have only one word of comment. Long before this question arose or at least before I knew that it would arise I took the ground in the case of the Indiana Post Office, that one member of the Cabinet ought to defer always to the opinion of another in regard to local appointments in the state of the latter. So I have refrained from any interference [*out of a*] in other states.

If the magnitute of New York City and its Custom House patronage, render an exception necessary, or politically wise, I do not, as you know dissent, because 1st, it was understood that it should be so, & 2d because I can count no especial disappointment.

But when Mr Chase out of his department demands as a personal favor an appointment in my state humiliating to me, or the Attorney General assures that he can better determine who should be a marshal in the very district in which I live, [*they*] the thing becomes a scandal, which I cannot digest, and so far as I know it is without precedent. I would sooner attack either of these gentlemen in the open street, than consent to oppose any local appointment they might desire to make in their respective states. *Mr Bates never has consulted me*

But my dear Sir, I shall cheerfully bear, whatever you require, and shall complain of no one

Faithfully yours,
William H. Seward

The President

[In pencil:] *March 30, 1861*

SOUTHERN FORTS.

Octr. 30, 1860, I emphatically called the attention of the President to the necessity of strong garrisons in all the forts below the principal commercial cities of the Southern States, including, by name the forts in Pensacola harbor.– Octr –31, I suggested to the Secretary of War that a circular should be sent, at once, to such of those forts as had garrisons, to be on the alert against surprizes & sudden assaults. (*See my "Views", since printed.*)

After a long confinement to my bed, in N. York, I came to this city (Washington) December 12. Next day I personally urged upon the Secretary of War the same views, viz;–strong garrisons in the southern forts–those of Charleston & Pensacola harbors, at once;– those on Mobile Bay & the Mississippi, below N. Orleans, next, etc. etc. I again pointed out the organized companies & the recruits, at the principal depôts, available for the purpose. The Secretary did not concur in one of my views, when I begged him, to procure for me an early interview with the President that I might make one effort more to save the forts & the Union.

By appointment, the Secretary accompanied me to the President, December 15, when the same topics, secessionism etc, were again pretty fully discussed. There being, at the moment, no danger of an early secession, beyond S? Carolina, the President, in reply to my arguments for immediately reinforcing Fort Moultrie & sending a garrison to Fort Sumter, said,—"the time has not arrived for doing so; that, he should wait the action of the convention of S? Carolina, in the expectation that a commission would be appointed & sent to negotiate with him and Congress respecting the secession of the State & the property of the U. S. held within its limits; & that, if Congress should decide against the secession, then he would send a reinforcement, & telegraph the commanding officer (Major Anderson) of Fort Moultrie to hold the forts (Moultrie & Sumter) against attack."

And the Secretary, with animation, added—"We have a vessel of War (the Brooklyn) held, in readiness at Norfolk, & he would then send 300 men, in her, from Fort Monroe to Charleston." To which I replied, first, that so many men could not be with-drawn from that garrison, but could be [*drawn*] taken from N. York;—next that it would then be too late, as the S? Carolina commissioners would have the game in their hands—by first using, & then cutting the wires—; that as there was not a soldier in Fort Sumter, any handful of armed secessionists might seize & occupy it, etc, etc,—

[Here the remark may be permitted, that if the Secretary's 300 men had then (or [*in the next 2 months*] some time later) been sent to Forts Moultrie & Sumter, *both* would now have been in the possession of the U. S.—& not a battery, below them, could have been erected by the secessionists. Consequently, the access to those forts, from the sea, would now (the end of March) be unobstructed & free.]

The same day, December 15, I wrote the following note:—

"Lieut. General Scott begs the President to pardon him for supplying, in this note, what he omitted to say, this morning, at the interview with which he was honored by the President:—

"Long *prior* to the *force-bill* (March 2, 1833;)—*prior* to the issue of his proclamation, &, in part, *prior* to the passage of the Ordinance of nullification—President Jackson, under the act of March 3, 1807

—"authorizing the employment of the land & naval forces"—caused re-inforcements to be sent to Fort Moultrie, & a sloop of war (the Natchez) with two revenue cutters, to be sent to Charleston harbor, in order, 1. To prevent the seizure of that fort by the nullifiers, & 2. To enforce the execution of the revenue laws. Genl Scott, himself, arrived at Charleston the day after the passage of the Ordinance of nullification, & many of the additional companies were then en route for the same destination.

"President Jackson familiarly said, at the time, that, by the assemblage of those forces, for lawful purposes, *he* was not making war upon So. Carolina; but that if So. Carolina attacked them it would be So. Ca. that made war upon the U. States.'

"Genl S. who received his first instructions (oral) from the President—in the temporary absence of the Secretary of War (Genl Cass) remembers those expressions well.

"Saturday Night
"Dec. 15, 1860".—

Dec. 28. Again, after Major Anderson had gallantly & wisely thrown his handful of men from Fort Moultrie into Fort Sumter—learning that, on demand of So C—there was great danger, he might be ordered by the Secretary, back to the less tenable work, or *out* of the harbor—I wrote this note:—

"Lieut General Scott (who has had a bad night & can scarcely hold up his head this morning) begs to express the hopes to the Secretary of War—1. That orders may not be given for the [*organ*] evacuation of Fort Sumter; 2. That 150 recruits may instantly be sent from Governor's Iland to re-inforce that garrison with ample supplies of ammunition & subsistence, including fresh vegetables, as potatoes, onions, turnips, & 3. That one or two armed vessels be sent to support the said fort.

"Lieut. Genl S. avails himself of this opportunity also to express the hope that the recommendations heretofore made by him, to the Secretary of War, respecting Forts Jackson, St Philipe, Morgan, & Pulaski, & particularly in respect to Forts Pickens & Mc Ree & the Pensacola Navy Yard, in connection with the last two named works, may be reconsidered by the Secretary.

"Lieut Genl S. will further ask the attention of the Secretary to

Forts Jefferson & Taylor, which are wholy national—being of far greater value even to the most distant points of the Atlantic Coast & the people on the upper waters of the Missouri, Mississippi & Ohio rivers, than to the State of Florida. There is only a feeble company at Key West for the defence of Fort Taylor, and not a soldier in Fort Jefferson to resist a handful of fillibusters, or rowboat of pirates; & the gulf soon after the beginning of secession or revolutionary troubles, in the adjacent states, will swarm with such nuisances."—

December 30. I addressed the President again, as follows.

"Lieut-Genl Scott begs the President of the United States to pardon the irregularity of this communication. It is Sunday; the weather is bad and General S. is not well enough to go to church.

"But matters of the highest national importance seem to forbid a moment's delay, & if mislead by zeal, he hopes for the President's forgiveness.

"Will the President permit Genl. S. without reference to the War Department, & otherwise as secretly as possible, to send two hundred and fifty recruits, from New York Harbor, to reinforce Fort Sumter, together with some extra muskets or rifles, ammunition & subsistence?

"It is hoped that a sloop of war & cutter may be ordered, for the same purpose, as early as tomorrow.

"Genl. S. will wait upon the President at any moment he may be called for."

The So. Carolina Commissioners had already been many days in Washington & no movement of defence (on the part of the U. S.) was permitted.

I will here close my notice of Fort Sumter by quoting from [*my*] some of my previous reports

It would have been easy to reinforce this fort down to about the 12th. of February. In this long delay Fort Moultrie has been re-armed & greatly strengthened in every way. Many powerful new land batteries (besides a formidable raft) have been constructed. Hulks too, have been sunk in the principal channel, so as to render access to Fort Sumter, from the sea, impracticable, without first carrying all the lower batteries of the secessionists. The difficulty of reinforceing has thus been increased 10 or 12 fold. First, the late President refused to allow any attempt to be made because he was holding negotiations with the S° Carolina commissioners.

Afterwards, Secretary Holt & myself endeavored, in vain, to obtain a ship of war for the purpose & were finally obliged to employ the passenger steamer, the *Star of the West*. That vessel, but for the hesitation of the master, might, as is generally believed, have delivered, at the fort, the men and subsistence on board. This attempt at succor failing, I next, verbally, submitted to the late Cabinet either that succor be sent by ships of war, fighting their way by the batteries (increasing in strength daily) or that Major Anderson should be left to ameliorate his condition by the muzzles of his guns; that is, enforcing supplies—by bombardment, & by *bringing to* merchant vessels, helping himself (giving orders for payment) or, finally, be allowed to evacuate the fort, which in that case, would be inevitable.

But before any resolution was taken—the late Secretary of the Navy making difficulties about the want of suitable war vessels—another commissioner from S° Carolina arrived, causing further delay. When this had passed away, Secretaries Holt & Toucey, Capt. Ward of the Navy & myself, with the knowledge of President Buchanan, settled upon the employment, under the captain (who was eager for the expedition) of three or four small steamers belonging to the Coast Survey. At that time (late in January) I have but little doubt Capt Ward would have reached F^t Sumter with all his vessels. But he was kept back by something like a truce or armistice embracing Charleston & Pensacola harbors, agreed upon between the late President & certain principal seceders, here, of S° Carolina, Florida, Louisana etc, & this truce lasted to the end of that administration.

That plan & all others, without a squadron of war ships & a considerable army, competent to take & hold the many formidable batteries below Fort Sumter, & *before* the exhaustion of its subsistence, having been pronounced, from the change of circumstances impracticable, by Major Anderson, Capt. Foster (chief engineer) & all the other officers of the Fort, as well as by Brig. Gen! Totten, Chief of the Corps of Engineers;—& concurring in that opinion—I did not hesitate to advise (March 12) "that Major Anderson be instructed to evacuate the fort so long gallently held by him & his companions, immediately on procuring suitable transportation to take them to New York. His relative weakness has steadily increased in the last eighteen days.

It was not till Jan. 3 (when the first commissioners from S° C. withdrew,) that the permission I had solicited, Octr. 31, was obtained,—to admonish commanders of the few southern forts, with garrisons, to be on the alert against surprises & sudden assaults (Major Anderson was not among the admonished, being already straitly beleagured.)

Jan. 3. To Lieut Slemmer commanding in Pensacola Harbor:—

"The General-in-Chief directs that you take measures to do the utmost in your power to prevent the seizure of either of the forts in Pensacola Harbor, by surprise or assault—consulting first with the Commander of the Navy Yard, who will probably have received instructions to co-operate with you." (This order was signed by Aide-de-Camp Lay.)

It was just before the surrender of the Pensacola Navy Yard (Jan 12) that Lieut Slemmer, calling upon Com. Armstrong, obtained the aid of some thirty common seamen or laborers (but no marines) which, added to his 46 soldiers made up his numbers to 76 men, with whom this meritorious officer has since held Fort Pickens & performed (working night and day) an immense amount of labor in mounting guns, keeping up a strong guard, etc. etc.

Early in January, I renewed (as has been seen) my solicitations to be allowed to reinforce Ft. Pickens; but a good deal of time was lost in vacillations. First the President "thought if no movement is made by the U. S., Fort Mc Ree will probably not be occupied, nor Fort Pickens attacked. In case of movement by the U. S., which will, doubtless be made known by the wires, there will be corresponding local movement, & the attempt to reinforce will be useless." (Quotation from a note made by Aide-de-camp Lay about Jan. 12,- of the Presidents' reply to a message from me.) Next it was doubted, whether it would be safe to send reinforcements in an unarmed steamer, & the want, as usual, of a suitable naval vessel—the Brooklyn being long held in reserve, at Norfolk, for some purpose unknown to me. Finally, after I had kept a body of 300 recruits in N. York harbor ready, for some time, & they would have been sufficient to reinforce, temporarily, Fort Pickens; & to occupy Fort Mc Ree, also —the President, about Jan. 18, directed that the sloop of War, Brooklyn, should take a single company (90 men) from Fort Monroe (Hampton Roads) & reinforce Lieut Slemmer, in Fort Pickens, but without a surplus man for the neighboring Fort Mc Ree.

The Brooklyn, with Capt. Vogdes' company, alone, left the Cheapeake, for Ft. Pickens, about Jan 22, & on the 29th, President Buchanan, having entered into a *quasi* armistice with certain leading seceders, at Pensacola & elsewhere, caused Secretaries Holt & Toucy to instruct, in a joint note, the commanders of the war vessels off Pensacola & Lieut Slemmer, commanding Fort Pickens, to commit no act of hostility, & not to land Capt Vogdes' company unless that fort should be attacked.

[That joint note I never saw until March 25, but supposed the armistice was consequent upon the meeting of the Peace Convention at Washington and was understood to terminate with it.]

Hearing, however, of the most active preperations for hostilities, on the part of the seceders at Pensacola, by the erection of new batteries & arming Fort Mc Ree,—that had not a gun mounted when it was seized,—during the Peace Convention & since—I brought the subject to the notice of the new administration, when this note, dated March 12, to Capt Vogdes, was agreed upon, Viz: "At the first favorable moment you will land, with your company, reinforce Fort Pickens & hold the same 'till further orders." This order, in duplicate, left New York, by two naval vessels, about the middle of March, as the mail & the wires could not be trusted. And detached officers could not be substituted; for two had already been arrested & paroled, by the authorities of Pensacola; despatches taken from one of them, & a third, to escape like treatment, forced to turn back when near that city. Thus those authorities have not ceased to make war upon the United States since the capture, by them, of the Navy Yard—Jan. 12.

Respectfully submitted
Winfield Scott.

Head Qrs. of the Army,
Washington, March 30, 1861.

COPY

Executive Mansion
April 1st 1861.

Lieut General Scott:

Would it impose too much labor on General Scott to make short, comprehensive daily reports to me of what occurs in his Department, including movements by himself, and under his orders, and the receipt of intelligence? If not I will thank him to do so.

Your Obedient Servant
A. Lincoln

For the President.

It is known today, thro satisfactory unofficial letters that the sloop of war, *Brooklyn,* before leaving her station, off Fort Pickens, shifted Capt. Vogdes' company, on board [*to*] the *Sabine,* another vessel of war cruising before Pensacola Harbor. The private letter adds that the company expected, hourly, an order to land.

Such order was issued by me at the instance of the War Department, but at my suggestion, & in *duplicate,* about the middle of March, & the two copies were despatched by two naval vessels from New York. No previous safe conveyance had presented itself in that month. The mail & the wires had, some time before, been turned against us, & we could not, without great hazard, employ officers as despatch bearers. Major Towers was stopped this side of Pensacola, & Lieuts. Prime & Saunders captured & placed on parole.

Some progress has been made, today, towards setting on foot an expedition etc. To science, numbers & valor, there are, in war, but few impossibilities. The object it is now proposed to attain, is certainly not one of them. I will only add that the difficulties to be conquered have been, perhaps, quadrupled in the past month. In that time the adverse forces which took the Navy Yard & then dispersed have been (since the 12th of March) augmented to about 5,000 men, under a very able commander—Genl. Bragg. In the same time, Fort McRee, which had not a mounted gun, when seized by the enemy, & was only occupied by a guard over convicts, delinquents & prisoners of war, from that event till recently, has now a formidable armament, commanding the entrance to the Harbor, bearing on Ft. Pickens & sweeping the beach south of the latter. As has been already intimated, these obstacles are not insurmountable: but it is deemed better to estimate & provide for them in advance, than to mourn over them in disaster.

In compliance with the wishes of the President, respectfully submitted.

Winfield Scott.

Apl. 1, 1861.

[On back of letter:] No. 1

Head Quarters of the Army,
Washington, April 1, 1861.

Memorandum of expedition of Major Porter, asst. Adj't. Genl. in the Steamer "Daniel Webster", from New York to Texas, to bring out the Companies of Artillery and as many as possible of Infantry, for which orders were given before the secession of Texas was known.

The Daniel Webster sailed from New York February 15, landed 62 Recruits for the garrison of Fort Taylor (Key West) and supplies of provisions and ordnance for that post and Fort Jefferson, (Tortugas) the 23d and 25th February, Landed at Indianola March 2, & sent forward despatches to Col. Waite, Commanding the troops in Texas, in relation to putting the companies of Artillery in march for Brazos.

Arrived at Fort Brown 12 o'clock the night of March 3, But, Major French (commanding a company of Light Artillery) arrived at Fort Brown March 8, with three companies of Artillery which were embarked from the mouth of the Rio Grande the night of March 19. The Texas Volunteers then occupied the Brazos.

The 13th March, Major Porter chartered, in the Harbor of Brazos Santiago, the Steamer "Genl Rush," to convey a part of the companies and batteries thence to Key West. His measure expedited the movement of the companies, probably two weeks.

The garrisons of Forts Taylor and Jefferson were re-inforced by two companies each (making three in each) the 24th March. Those posts have been put in as complete a state as the resources of the Officers would permit, and are prepared against surprise and seige. Fuel and 160,000 gals of water have been collected in Fort Taylor (Key West). The daily supply is drawn from the Barracks on shore. At the Fort there is but a small surface from which water is collected in the rainy season. At Fort Jefferson there are over 200,000 gals water used only for drinking & cooking, besides a large quantity under each casemate, somewhat brackish, and used for washing. Fuel is scarce at this post, and Major Porter recommends that apparatus for cooking with coal be sent there; & that when supplies are sent to the post, coal should be included.

Respectfully submitted to the President:

Winfield Scott.

P. S. Made for me by a staff officer—More in detail than necessary—Error not to be repeated. *W. S*

No 1

[Endorsed in Mr. Lincoln's hand:] Genl Scott's daily report— No 1—

Head Qrs. of the Army.
Washington April 1. 1861

Dear Sir

The immediate departure of a war steamer with instructions to enter Pensacola Harbor & use all measures in his power to prevent any Attack from the main land upon Fort Pickens is of prime importance.

If the President as commander-in-chief will issue the order of which I enclose a draft, an important step towards the security of Fort Pickens will be taken.

I am, Sir, verry respectfully
Your most obdt. servant
Winfield Scott.

Hon W. H. Seaward(!),
Secy. of State,
etc etc.

[Endorsed in Mr. Lincoln's hand:]
Gen. Scott's report
No. 2. & other document.
[In pencil and in another hand:] April 1 1861

For Mrs. Mary Doubleday
care of A. K. Hewitt Esq.
Bank of The Metropolis Washington D. C.

Fort Sumter. S. C.
My Dearest *April 2d 1861*

We have no news as yet, I will keep this letter open until the mail is about to close, in hopes a messenger may be here. At present every thing seems uncertain. The dysentery has broken out among the men and the Doctor is afraid it will spread. We have three cases this morning.

Nothing from the North came yesterday as there is but one mail on Sunday. To day I hope to hear from you again.

Every one is weary of the confinement here. It is nothing but walking around the parapet, eating and sleeping.

I cannot see how this national quarrel is going to end. Every thing looks dark and yet I feel as if it would all come out right at last.

The action of Virginia in refusing to let the U. S. have its own cannon is most extraordinary as that state has not seceded. How we can get along without fighting in the midst of all this lawlessness it is impossible for me to see. The only effectual aim the South has would appear to be piracy or privateering. She threatens to sieze all defenceless merchant vessels belonging to the United States & confiscate the cargoes. The North cannot retaliate as the South has few or no vessels of its own, almost all in use being hired from the North.

—The mail is just in. The question of Fort Sumter does not seem to have been decided.— In haste

With kisses & love
Your aff husband
A. D.
[Abner Doubleday]

For the President.

I omitted to say, yesterday, that an officer, at Key West, writes—"it is expected that Judge Marvin will resign his office in May, & that this will take away most the moral force from the Island. His marshal & clerk had already resigned." Judge Marvin will be a great loss to the U. S. No legitimate judicial authority will then remain at Key West—none but Florida judges; & it is suggested that Col°. B. be authorized to send them away, at once, together with all [*men*] holding commissions from Florida, & other disaffected persons from Key West & Tortugas. Cut off, as they are, from any State, by the sea & sesession, they are without any civil goverment, & can only be held & protected, for the time by martial law.— I have, accordingly, desired Col. B. to take the views of the President, thro' the Secretary of State, on the subject, & govern himself accordingly. [This I am happy to say has been placed on (I may presume to say) the right footing.]

A marshal (& if Marvin resigns) a new judge, for Key West, ought to be early appointed.

Respectfully submitted to the President.

Winfield Scott,

Ap^{l}. 2, 1861.

[Endorsed in Mr. Lincoln's hand:]
Gen. Scott's daily report
N°. 2.
[In pencil and in another hand:] April 2 1861

Chillicothe Ohio April 2nd 1861

Hon Abraham Lincoln
President of the U. S.

Dear Sir I have this day sent to you per the Adams Express Co one Box inclosed you will find one pair of Slippers worked by my Little Daughter as a presant for you from her—you will also find a few Lines inclosed in Box Well now in regard our National trubls= I Sometimes think we are giving them Traitors too much time they are working with a will to do and in a Short time will I fear be the Strongest Goverment of the two—though I Still hope that you may Be able to restore the Goverment But if the Country is Lost the Democratic Party must bare the blame for it is them that made all this truble we know you have a hard time of it and I often think of you in those trublesome times and Pray God that he may give you Wisdom and Strenght to guide the Ship of State into the harber of Safty—

I am but a poor humble Mechanic and Seek no office But I Love my Country and would Die in its Defence though I must not intrude on your time with a Long Letter will you please let me know if you receive the package and oblige

yours truly
S. Shreckengaust

To A. Lincoln
President U. S.

[Notation on margin:] Slippers
1861

New York April 3d 1861

Mr Lincoln
Dear Sir

I voted for you thinking that *in* you the country would find a defender of its rights & honour. I am totally disappointed. You are as destitute of policy, as weak, and [*as*] vassalating as was your predecessor when he begged the enemies of the country to defer the execution of their schemes of wickedness until he was out of office. Dou you imagine your course is meeting the favor of republicans—even in New York? No Sir! Democrats rejoice over it, knowing that it will demoralize & overthrow the party, Give up Sumpter, Sir, & you are as dead politically as John Brown is physically. You have got to fight. Issue a proclamation to the Union loving men of the Slave States & tell them, it is not them but their *enemies*—who would subject them to grievous taxations to support over them a military despotism—that you fight, You have got to *do* this thing Sir, else the country will do it *without* you, Do you think New York is going to sit quietly by & see its commerce diverted to Southern ports—foreign imports sent into the West & North West—*duty free* through the ports of of the South? No Sir, As the New York Times says this morning—"Your want of *policy* & *action* has demoralized the country more than all of the 3 months of Buchanans imbecility did all together"———

As a republican I am sorry to have to *say* these things. But *facts vindicate* this statement, Either *act, immediately* & *decisively* or resign & go home,

A Republican

For the President.

Report from Major Anderson recd which the President has seen.

The company of Sappers & Miners—called *Engineers Company*—left Washington this morning, for New York harbor, to embark tomorrow. Three companies will leave here, tomorrow morning, of the same expedition. These companies are: —Barry's horse-artillery; Brooks' foot artillery, & Allens' foot artillery.

There will remain in Washington, a detachment of cavalry; recruits, from Carlisle, recruiting depôt, about 80 men & horses;—Magruder's horse artillery; Griffin's, do belonging to the Military Academy show needed there; Elsey's foot artillery & Haskins' do

The companies of *foot* artillery are acting as infantry.

The number of Marines, at the Washington Navy Yard, varies. We heard today, that the number now there is some 200.

There is not another company of regulars, within reach of Washington, except seven at Fort Monroe, making about 400 men—the *minimum* force needed there, under existing circumstances,—one company at the Fayetteville Arsenal, No C., to guard arms & ammution against a thick population of blacks;—a garrison of recruits, (50) at Ft Washington, 10 miles below us; a garrison of 100 recruits in Ft Mc Henry, Baltimore; about 750 recruits, in N. York Harbor; 220, do at New Port Barracks, opposite to Cincinnati, & about 350 men, at Jefferson Barracks & the St Louis Arsenal, near by, mostly recruits.

Lieut. Gilman from Ft Pickens has just arrived with a full report from Lieut. Slemmer—too long to be abstracted—& I have sent him with the report, to the Sec. of War.

I have sent for, & am waiting to see Wm Fox, when instructions will be ready to effect his objects, in N. York, so far as may depend on the Army.

Respectfully submitted.
Winfield Scott.
Ap^{l}. 3, 1861.

[Endorsed in Mr. Lincoln's hand:] Gen. Scott's daily report N° 3,

PRIVATE

Springfield Illinois
April 3rd 1861

Dear Lincoln:

I have recieved your favor of the 30th ultimo. I would not let the case of Cousin Lizzie trouble me if I were you No one will complain of you if you do not give her the appointment while very many doubtless would complain of her appointment and would have much show of reason because the appointment of a lady would be unusual. All I feel that I can properly say now is what I said to Cousin Lizzie that the emoluments of the office would be a great source of comfort to her and to Uncle & Aunt. If they live a few years they will be dependent In my letter to Cousin Lizzie I said that I did not expect you would give her the appointment

So far as the election is concerned (I mean for Postmaster) it will amount to nothing. I understand that all the applicants but Ellis are opposed to submitting to a vote and it is charged that Ellis' friends on the North Side of the town are anxious to have Ellis appointed so as to remove the Office to that side of the town I have no reason to believe that there is any truth in that I only refer to it to show the feeling—There is a good deal of feeling among the different Candidates and their friends and no appointment you can make would be very satisfactory and if I were you I would please *myself*.

All that I can say is that I cannot urge upon you her appointment yet I would be glad if she is appointed. I do not feel that her appointment would subject you to [*less*] more remarks than any one else while a very large portion of our community would be very much gratified by it—

I hope you will give Dr. Wallace some good appointment and the appointment of both will do you no great harm I believe I have said enough to explain my feeling on that subject—

I wish to say one thing more that my personal attachment and respect for you which I have maintained for thirty years—is as sincere now as it ever was—notwithstanding our difference in politics and I hope you every success [*you*] for you and our common country

Yours truly *John T Stuart*

(CONFIDENTIAL)

Fort Taylor
Key West. Fla.
Apr. 4. 1861.

Gen. J. G. Totten.
Chief Engineer.
Washington. D. C.
Sir.

I suppose it is my duty as a faithful sentinel on the extreme Southern Outpost to report to you whatever may in my opinion concern the national interests, having in view only the good of the whole country & not hedging myself by mere technical lines. The time is near at hand, apparently which must definitely fix the status of these Forts & this line of Keys & Reefs. I enclose a copy of an article which I prepared so long ago as in Decr. last, & which in the main, still expresses what seems to me the proper course of policy concerning the subject treated. There are some points on which I will now add a few comments as present circumstances require. That the public establishments here are to be retained by the U. S. in any adjustment to be made with the seceding states, I have not permitted myself to doubt. The exact mode of adjustment I have not much considered, but on the whole, I cannot see how any jurisdiction can be here conceded to the Southern Confederacy unless it is to have all. To hold the Forts & leave to this C. S. A. government. the Admiralty jurisdiction which by a special law creating an Admiralty Court [*here*] of Key West, it has assumed, is to leave the U. S. here shorn of most of the substantial power & a costly mockery. There can be no enduring & peaceful division of jurisdictions here. Either the U. S. must withdraw entirely or it must dispossess, in the end the S. C. A. from all pretense of jurisdiction on this Key. The case is [*none*] one involving serious complications. The U. S. Court is now disabled, having no Marshal, & it is also fully determined by Judge Marvin, soon to resign his place & transfer his residence permanently to N. Y. He is brought to this conclusion partly by considerations of health & family, & partly by the conviction that he could not execute the laws without resort to force, which he could not now legally call into action & to which he has a a most natural aversion.— He regards this as but a small outpost of a great question & that it would be wrong & injudicious to create here any complications which might obstruct the pacific solution of the greater questions, which once duly solved will carry all local questions as corollaries with them.— On the part of the Military & naval forces here, it is clear that no act of force must be exercised, except under due process of law, just as in ordinary times, except under the *extreme* resort of a proclmation of martial law; itself, under the circumstances an act of hostility & thus contravening what is believed to be the desire of the U. S. Government. There the Court provided with a Marshal & otherwise completed for work, the consignees could legally perhaps carry most of the wrecking business into the Fa. Court, & possibly into the S. C. A. Admiralty Court— It is doubtful if the Collector can exercise his functions, unbacked by a U. S. Court & it is stoutly declared that any attempt of Mr. H. . . ., newly appointed as Collector, to execute the duties of the office, will lead to resistance, nor can the U. S. forces be used to aid him without due process of law, which cannot now be had. Thus the fundamental difficulty seems on every attempt to vindicate the U. S. laws here. in their application to the town. It is therefore a question to be decided once for all by *general* action of the Government, whether the laws shall be enforced. at the expense of collision. & if so. the U. S. court must be completely organized. & there should be an authentic proclamation of the designs of the U. S. Government. Citizens of Key West cannot in justice to themselves accept offices. unless they are positively assured that the U. S. will retain the town as well as the Fort. & will vindicate the execution of the laws by a forcible posse under the laws, if necessary. Such a proclamation would probably at once settle all local opposition for it is I believe nearly certain that a half or two thirds of the K. W. people really prefer the U. S. authority to any other. & a positive & conclusive settlement of the question would find well nigh all, perfectly reconciled to the U. S. There is an interest. which plainly speaking. is I believe striving to open this Fort for the slave trade & which has stimulated most of the secession feeling of the town, & [*has*] worked actively to procure the overthrow of U. S. jurisdiction here. They have stimulated hopes of a more profitable administration of the wrecking business. by a change. & the new Judge McIntosh is expected to decree more literal salvages—He is expected by the boat due to-morrow. & a cotton wreck has been nursed along to inaugurate his court upon.

On the whole it seems to me that the Government should make a complete disposal of the main question before any petty entanglements arise. & this once decided, will remove all probable collisions.— It may require some time for this main question to be properly closed, but it must be met sooner or later. Until then, half way measures, can only embroil, or place officers in false positions—As soon as a final decision can be reached. then the U. S. court should be fully reestablished & all needful measures taken for a complete vindication of the U. S. authority.

In any arrangement with the C. S. A. I believe that the complete tenure of the line of Keys could be peacefully secured to the U. S. as a counter guaranty of the Missi. R. commerce, in which the U. S. has still the chief interest. What should be the Status of this line of Keys is hard to say. but this might by consent be made a County of

Del. for instance, or made a special judicial District with power of local legislation.— The subject is difficult & exhaustless, nor am I fitted to suggest very wisely concerning it.

As to local officers, I am confident they could be appointed from town, after the ultimate decision of the U. S. to hold on is known. though the Judge & Marshal may probably best come from some border State.- There should be a good District Att^y. here, but the pay will not induce a proper man to take the post.

I will not now enter farther into the subject discussed. as I have only meant to *indicate* a *hint.* what seemed to me proper considerations under the circumstances. This I have done, that you may make such use of the ideas offered as you may think proper. Though the community & interests involved are seemingly small, the questions implicated are the very ones, so oppressive in their magnitude under which our ablest statesmen stagger. & it is not for the officers here to act out a decision on their own responsibility, & without full concert —I might well excuse myself from this presentation, but as I care too much for the just appreciation of the matters involved to leave them subject to mischance. you will correctly estimate what may seem gratuitous zeal—

I have just learned that the cotton wreck before referred to: has today been submitted to Judge Marvin for *arbitration.* & this may leave Judge McIntosh some time without chance of asserting his Judgeship.

Very respectfully
Yours etc
E. B. Hunt.
Capt. of Eng^s

[Endorsed:] Rec^d April 13th

(PRIVATE.)

Cincinnati O. April 4/61.

To President Lincoln:

Thirty days more of *"Peace Policy"* at Washington—and not only the Republican Party, but the Government itself will be gone to destruction or placed beyond remedy!

We have been beaten in our City election—the same in St. Louis—Cleveland—Rhode Island—Brooklyn—and lost two Members of Congress in Connecticut—all from the demoralization and discouraging effect produced by the apparent *inaction* and *temperizing* policy of the new Administration, and the *impression* that *Fort Pickens* was going to be given up also to the rebels!

The only *possible* salvation of the Administration—of the Government, and of the Union, depends upon a *firm stand* against Secession, and by all means and above all, upon the *re-enforcement and holding against all opposition* of *Fort Pickens*! That is the *Key* to this whole secession business! Hold that—and you hold everything within your own grasp, and everything *"steady"*, until the *disease runs* its *course, and* either *kills* or *cures* itself—as it surely will in less than one year. If it be *possible* (no matter what the cost of money or life)—*Fort Sumpter* should be *supplied with provision.* It should be done by *strategem.* IT CAN BE DONE. *Afterwards,* it could be re-enforced with troops. But it will be better, a thousand times, that the Fort be attacked, *Captured,* and Anderson and his men made prisoners of war, or all killed—than that it be *evacuated!* But if it *must* be abandoned, let it be done; we can bear it—provided Fort Pickens is held and reenforced for any emergency.

The most fatal infatuation that ever did or can possess a statesman is the idea of a *Peace Policy* in the present emergency! It only encourages and strengthens the enemy, while it disheartens the friends of the Union in the seceded States, as well as the *real* friends of the Union every where!

A"Peaceable Separation"—is *an impossibility!* Besides—*that* is not what is aimed at by the Secessionists and their abettors. All they want is to get the Administration, and the Republican Party committed to a "Peaceable Secession", and that moment the question will be sprung upon us—*"Reconstruction, on the basis of the South-*

ern Constitution, or Disunion"! and *we* will thus be placed on the side of disunion,—*and beaten to death*! The love of the "*Union*" in this Country is stronger than hatred to *Slavery*; and whatever that question—that issue comes (and it *is coming*)—the dissolution of the Union, on the adoption of the Jeff. Davis Constitution by all the States—*the whole South,* and the whole Democratic and Bell-everett Parties at the North, with a large portion of the commercial and Manufacturing interests besides—*will be against* us, and *will carry us into the Southern Confederacy!*

This scheme must be broken up—and at once!

1 Reenforce Fort Pickens. Let them attack it, if they will. (Who *knows* that they will?) If they *do*—the *balls* which they fire against its walls will *rebound* and *strike them—kill them; that is all!* No body, out of the range of the Forts' guns will be hurt! There need be no *invasion*—consequently no "Civil war". But we better have *twenty years* of civil war, than let the Government *go to pieces*—or than "recognize" the "Southern Confederacy",—which would be *recognizing* the *Right of Secession*—etc.

2—The Administration *ought* to do all it can—in the line of its legitimate duty—to *encourage an attack* or *attacks* by *the Confederates*: It should *court* and encourage, and bring it about, if possible. *This*—in order to induce them to raise, equip, and keep up *a large military force, thus increasing their expenses, tax levies,* etc, in order the sooner to *break them down*—force a *reaction* among the *people*—and in this way the thing would soon be *crushed out.*

3—Call Congress together—modify or *abolish* the Tariff: Raise an army of *60,000:* make southern Kansas, the Indian Territory & West. Arkansas, the *base* of operation of our division of say 20,000 men, Send 5,000 to 10,000 down the Mississippi, to clear out the obstructions to commerce & navigation along that river. Hold 20 to 30,000 in and near Washington—Fill Fort Monroe & & Gosport Navy Yard as full as they can hold: Then *hold things steady*—Collect the revenue on shipboard, or blockade the ports—and while all the *war munition manufacturies* in the U. States are put to work, day and night, to their utmost—let the "Model Government" of the Confederate States flourish, for a few months,—giving its leaders as well as *all the people of* both the seceded States and those that *talk* of seceding, that after giving them sufficient time for reflection and a return to their loyalty in the Union if they *dont do it,* you intend to *make them do it!* [500,000,000] *Five hundred thousand* of the men who voted for you are ready, willing, and *anxious,* to back you—in this course—in maintaining the *integrity* of *the Union* —the *old Constitution as it* is, and the *enforcement of the Laws.* But for God's sake! *Give not an inch*—and *dont* be afraid of *war! Do what you will—War,* (to some extent) *is inevitable!*

Truly Yours.
J. H. Jordan.

For the President.

There is nothing of special importance in the military service to be reported to day, that will not reach the president thro' the Department of State, & no doubt certain details from Fort Sumter will be reported from the Secretary of war. There are some other small details from Pensacola; but I am too sick to abstract them.

Respectfully submitted.
Winfield Scott.

Head Qu. of the Army,
Washington, Ap[l]. 4, 1861.

[Endorsed in Mr. Lincoln's hand:]
Gen. Scott's daily report
No. 4—

For the President

I have nothing of special interest to report today; but that machinations against the Government & this Capital, are secretly going on, all around us—in Virginia, in Maryland & here, as well as farther

South—I have no doubt. I cannot, however, say that they are, as yet, formidable, or are likely ever to come to a head. I have no police man at my service, & no fund for the payment of detectives. But, under the circumstances, recommend that such agents should be, at once, employed in Baltimore, Anapolis, Washington, Alexandria, Richmond & Norfolk.

For the reasons stated, I am not prepared to suggest that a militia force should be called out to defend this Capital—under section 2, of the militia act, passed Feb. 28, 1795. The necessity of such call, however, may not be very distant.

Respectfully submitted.
Winfield Scott.

Head Qrs. of the Army,
Washington, Apl. 5, 1861.

P. S. The President cannot call, direct, for volunteer companies, or battalions; but Governors of States frequently substitute volunteers to make up the quota called for, in lieu of regular militia drafts.
W. S.

[Endorsed in Mr. Lincoln's hand:]
Gen. Scott's daily report
No. 5

Washington, D. C. April 5th. 1861.

Hon Wm H Seward
Secretary of State
Sir;

On the subject of which we conversed this morning, the following has been communicated to me.

Mr Forsyth, one of Mr. Jeffn Davis' commissioners asserted on Wednesday to Dr Mackie, clerk in the State Department, that within sixty days, the Government of the Confederate States would embrace this city and all the States north as far as New York—That said States would extend their protection thus far, but would cut off those damned puritan States east, and never let them come in.

A lady recently arrived from Montgomery, states that she called on Mrs Jeff^{n} Davis before leaving, and on taking leave asked Mrs. D. what she should say to her friends at Washington—That Mrs Davis replied; "tell them I shall be happy to see them *in the White House at Washington in June.*"

This statement comes from Mr. Wood, clerk in the office of the Secretary of the Treasury.

Mr. George Taylor, of Georgetown, who was frequently brought to my notice during the past winter as a hot headed young secessionist, stated a few days since to a gentleman from Tennessee, that the Southern Commissioners, at the National Hotel in this city, are securing as many men as possible for action here and in the adjoining states.

That they did not wish to have men go south, but wanted them to be ready *here*—

A young man formerly employed by Gilman, the Druggist on P^{a} Avenue, stated that there were thousands of men in Virginia, here and in Baltimore ready to rise up armed at a given signal by Mr Davis—That the attack on Fort Sumpter would be the Signal for action here, and plenty of men would rise to seize and hold the Capital until the Southern army could reach here.

He further stated that he himself would lead a company to take the Presidents House, and that the President, Cabinet Officers and General Scott would be made prisoners at the outset.

Taking into consideration the intense activity of the Secession leaders in Virginia, the meetings which have been called in the eastern portion of the State, the presence of that active & bold revolutionist Ben. McCulloch in different parts of Virginia on different days when his presence in Texas would be so valuable to the interests of the Secessionists there,—also the ease with which the large bodies of troops now concentrated and concentrating at Charleston and Pensacola could be transported by rail to the heart of Virginia before news of this approach could reach this City, it would not to me be an improbable conception, that those who now rule the southern state intend to secure to themselves the prestige of possessing this Capital, and forcing a revolution here and in the middle States

Very respectfully I am,
Sir,
Your mo. obt. Servt
Charles P Stone
Insp Gen[l] D C.m.

For the President

The information brought today, by Capt. Talbot & Lieut. Bell from, respectively, Fort Sumter & Texas, has, no doubt, been fully communicated to the President by the Secretary of War.

A second steamer will arrive, from Texas, at N. York, in a day or two, with six troops of dismounted cavalry. In advance, I have ordered two of those companies (or troops), [*from the ship*] to proceed, from the ship, to this place, [*to this place*] to be filled up with men (cavalry recruits) here, & to be partially mounted out of the 80 horses in the use of those cavalry recruits. The additional horses (some 35) can be purchased here. The other four troops of cavalry, I have ordered to proceed, from the ship, to Carlisle Barracks, Pennsy[*i*]lvania, to be remounted there, whence they can be readily brought here—if deemed necessary.

Whilst writing the foregoing (½ past 3 o'clock) Lieut. Smead, belonging to Vogdes' company, arrived with despatches from Cat. V. & Com. Adams of the Sabine, from which, as will be seen by the correspondence between the two (which I have not time to abstract), Commodore Adams refueses to put the company ashore—notwithstanding my order to Capt. Vogdes!!

I have no time to comment on this extraordinary conduct. Lieut. Smead brings no other material information.

Respectfully submitted,
Winfield Scott
Apl. 6, 1861.

[Endorsed:] *Confidential* Gen. Scott's daily report No. 6

(In pencil: April 6, 1861)
For the President,
Thro' the Sec. of War,
From Lieut. Genl Scott.

Orrstown
April 8„ 1861

Mrs Abraham Lincoln
Dear Madam

after my compliments to you Honered Madam, I take the liberty of addressing you, hoping you will not consider it presumption, I have a very interesting little Daughter four months *Old,* And we were anxious to call her after our President not knowing her Maiden name we gave her the name Linie for Lincoln, untile such time as we could know, would it be asking to much of you to please let me know by letter or some other mean's which you see proper you will oblige you obedient Servern't

Anna L. Mackey

PS) Please Direct
Mrs Anna L Mackey
Orrstown
Franklin Co
Penn[a]

[Notation on 4th page:]
Mrs Mackey
wants to name her
little girl for Mrs L

For the President.

The Secretary of War, will, no doubt, make the President acquainted with Major Anderson's report received today. There is nothing official from Ft. Pickens or the expeditions, out of New York.

For the defense of the government more troops are wanted. The steamer with the dismounted cavalry (six companies) from Texas, must be in N. York, today or tomorrow, to be followed by another steamer, with about the same number of troops, from Texas, in a week. There is a growing apprehension of danger here, in the meantime. I rely on the presence of a third battery of flying Artillery (Sherman's) by sea tuesday next. It is coming from Minesota. Three other companies of artillery, on foot, serving as Infantry, will be, at New York, from the same quarter, in 14 days. All these reinforcements, excepting Sherman's battery, may be too late for this place. For the interval, I have sent Colo. Smith (the immediate commander of all the forces in the District of Columbia to learn what numbers of *reliable* volunteers can be obtained in this city, I have also desired him to see whether the companies already here, may not be advantageously concentrated near to the President's Square.

I beg leave to suggest that a small War Steamer, to cruise between Alexandria & the Long Bridge, over the Potomac, would be of great importance to the system of defense that we are planning.

I ought to report that officers who, notwithstanding their oaths of fidelity to the U. S., ask to be excused from duty, *in the South,* lest they should come into conflict with the forces of the Montgomery Confedracy, are invariably refused & told to remember their oaths. Capt. Johns (born in the District) & Lieut. Smead (born in Georgia)—the same who arrived, Saturday, with despatches from Captain Vogdes & Com. Adams—have been so answered this morning.

Major Anderson—an officer of the highest honor, valor, patriotism & morals showed some nervous irratability in his letter received this morning—arising from partial sickness, long confinement & a sense of neglect, in respect to the denial of the brevets that he knows I asked for him—first in the time of President Buchanan, & once, since. The last cause of soreness is wholly conjectural; for, no matter how deeply wounded, I know that he would sooner die than utter a word of complaint. A little nervousness will, I am sure, be, under the circumstances, excused in a noble soldier.

Respectfully submitted.
Winfield Scott.

Head Qrs[.] of the Army,
Washington, Apl. 8, 1861

[Endorsed in Mr. Lincoln's hand:]
Gen. Scott's daily report
No. 7.

New York,
April 8th 1861.

Hon. Abraham Lincoln:–
Presd't U. S:–
Dear Sir:–

In the present crisis, and distracted state of the country, if your Honor wishes colored volunteers, you have only to signify by answering the above note at 70 E. 13 St. N. Y.C., with instructions, and the above will meet with prompt attention, whenever your honor wishes them.

Your very Obedient
and Humble Servant.
Levin Tilmon.

His Excellency *Quincy, Ills—Apl. 9. 1861*
A. Lincoln
President of the U. S. A.
Dear Sir

Since the announcement of the death of Judge Mc Lean very many of my friends in this part of the State have asked permission to present my name for appointment as his successor. I have refused to permit petitions to be gotten up and circulated, thinking it incompatible with the dignity of the office, and the dignity of character which ought to be maintained by any one fitted to fill it, that it should be sought in that manner.

Upon mature consideration of the subject I have concluded to write you frankly, and candidly to express to you my wishes, and there leave the matter to be disposed of as, to you, may seem right and proper.

It is not without a great deal of embarrassment and hesitation that I have determined upon this course, but, having determined upon it, I do not propose to offer any apologies for addressing myself to the task. You know me about as well as I know myself; and in regards to my fitness for the office you know me better—for you occupy a far better stand point for the formation of a fair and impartial judgment than I do. If, then, you shall think me competent to the duties of the office, and shall be at all inclined to gratify me in any thing, I say frankly, and without any sort of disguise, or affectation, that there is nothing in your power to do for me which would gratify me so much as this. It is an office peculiarly adapted to my tastes, and the faithful and honest performance of the duties of which would be my highest pride and ambition.

For twenty years, and more, I have been fighting the political battles of my party, and my Country under circumstances of exceeding difficulty, and without hope or expectation of reward.

I have very little political ambition, and have not sought high political honors. In the line of my profession I confess to a large ambition—yet I do not think it passes the bounds of what is laudable. I do not think it is inordinate. And this ambition, I say without hesitation, cannot be so gratified in any other way as by the success of the application I now make.

Heretofore I have neither asked, nor received, and whether this is granted or not I shall not ask again.

I have asked no body to aid me—have, in fact, refused to permit petitions to be gotten up by others. I felt that the relations between us justified me in addressing myself to you directly, and in giving full and free utterance to my sentiments—and this course is less humiliating to me than the other.

I am willing *you* shall know that I do desire the office—I am *not* willing that the world shall.

I think Illinois is entitled to the office. She is now one of the first and most important States in the Union, and has never been honored with such an appointment. Ohio has had it for thirty years and has no right to claim it again. If it is to be given to Illinois I do not think it egotism to say that my claims are, at least, equal to those of others.

You will doubtless be beset by many whose claims will be more earnestly and more powerfully urged—yet I know that you can do as you please, and that the great body of the people will not care a fig who the appointee is, so that he acquits himself of the duties of the office with integrity, fidelity, and a reasonable degree of ability.

I do not think I would dishonor the position; but, as before remarked, you are more competent to judge than I am of my qualifications.

One request, in conclusion, I make upon your friendship—that if you reject my application you will not subject me to the mortification of letting it be known that I personally solicited the office and was refused. I have not written a line to any other person upon the subject—not even Mr. Bates—nor do I intend to, altho' I have been much urged to do so. I am willing to expose my wishes and feelings to you. I am not willing to exhibit them to others. The whole matter is in your hands. Will it be too much to ask, that, at some convenient moment, you will give me a line in reply.

Respectfully and Truly
your friend
O. H. Browning

[Endorsed:]

Hon. O. H. Browning
Asks for Judgeship
vacated by death
of Judge Mc Lean
1861

For the President.

There is no news, of interest, today, (as far as I know) from any quarter.

I suggested to the Secretary of War yesterday, the calling out (say) ten companies of the militia (or by substitution) uniformed volunteers of this city to aid in the defence of the public buildings & other public property of the Capital, against "an invasion or insurrection, or probable prospect thereof." [*Calan's Mil. Laws* (Edit. of 1858) *p.* 125.] The necessity for this additional force & the manner of employing it, were, yesterday, pretty fully discussed, before the Secretary of War, by Col? Smith, Col? Stone (two most excellent officers) & myself Col? Stone, Inspection General to Major General Weightman's division, thinks that twice that number of loyal volunteers can be properly furnished by the division, & I appreciate that the twenty companies may be deemed necessary in a few days. I hope that the President may give the Secretary of War the authority to make the call for ten companies at once.

The act "more effectually to provide for the organization of the Militia of the District of Columbia" (referred to above) is quite distinct from the general Militia law, same book, p.77. The District law gives the President all the power that he wants in the proposed case.

With the ten volunteer companies & (as yet) handful of regulars, [*as yet*] we can can give a guard of one company to each of the Department buildings, nightly, & keep small guards (alarm posts) at the principal entrances into the city—besides looking to the safety of the President's house.

[I have, this moment, received the President's instructions of this date thro' the Secretary of War on the Safety of this District.]

The first step now to be taken is to call out the ten companies. This shall be attended to as soon as I can communicate with the Secretary of War, Gen! Weightman, Col? Smith & Colo. Stone.

Respectfully submitted.

Winfield Scott.

Ap! 9, 1861.

[Endorsed in Mr. Lincoln's hand:]
Gen. Scott's daily report
No. 8

THE MAGNETIC TELEGRAPH COMPANY

13 Dated Charleston Apl 9th 1861

Rec'd, Washington Apl 9th 1861, ____ o'clock, ______ min. M.

To. W W Wallach

Editor Star

Sanguinary fight this
evening between the Gov &
S C Troops four (4) vessels
sunk the balance went
out sea disabled, Gov't
troops suffered severly
loss S C troops slight.

Jno W Martin

30–200
pr

OFFICE GLOBE IRON WORKS.

Lewis Worthington Joseph Kinsey

WORTHINGTON & CO.

Cincinnati, Apl 9 1861.

A Lincoln President

Having received much benefit from the occasional moderate use of my wine I am induced to Send you a case of it made from the Pure Juice of "Catawba Grapes" off vines of my own planting The severe tax upon your Phisicul Strength at Present under the heavy cares of State must produce great exhaustion
In this Pure wine I send you will find a quick and wholesome nourishment. but if your veiws of temperance forbid the use of it

please hand it over to my friend Honr D P Holloway Com of Patents who I know to be a good temperance man and will make proper use of it. Please excuse this liberty I have taken and believe me a true friend to the Present *active indication* for Preserving the union very Resply

Joseph Kinsey

His Excellency, Abraham Lincoln,
President of the United States.

Sir.

I respectfully renew a tender, made some time since, of the services of two Regiments of Philadelphia Volunteers, for any duty to which they may be called, in the present unfortunate, but not appalling condition of public affairs. One Regiment is composed of citizens of German birth or descent,—the other of Americans. Both,—numbering from eight to sixteen hundred men,—may be put in marching condition in a few days, and may be safely relied upon in any emergency.

If their services can not now be accepted, I respectfully solicit an appointment in the Army, and take pleasure in referring to the Honorable Secretary of War for evidence of my present position and past services. I served as a Captain in the First Pennsylvania Volunteers, in Mexico, and have since held the commission of Brigadier General. I now solicit an appointment as a Field officer in the Infantry or Cavalry. It would gratify me much to raise a Regiment of Infantry in Pennsylvania, as, I am sure, I could collect one of the best.

Truly Yours
Wm F. Small
Phila: April 9th, 1861

Mr. President

Give these South Carolina ruffians h–l, and we will Support You

A member of the
7th Regt. National Guard

For the President

No important military intelligence has reached me today, but no letter being received from Major Anderson, this morning, confirms the news-paper report that his communications, with Charleston, are cut off. And there is an untraceable rumor, in the streets, that some unknown person has received a telegram stating that the hostile batteries had opened fire upon F[t] Sumpter. This is improbable, as it must, in Charleston, be well known that Major Anderson is nearly out of subsistence.

The storm of the last two or three days must have been of great violence on the Sea-coast, & I am afraid that some of our transport steamers have been incommoded—perhaps damaged by the gale

The mustering of volunteers into the Service of the U. States is going on in the District. Before the ten companies already called for have been received, it is probable that I may have to ask for as many more.

Respectfully submitted,
Winfield Scott,

H[d] Qrs. of the Army
Washington, Apl. 10, 1861

[Endorsed in Mr. Lincoln's hand:]
Gen. Scott's daily report
N[o] 9.

Baltimore April 11.1861

To Abe^m. Lincon Esqr

Dear Friend I take this method of informing you that you better prepair yourself for an asailing mob that is organizing in Baltimore as far as i can inform myself is about 12000 m. strong they intend to seize the Capitol and yourself and as they say that they will tar & put cotton on your head and ride you and Gen Scot on a rail this secret organization is about 70000 m members in Maryland and Virgina and thay can be all brought to gether in five days, the person that rits this was a member and is bound by a strong oath which if they now ho i was i wold not be suffer to live but justis to you and my country make me do this

IMPORTANT

Office of the Board of Trade,
Philadelphia, April 11th 1861

His Excellency:
The President,

I had the honor to telegraph to you yesterday *thus. "Your course-secures*-a *reaction-Northern support. Secure—border States by a comprehensive view of their claims in your Councils. A Convention —treason States represented—settles the rest."*

At this time of darkness & confusion—*stand alone firm*—Each day will prove to you the fallacy of human reason & the inadequacy of human power to arrest the Calamities into which demagouges have brought the Country. Their now remains but one extremity. The South seem willing, indeed determined to maintain what they deem their rights & bear the burden *& odium*—as we term it—of Slavery. Now let them try it—for means & result—trust to the *invisible Cabinet*—who will bring the Country to a place of safety—a haven of rest. One by one the border & Western States will fall into the right chain. The Colonies or New England States be seen as the North—Geographical limits not seperate to government & those who cling to old puritanical ideas of freedom will enjoy it, by attempting to bring all others to their standard—which in itself is tyrany of the meanest —and most bigoted stamp.

The Commissioners will return South—*unsatisfied*—as they will remain in Europe—*unhonored.* With the *Consttition—Union & right* —you hold an impenetrable sheild. The immortal Clay—said "I had rather be right than—be President. Truth is mighty & public justice certain".

Sumpter *re-inforced*—Washington *strongly armed*—quiet will be restored—by your showing the government prepared for all & every emergency.

I wrote to *my friend & reference*—Commodore Vanderbilt—to day *thus*—

"I cannot believe the report you are disposed to aid the South—
"If the treason States *make war against a humane policy*—let them
"take the consequences of a just support from the North. Tender to
"the government your Steam force—from duty—interest & the crown-
"ing joy and pride of a declining life—*to sustain the Union. You*
"*know I am seldom wrong*—I defeated the Monster National debt
"Pacific Rail Road bill—saving you Millions—I DID IT NOT—FOR YOU—
"NOR—*that type of inhumanity* my father-in-law—Commodore Garri-
"son—BUT FOR MY COUNTRY. I scorn reward—my motto is "*right for*
"*the sake of right*". I now ask you to sustain the Government by
"your powerful force of Steamers—if not for your Country—your
"own interest——Do the former—crucifying self—aid the South in
"an unholy course—*the end a just retribution, your loosing all.*"—

Asking you to write one line—"all your letters are recd" as without —*all*—the chain is broken. I remain

Your friend ObtS
W.C. Jewett
of Colorado.

[Endorsed:]
PRIVATE—*only to be opened*
by the President
His Excellency
A. Lincoln
President of the
U States

For the President

The mails, this morning, fail to bring me any military news of special interest, except that Sherman's battery, on the Minesota, & three companies of foot artillery in the same district—all ordered to Washington—have been delayed by ice or snow a week or more.

It was only yesterday that I learned Captain Talbot had been ordered back to Fort Sumpter, some days before; but with what instructions, to Major Anderson or himself, I am officially ignorant.

Several companies of District volunteers were mustered into the pay & service of the U. States, yesterday & this forenoon, & the process is still going on.

A few individuals, in several companies, declining to take the oath of allegiance to the U. States, were, of course rejected,—but I am happy to report that five or six other companies have sworn allegiance without excepting a man.

The stripping of the rejected men, yesterday, of their arms, accoutrements & uniforms, by their own officers, has, I learn, had a fine effect upon the patriotism & devotion of the entire militia of the District.

A fine company, not one of the ten called for, [*yesterday*] having presented itself, this morning, of its own mere motion, & requested it might be accepted, I did not hesitate to consent & hope for approval. Before night, we shall have probably eleven companies sworn in.

The Clerk of the House of Representatives, having, thro' the Secretary of War desired that a company might be assigned to guard the Capitol, I shall instruct Col^o Smith to comply with that reasonable request—

Respectfully submitted
Winfield Scott.

H^d Qrs. of the Army,
Washington, Ap^l. 11, 1861

[Endorsed in Mr. Lincoln's hand:]
Gen. Scott's daily report
No. 10

STATE OF RHODE ISLAND, &C.

Executive Department
Providence, April 11. 1861

Sir.

During the anticipated attack on Washington previous to your inauguration I had a messenger in constant communication with Genl Scott giving a minute detail of our military organization and requesting him to make such demands for them as the exigencies of the case should demand. I should not now be correctly representing the public sentiment of the people of this State did I not assure you of their loyalty to the government of the union, and of their anxiety to do their utmost to maintain it. I have just returned from N Y from an interview with Gov Corwin, and now take pleasure in saying that we have a Battery of Light Artillery, Cps, Horses & men complete, and a force of 1000 men completly disciplined & equipped, unequalled, or at any rate not surpassed by a simular number in any country, who would respond [*to any call*] at short notice, to the call of the government in defence of the Capitol. The Artillery especially, I imagine would be very serviciable to take the place of a similar number required elsewhere. I should be ready to accompany them. That God will grant his protecting care and guidance to you, Sir, in your trying and difficult position and a safe deliverance from our unhappy difficulties, is the constant prayer of,

Your obdt svt,
Wm Sprague,

To The President.
Washington
DC.

Pellham Farm April 12th 1861

To the Cabinet at Washington
Gentlemen.

A dark cloud is about to burst on our land, that will sink everything in its descent, I hoped and prayed, that through you, our

Country would have been saved from a cruel war; but I fear it is now inevitable; the last link is broken, the last wedge that sustained the Union is gone; and nothing left but destruction and desolation, the demon of discord will stalk forth throughout the length and breadth of America; and all because, you gentlemen, have permitted your feelings to overcome the common interest you should feel in our beloved country; and the only possible way it can be brought back into the past state of happiness, is to become once more united in the bond of paternity with our irritated friend and countrymen by showing them a little kindness, What have you done to conciliate, not a single thing, have you even offered to call an extra session of congress No, have you offered to call a convention to alter the constitution, No—have you consented that they should enjoy the Territories with you, No—Are you not now using every means in your power to irritate them, Yes. Are you not sending useless fleets to beard them, Yes, Do you not talk of sending armies into their sickly climate to be killed by thousands, Yes.

I pray you for the sake of God and humanity, Oh Northern men to look what you are doing; some of you no doubt, as well as myself, are opposed to slavery, having been brought up to look at it as an institution repugnant alike to God and man. But gentlemen suppose the south would give up slavery, how could you return them an equivalent; do not I beg of you be fanatical, but remember that the wealth of the south lies in her planations, and that white men cannot work them. You might judge by the negroes of the north, how perfectly unable they are to take care of themselves, and could there be a greater curse entailed upon us, than to have the 4000000 Southern negroes freed, and set loose among us. Can the north expect the south to give up its breath, its substance, to oblige the north because a few fanatics desire it. You sail altogether too much on the word Negro; believe me, he is much better off there, where he receives kind treatment; and nine out of ten of them would not leave their masters if they had the opportunity—notwithstanding they all imagined they would be free if Lincoln was elected, have they shown the least disposition to rise—And still all our troubles have been brought upon us by this cursed race, I would not shed the blood of a single high toned southern gentleman, for all the negroes south of Mason and Disons line. Remember that it is no matter how right our systems may be, they are not in union with the south, and though you may look upon them as superior to all others in every respect, the southern people cannot be brought to think so; for that reason you must bear with them in their waywardness, and believe me when I say that it is not the intelligent classes on either side that are augmenting the war.

I call upon both north and south by every tie that binds you to be linked once more under the same flag, let us unfurl our proud banner to the winds [*of heaven*] and bring back to its azure heaven those stars that have left it.

Remember you are brothers, bound together by the ties of blood, goodness, and humanity; then do not bring war and bloodshed on our land; rather hear the earnest prayer of one insignificant raiser of cabbages and apples like myself, than the eternal and everlasting curse of millions now born, and to be born., If you bring on Civil War, the entire responsibility rests on you.

How can you hesitate for one moment, when you look at the position our glorious Country occupies—If you do, think of the deeds of our common ancestors, whose bones are crumbling to the dust, of the nobles who have passed from earth to heaven, and who if they could look down upon you, and speak; would say, conciliate the south within a week, or the curses of the widow and orphan will rise to heaven against you; for within that short period of time, all power, all control will have left you, and your Country will have passed beyond your reach.

Think of your own children, and think what after ages will think of you, you will stand on earth unloved by any, and descend to the grave with none to morn or weep your loss, can your souls be so dead that you cannot see the state your Country stands in, *if so God help you*—

Respectfully Yours

Robt L Pell

For the President.

The steamer expected from Texas with the six companies of Cavalry (dismounted) arrived at N. York yesterday. Tonight, two of those companies will be here & the others at Carlisle. A company of Infantry (making seven) came on board the same steamer. I shall bring it here & send a company of foot Artillery (Haskin's) to garrison Fort Washington 10 miles below

Another steamer will bring from Texas, to N. York, about 600 men in 10 or 12 days.

After a sharp attack of cramp, last night, I can scarcely hold a pen.

Respectfully submitted
Winfield Scott

Head Quarters of Army
April 12. 1861.

[Endorsed in Lincoln's hand:]
General Scott's daily report
No. 11

Augusta Ga. Apr. 12th 1861.

Mr Abraham Lincon

President of U.S. *Sir.* I propose to bet you or any other Black Republican five hundred dollars (500) that you nor your government will fight the Southern Confederacy. I also propose to bet you or any other Black Republican that if you do fight us we take your scalp in 12 months after the war commences, fifty thousand dollars to be bet on the last point, and the money to be put up in the Farmers Bank of Virginia. I refer you to Wm Toombs & Wm Stephens & Ex. Gov. Crawford.

Respectfully
Wm M. Thomas.

P.S. Both bits to be taken together

W.M.T.

John A. Campbell, an associate justice of the Supreme Court, appointed from Alabama, was an intermediary between the Southern commissioners and Secretary Seward.

RECD 13. AP: AT 4 P. M.

Washington City
April 13, 1861

Sir—

On the 15th March ult, I left with Judge Crawford, one of the commissioners of the Confederate states, a note in writing to the effect following;

"I feel entire confidence that Fort Sumter will be evacuated in the next five days. And this measure is felt as imposing great responsibility on the administration.

"I feel entire confidence that no measure changing the existing status prejudicially to the Southern Confederate States is at present contemplated.

"I feel entire confidence that an immediate demand for an answer to the communication of the commissioners will be productive of evil and not of good. I do not believe that it ought at this time to be pressed. The substance of this statement I communicated to you the same evening by letter—

Five days elapsed and I called with a telegram from Genl.. Beauregard to the effect that Sumter was not evacuated but that Major Anderson was at work making repairs.

The next day after conversing with you I communicated to Judge Crawford in writing, that the failure to evacuate Sumter was not the result of bad faith, but was attributable to causes consistent with the intention to fulfil the engagement, and that as regarded Pickens, I shall have notice of any design to alter the existing status there— Mr Justice Nelson was present at these conversations, three in number, and I submitted to him each of my written communications to Judge Crawford, and informed Judge C, that they had his (Judge Nelson's sanction. I gave you on the 22d. of March a substantial copy of the statement I had made on the 15th.

The 30th March arrived, and at that time a telegram came from Gov Pickens inquiring concerning Col Lamon & his visit. I left that with you, and was to have an answer the following Monday (1st of April)—On the 1st of April, I received from you the statement in writing. ("I am satisfied) the Government will not undertake to supply Sumter without giving notice to Gov P." The words "I am satisfied" were for me to use as expressive of confidence in the remainder of the declaration ==

The proposition as originally prepared was "The President *may desire* to supply Pickens, but will not do so &c. and your verbal explanation was that you did not believe any such attempt would be made. and that there was no design to reinforce Sumter.

There was a departure here from the pledges of the previous month, but with the verbal explanations I did not consider it a matter then to complain of, I simply stated to you that I had that assurance previously—–

On the 7th April I addressed you a letter on the subject of the alarm that the preparations by the government had created and asked you if the assurances I had given were well or ill founded.

In respect to Sumter your reply was "Faith as to Sumter fully kept—wait and see—"

In this morning's paper I read—"An authorized messenger from President Lincoln informed Gov Pickens and Genl. Beauregard that provisions will be sent to Fort Sumter peaceably, or otherwise *by force*—" This was the 8th of April, at Charleston, the day following your last assurance, and was the evidence of the full faith I was invited to wait for and see. In the same paper I read that intercepted despatches disclose the fact that Mr Fox who had been allowed to visit Major Anderson on the pledge that his purpose was pacific employed his opportunity to devise a plan for supplying the fort by force and that this plan had been adopted by the Washington government and was in process of execution.

My recollection of the date of Mr. Fox's visit carries it to a day in March,—I learn he is a near connection of a member of the cabinet.

My connection with the commissioners and yourself was superinduced by a conversation with Justice Nelson. He informed me of your strong dispositions in favor of peace and that you were oppressed with a demand of the Commissioners of the Confederate States for a reply to their first letter and that you desired to avoid it if possible at that time.

I told him I might perhaps be of some service in arranging the difficulty—I came to your office [*entirely*] at his request without the knowledge of either of the commissioners. Your depression was obvious to both Judge Nelson and myself—I was gratified at the character of the counsels you were desirous of pursuing, and much impressed with your observation, that a civil war might be prevented by the success of my mediation—

You read a letter of Mr Weed to show how irksome and responsible the withdrawal of the troops from Sumter was— A portion of my communication to Judge Crawford on the 15th March was founded upon those remarks and the pledge to evacuate Sumter is less forcible than the words you employed—Those words were "Before this letter reaches you (a proposed letter by me to President Davis) Sumter will have been evacuated.

The Commissioners who received those communications conclude they have been abused and overreached— The Montgomery government hold the same opinion— The Commissioners have supposed that my communications were with you and upon the hypothesis, prepared to arraign you before the country in connection with the President. I placed a peremptory prohibition upon this as being contrary to the terms of my communications with them.

I pledged myself to them to communicate information upon what I considered as the best authority, and they were to confide in the ability of myself aided by Judge Nelson to determine upon the credibility of my informant.

I think no candid man who will read over what I have written and considers for a moment what is going on at Sumter, but will agree that to the equivocating conduct of the administration as measured and interpreted in connection with these promises is the proximate cause of the great calamity.

I have a profound conviction that the telegrams of the 8th of April, of Genl. Beauregard and of the 10th of April of Genl. Walker, the Secretary of War can be referred to nothing else than their belief that there has been systematic duplicity practised on them through me. It is under an oppressive sense of the weight of this responsibility that I submit to you these things for your explanation

Very Respectfully
John A. Campbell

Hon W^{m} H Seward
Secretary of State

[Endorsed:] Despatches

Charleston April 8 1861

To Hon L P Walker Secretary of War; Montgomery

An authorized messenger from President Lincoln has just informed Gov Pickens & myself that provisions will be sent to Fort Sumter peaceably or otherwise by force

G–T. Beauregard

Montgomery April 10 1861

Gen Beauregard Charleston

If you have no doubt of the authorized character of the agent who communicated to you the intention of the Washington government to supply Sumter *by force* you will at once demand its evacuation, and if this is refused proceed in such manner as you may determine to reduce it

L.P. Walker

PRIVATE

New York April 13.1861

To
His Excellency A. Lincoln
President, United States
Dear Sir

I am in receipt of information, the authenticity of which I cannot doubt, that the secession leaders intend to make a sudden and desperate attempt to seize Washington City. When and how the attempt will be made is not known positively outside the city of

Montgomery, but as I communicated to Gen! Scott yesterday, the intention to make such attempt exists, and practical means for that purpose are being consumated by paid Agents at Washington city, and the cities of Virginia and Maryland, and here at New York.

Great expectations are indulged of success, because it is supposed that the Administration will hesitate to, and in fact will not call out, volunteers from the loyal states for the defence of the Capital. This not being done in February last, the hope with the conspirators is largely entertained that volunteers will not be called upon now, and they believe at this moment, Washington will be theirs in a few weeks without them.

It is not for me to presume to suggest to the Executive his course with regard to this important matter of preventing the seizure of the Federal Capital by direction of a band of conspirators. But owing to certain advantages which I possess of knowing the designs of the conspirators, and which in the dark days of last January I communicated to Gen! Scott, causing thereby a postponement of the attack, I hope that now when I inform you the struggle for the Capital of the Nation approaches, you will do all that the people, the loyal people of the loyal states, expect to be done in taking vigorous precautionary measures to destroy any such attack. If the force now in Washington is sufficient to resist and destroy *any force* which can be brought from the Southern States, then all is well, but I do not believe it is, neither do the Conspiracy leaders. If that force is not sufficient why hesitate longer to call upon the loyal states for volunteers for the defence of Washington? By doing so you would inspire a heartiness of loyalty in those states that would, in its influence, be irrestible to any infernal designs of the bad men of Montgomery. You would strengthen the Administration by such continuance of the energy and vigor displayed in relation to the Forts, and best of all, you would proportionally destroy the hopes and aims of those men who lead this secession movement.

By firmness, energy and reliance upon the liberal support of the people North, and upon the good sense of the people North and South, you will put down this treasonable movement. Be assured that either they, the conspirators, or you will go down in a few weeks, and I hope to God it will not be you.

Permit me to mention before closing what Mr Jeff Davis told a gentleman in this city lately from Montgomery. *The only thing he dreaded the Government at Washington might do would be to blockade all the ports of the seceding states.* That, said he, is perhaps more than they dare, but to do it even for a short time, would work their, (the Conspirators) certain destruction, because *it would cause great dissension, starvation and poverty in the great centres of secession.*

This you may rely on. It will be soon known if it must be adopted.

I am with great respect

Your obt. Svt.

Ja^s^ Henderson

For the President

Nothing of military importance has reached me to day except thro' the news-paper.

The two companies of dismounted Cavalry arrived last night as I had anticipated in my report of yesterday.

At my instance the Secretary of War has called for four other companies of District volunteers, which will make, in all, fifteen companies of this description for the defence of the Capital, besides six companies of regulars, the Marines at the Navy Yard, & (I hope very soon) the War steamer to cruise on the Potomak between the long bridge & a point little below Alexandria. The next regular reinforcements to be expected here, are:— Sherman's battery of flying Artillery from Minesota, & the companies of foot artillery from the same quarter—in five & seven days, & a portion of the troops expected in the next steamer from Texas. From the same steamer, I shall have the means of reinforcing Fort McHenry (at Baltimore) a most important point.

Respectfully submitted.

Winfield Scott.

H.d Qrs. of the Army,
Washington, Ap.l–13, 1861.

[Endorsed in Mr. Lincoln's hand:]
Gen. Scott's daily report
No. 12.

Springfield Ill. 13th

Friend Nicolay–

Reports here say the war has began. In case the President needs assistance we hope he will first call on Illinoi's–for we have fought for him once & won and will do it again–true muskets & ball are not torches and oil but we are ready with either. We were whipt out at the city election by traitors in our camp–some who are applicants for federal office are not true Republicans so their votes on the 9th say–Many of us Republicans here wish Lincoln would appoint Mrs Grimsley to the P.O. of this city. I believe there could be nothing said to it & think it will give general satisfaction. Of course Ln will do as he pleases & wouldn't take my advise. Senator Trumbull arrived here this A.M. Things remain Status-quo–no body getting married or dying–The Zouave Gray still flourish & are spoiling (some of them) for a fight. I think after Court I will put a shirt in my pockets & come down & see the City. What condition is John Hays black eye in? Give Lin my respects–excuse this scrawl and believe me–your brother soldier & friend

L. Rosette

[Endorsed:]
Springfield Ill 11 April 61.
L. Rosette writes to Mr. Nicolay
that he hopes the President will
make the first call for troops in
Illinois. That they are ready to
march

Mr. Lincoln dispatched a fleet to relieve Fort Sumter. Learning of its momentary arrival, the Confederate commander, General Beauregard, offered Major Anderson a last opportunity to evacuate. When this was not accepted, the Confederate batteries opened fire on the fort, beginning at half-past four in the morning of Friday, April 12. The bombardment continued for thirty-four hours; Anderson was obliged to surrender; the Civil War had commenced. Two days later Mr. Lincoln called out 75,000 militia.

THE MAGNETIC TELEGRAPH COMPANY.

4 Dated Wilmington Del Apl 13 1861.

Rec'd, Washington, 13 1861, o'clock, min. M.

To Abe Lincoln

President U–S.

Please inform me at once if any-body is hurt at Charleston

Wm J. Bayless

/12

/29

HB

THE MAGNETIC TELEGRAPH COMPANY.

43 Dated Savannah Apl 13th 1861.

Recd, Washington, Apl 13th 1861, o'clock, min. M.

To Mr A Lincoln

Fort Sumter has surrendered there is nobody Hurt

H W Denslow

Tr

8/130

THE MAGNETIC TELEGRAPH COMPANY.

23 Dated Charleston Apl—13 1861.

Rec'd, Washington, Apl 1861, o'clock, min. M.

To His Excellcy Abraham Lincoln

Prest U S or
Hon J Holt Late
secry of war

fort sumter has surrendered unconditionally & not a Carolinian hurt the stars & stripes were hauled down & the white flag raised precisely at half past one oclock

Isaac W. Hoyle
Late Envoy

283190
Lr

THE MAGNETIC TELEGRAPH COMPANY.

25
Dated Columbus Ga Apl 13 1861.

Rec'd Washington, 13 1861, o'clock, min. M.

To President Lincoln

Try it again, nobody hurt

J. E. Hurt

5–255 NOTICE DELIVERY PAID
(?)V

1861
Apr 13

FIVE. NYORK XIIITH. HON.WM.H.SEWARD. WASHN.
I HAVE THE HONOR TO TENDER TO THE PRESIDENT OF THE UNITED STATES THROUGH THE SECRETARY OF WAR A REGIMENT OF NEW YORK VOLUNTEERS TO SERVE EITHER AS LIGHT ARTILLERY OR CAVALRY WILL YOU KNOWING ME KINDLY MAKE THIS TENDER FOR ME. . H.S. LANSING,

---

The following was probably sent to the Secretary of War.

Please send over the F[t]
Sumpter Messenger at once.

Lincoln

EXECUTIVE MANSION

April 15. 1861

Lieu[t]. General Scott:
My dear Sir:

Co[l] Peter G. Washington tells me it is my duty to call an officer to the command of the District of Columbia Militia, now in the U. S. service, and that he, by rank in the District [*of*] Militia, is entitled to the place—

Is it my duty to call, or designate, such officer? And if yes, is Col. Washington, by military law, usage or courtesy, entitled to the place?

Please investigate & inform me.

Your Ob[t] Serv[t]
A. Lincoln

[Endorsed in Mr. Lincoln's hand:]
Gen. Scott— Extra—

Executive Mansion April 15/61
The President

Desires information concerning Col. P. G. Washington—

Col Washington was an officer of the old Organization of the Militia of the District: but that organization has been legally broken up. and replaced by a new one by the President Buchanan

Colonel Washington is not an officer of the present organization—
April 15/61 *Chas P. Stone*
Insp Genl

If Lieut. Col. Washington were legally in commission; we do not want him or any other field officer, with the District Volunteers mustered into the service of the U.S.—because those volunteers are all doing duty as seperate & independent companies, & require no field officer.

Respectfully submitted.
Winfield Scott
Apl. 15, 1861

Memo: of E. Bates, in Cabinet, April 15.1861—

Now that we are in open war, it is my opinion,

1. That the Mails ought to be stopped in the revolted States, forthwith.

2. That the Southern ports, at least, from Charleston to New Orleans, ought to be closed at once.

3. That the Mouth of the Mississippi ought to be effectually guarded, so as to prevent all ingress or egress.

4. That the approach to New Orleans by Lake Ponchartrain ought to be at our entire command.

5. That the Mississippi, at the Mouth of the Ohio ought to be commanded by the Government, so as to control the navigation and trade at that centre.

6. That the safety of St. Louis ought to be ensured.

7. That the seat of Government, of course, must be protected, cost what it may.

8. We must maintain command of the Chesapeake Bay,—as that locks up Virginia and Maryland and half of North Carolina—and to that end we must maintain Fort Monroe.

9. Harper's Ferry & Gosport, ought to be protected, if possible.

Note. Of course, I am for "enforcing the laws," with no object but to reinstate the Authority of the Government, and restore the integrity of the nation. And, with that object in view, I think it would be wise and humane, on our part, so to conduct the war, as to give the least occasion for social and servile war, in the extreme Southern States, and to disturb as little as possible, the accustomed occupations of the people.

The plan of practically closing the ports of the insurgent States, and cutting off all their sea-ward commerce, seems to me the easiest, cheapest & most humane method of restraining those States and destroying their confederation. Their people are high spirited, and ready enough to fight, but impatient of control, & unable to bear the steady and persistent pressure which we can easily impose, & which they have no means to resist. They are an anomalous people—the only agricultural people that I know of, who cannot live upon the products of their own labor, and have no means of their own to take those products to market.

Cotton & sugar, their only staples, must be exported and sold, in order to procure the very necessaries of life. They *must sell,* or sink into poverty & ruin; and if their ports be closed they must send their Northwards, to the ports of the states yet faithful. In that way their products will find their way into the markets of the world, and they will be compelled to receive their foreign supplies, through the same channels. And thus, our duties (somewhat diminished, it may be) will still be paid, and the people of the loyal States will get the profits of the trade. While they, getting no revenue from duties, must resort to direct taxation, and that, to an extent that their people cannot long endure.

This plan, it seems to me, if strictly and persistently enforced, while it would not necessarily lead to the shedding of a drop of blood, would, never the less, be very *coercive* and very promising of success. At all events it is the most feasible project for the accomplishment of our main end, that has occurred to my mind.

Others may think it wiser and better to adopt a line of action more bold & warlike, & to enforce the laws at the point of the bayonet, in the field. If that opinion prevail, then I have a suggestion to make as to the point of attack, which seems to me at once the most vulnerable and the most important.

On this hyposthesis, it is my opinion ought to take and hold with strong hand, the City of New Orleans. And that, I believe, can be done, without much fighting, provided the plan be judiciously matured, & the preparations be made with intelligence secrecy and celerity.

I suggest *some of the means,* not presuming to cover all the deails of a design so complicated, & so beyond the range of my habitual thoughts. And

1st. The naval force in the Gulf ought to be stronger than necessary for a mere blockade—and yet it would look like a mere blockading squadron, and the enemy might be made to understand it so,—and there ought to be on board the squadron, some of our best Artillery to cöoperate with the force to descend the river.

2. There is, up the river, a class of men, the hardiest on the continent—the boatmen—now, for the most part, not well employed, and likely to see worse times, as soon as the trade of New Orleans is stopped or crippled, by our squadrons in the Gulf. These men are hardy and bold, and will be ripe for such a brilliant enterprise.

I know several gentlemen who know these men perfectly, and can exercise a great influence over them. I think that 8 or 10 000 of these men could be promptly engaged, by using the proper agencies. These being equipped and concentrated at Cairo, might, with such other means as may be thought needful, run to the City of New Orleans in four days, or less, and these, cöoperating with the fleet, might, very probably, take the city without a serious struggle.

The success of such a scheme might make it proper to use some freedom, in stopping mails and telegraphs for a few days.

I do not propose this plan, for I greatly prefer to accomplish the end by blockade. But if regular war be inaugurated, in the valley of the Mississippi we MUST command the mouth of the river and ought to command also the mouth of the Ohio. This last would protect and control the commerce and navigation of nearly ten millions of our people.

Respectfully submitted.

Note 2. In order to ensure constant employment to the insurgent troops, our cruisers could frequently look in upon the enemies' forts, only to see that they are well manned and guarded, and now & then, make a show of force off the most exposed points of the enemy's coast.

CINCIN. APR. XVTH. HON. A. LINCOLN. WASHN.
MEN OF ALL GRADES AND AGES ARE ENROLLING
THE UTMOST ENTHUSIASM PREVAILS
THERE IS NO SYMPATHY FOR TREASON. GOD SPEED YOU.
R. M. CORWINE.

PEARL STREET HOUSE

Nashua N. H. April 15/61

Abraham Lincoln President of the U. S.

Dear Sir:

Why need I write you? Why should I? Indeed I know not—There are irrepressible feelings [*that*] beyond my controll that induce me to address you—Do not stop to read this—The eyes of twenty million of freemen are upon you—the illustrious spirits of the departed dead, hover around you, the hopes of the word, the eternal future all centers on you—May God sustain you—I am a humble citizen of the granite state, unknown to fame with no ambition save to live hapely in the embraces of my family, in a *Free Country* under the Glorious Union, under the Stars & Stripes, that wave over our houses—Sixty miles from here, at my home in Alexandria N.H. now hangs in my hall, the Flag of our Country under it our Fathers conquered, under it & on it your name inscribed and carried the town, the State, the nation for Liberty Nor last—under it we will die—

Tomorrow I return home—I have but one son of seventeen Summers, he our only child, a man in stature—We are ready to volunteer, to fight for the integrity of the Union—These rugged hills of New Hampshire overlook strong arms & brave hearts—

I left my home thirty days since, as An Agent of the "Pilgrim Monument Society" to collect funds to build a Monument to the Pilgrim Fathers at Plymouth Mass—I have been successful; the friends of the Pilgrims are your friends; they all love their Country .

Under ordinary circumstances I would have been thrice happy to have had your name on my book but I forbear inviting your cooperation in this momentous crisis—Please accept the enclosed Honorary Certificate of Life Membership to the Pilgrims Monument Association—Remember from one who knows the minds of men, that we expect to kill of the rebels, hang the traitors & that New England alone will furnish fifty thousand men & bayonets to return the "poisoned chalice" to the lips of seceders & cause the poisenous serpents to fasten their deadly fangs into the vitals of traitors .

Flinch not—"demand nothing but what is right & submit to nothing wrong"—God & your country men will sustain you—

I have the pleasure of remaining your humble Svt

Renewick Dickerson

Abraham Lincoln)
)
President of the U.S.)

STATE OF CONNECTICUT,
EXECUTIVE DEPARTMENT

Norwich, April 15 1861

Sir

I beg leave to assure you that the Government and citizens of this state are loyal to the National Union, that they appreciate the efforts you are making to hold and possess the property of the United States and will be happy to render any service in their power to enable you to enforce the laws.

Our General Assembly will convene on the 1st day of May and any communication which you will make relating to your purposes which may require our cooperation I shall be happy to receive and will hold such communication in as much confidence as the nature of the case will admit.

I am dear sir your
with high considerations
Wm A Buckingham

To Abraham Lincoln
President of the U S
Washington

THE MAGNETIC TELEGRAPH COMPANY

50 Dated N York Apl 15th 1861.

Rec'd, Washington 15th 1861, ___ o'clock, ___ min. M.

To Hon S Cameron

Will I be sustained by the Government in seizing small
arms in the Hands of the Carier on their way from
Connecticut to any place south of Washington

John A Kennedy
Supt Police

CR 29–COLL
140

For the President

I have but little of special interest to report today, except that Col° Smith, the commander of the Department of Washington, like myself, thinks our means of defence, with vigilance, are sufficient to hold this till reinforcements arrive.

I have telegraphed the commander at Harper's Ferry Armory to say whether he can station, to advantage, for the defence of that establishment, additional recruits from Carlisle? The ground about the Armory is very contracted & rocky.

Respectfully submitted.
Winfield Scott

Head Qrs. of the Army
Washington, Ap[l]. 15, 1861.

[Endorsed in Mr. Lincoln's hand:]
Gen. Scott's daily report
N° 13.

OFFICE OF DAILY TRIBUNE,
51 Clark Street,
Chicago, April 15 1861.

President Lincoln

There is but one opinion in Chicago—Douglas Dems and Lincoln Rep's are a unit, and that is that *Sumter must be retaken*. Moultrie retaken, Pinckney retaken, the custom house retaken, and the Stars & Stripes—the National Emblem, must float over the Federal property in Charleston. Chicago will send you a gallant regiment on call, and Illinois fifty more England and France met Russia at Sebastipol—localized the war and whipped her there. She has been tame and quiet ever since. Charleston, of all spots, is the place to settle our national difficulties. There meet the secessionists and there crush them. If 50,000 men is not enough call for 100,000, and if that is not sufficient call for 500,000. But crush the head of the rattle-snake. There is where the trouble was hatched. The tories live there—let them die there. The North West will back you with their best men dollar and bushel of corn. The authority of the Govt. must be made good. Do your duty; the people are with you.

J. Medill

For the President.

He has, no doubt, been informally made acquainted with the reply of the officer commanding at Harper's Ferry yesterday, viz; that *he wants no reinforcement.* Nevertheless, as soon as the Capital, the rail-road to the Delaware, at Wilmington, & Fort Monroe are made secure, my next object of attention will be the Security of Harper's Ferry—proposing, in the mean time, or rather suggesting, that the spare Marines from the Navy Yards of Philadelphia, Brooklyn & Boston, be promptly sent to the Gosport Navy Yard. This relief may serve—by compelling the secessionist to enlarge their preparations—to give us time to send a regiment of volunteers to that important point in advance of any formidable attack, upon it .

With the authority of the Secretary of War we are engaged in mustering into the service eight additional companies of District volunteers. These, I think, place the Capital a little a head of impending dangers & we will maintain, at least, that advantage, till by the arrival (in a week) of regulars & abundant volunteers our relative advantage will, I trust, be more than doubled.

Respectfully submitted.

Winfield Scott.

H^{d} Qrs.of the Army
Washington, Ap^{l} 16, 1861

[Endorsed in Mr. Lincoln's hand:]
Gen. Scott's daily report
N° 14.

APRIL 1861

PRIVATE AND CONFIDENTIAL

New York April 16/1861

To His Excellency A. Lincoln
President, United States
Dear Sir

It was with feelings of great satisfaction that I read your proclamation yesterday morning. The Administration is rising up to the Dignity of the times' requirements. That proclamation and the glorious results now developing in the enthusiasm of the Free States will fall most unexpectedly in the conspirators' camp.

On Saturday last I took the liberty of writing you of the pressing necessity to secure Washington from an attempt at seizure. Today from important communications just received from Charleston and Montgomery dated last Wednesday, I am able to inform you that it was the intention of the conspirators to march on Washington, *rendezvousing* at Richmond V^{a}, immediately after Fort Sumpter was evacuated, of which by the way they consider a certainty. The rapidity of movement on the one side, and expected demoralization on the other side of the North from loss of Sumpter, (in which they are signally mistaken) contain according to the plans of conspirators, the element of success so as to secure Washington city and perhaps force Border Slaves States into Secession. They inform me also that there are 5000 men in Virginia, 3000 in Maryland, and 1000 in Washington city, (several hundred in employ of government) who are ready to assist in movement contemplated by the conspirators. How affairs at Fort Pickens, and your proclamation and its glorious results, will alter their plans I know not. My impression is that Washington will be attacked this week by some force not far from 15,000 men. Martial Law should at once be declared in the District, and as many volunteers concentrated at the Capital immediately as can be at once acomodated. This may prevent the attempt if you do. This Crisis I take it occurs this week. This week the conspirators are stronger—on land, and next week they will probably be weaker than the Federal forces. Are they likely to postpone? Let me beseech you then to do all that you can most energetically, all that you can most effectually to prevent the horrid

calamity to our Nation, our Government and Union of the seizure of the National Capital by Rebels. If we should lose Washington who can estimate our unfortunate position?
So much are the conspirators convinced that without Washington city they are bound hand and foot, and so much do its possession enter into their schemes to confirm their bogus Government, that I am prepared to say your administration has more than half triumphed over this fearful conspiracy to destroy the Government when Washington is secured against any possible attack. Permit me to ask will not closely blockading the ports of the seceding States, and cutting off their mails, for a time, do most of the balance?
You have a noble task before you, which I believe you will accomplish. A virgorous and determined policy, I can assure you, was never contemplated by the Conspiracy leaders and their friends on the part of the Administration. You will baffle them, I hope, as Genl Scott baffled them last winter. If Washington formed the Union we will say hereafter, Lincoln consolidated it and made it perpetual.
One word of myself. I consider that in the trying times of our free institutions, and of our national character every man may share in the great work of perpetuating the one and preserving the other. At some risk and expense I learn the plans and designs of the Conspirators only to expose them to those in power, and if possible to prevent their accomplishment. I do my duty. May God endue you and the able men around you to do yours.

I am with great respect
Your obt Svt.
James Henderson

P.S. I would respectfully suggest two things. 1st you take needful precaution against personal violence, though that is not discussed now by the leaders. 2nd That as far as possible the Press may not be able to communicate important information to the enemy too soon.

For the President.

I repeat, in writing, some details which I had the honor to submit, verbally, to the President, this forenoon.

Three or four regiments from Massachusetts (*believed* to be the first ready under the recent call) may be expected (three of them) to arrive here, & (one of them) at Fort Monroe in two or three days. One of the three may, I think, be safely spared for Harpers' Ferry—if the danger there (& I shall know tomorrow) shall seem imminent. Captain Kingsbury, a most capable officer of the Ordnance Department, goes up this afternoon for that purpose, & *to act*, a few days, as Superintendant—that is, till a new appointment (of a civilian) can be made.

Two of the Massachusetts regiments are needed here. One of them shall endeavor to intercept at Baltimore & direct it to Harpers Ferry.

As soon as one of the four reaches Fort Monroe, it, perhaps, may be safe to detach thence, for the Gosport Navy Yard, two or three companies of regulars to assist in the defence of that establishment. By tomorrow, or certainly the next day, we shall have Colonel Delafield here, an excellent Engineer, to send to Gosport, (with a letter from the Secretary of the Navy giving the necessary authority) to devise, in conjunction with the Naval Commander there, a plan of defence. Col. Delafield will take instructions to call for the two or three companies of regulars as mentioned above. Excepting the reinforcement of Marines (suggested yesterday) & until the arrival of more volunteers, I know not what else can be done for the security of the Gosport Navy Yard.

Tonight, all the important avenues leading into Washington shall be well guarded.

Respectfully submitted.
Winfield Scott.

Head Qrs. of the Army,
Washington, Ap! 17, 1861

[Endorsed in Mr. Lincoln's hand:]
Gen. Scott's daily report
No. 15.

His Excellency Abraham Lincoln Esq
President of the United States
Dr Sir

Allow me to suggest to your excellency the propriety of using a portion of the secret service money placed at your disposal, to discover the parties connected with a secret Society called the Knights of the Golden Circle. There are strong suspicions of their existence in this City—I am informed W[m] B. Mann Esqr District Attorney of this City entertains the like opinions with myself as to the existence of such a combination among us—Being personally unknown to you I beg leave to refer to the Hon Simon Cameron Secretary of War for my character & personal antecedents [.]

Respectfully &c
Rob Bethell
Philad[a] April 18 1861

MAYORS OFFICE
CITY HALL

Baltimore April 18th. 1861

Sir

This will be presented to you by [*the Hon. Robert M. McLane and*] the Hon Hugh Lennox Bond and George W. Dobbin and John C Brune Esquires who will proceed to Washington by an Express train, at my request, in order to explain fully the fearful condition of affairs in this City

The people are exasperated to the highest degree by the passage of troops, and the citizens are universally decided in the opinion that no man should be ordered to come.

The authorities of the City did their best to day to protect both strangers and citizens and to prevent a collision, but in vain and but for their great efforts a fearful slaughter would have occurred.

A Confederate "Bull Battery" in the early summer of 1861. Pencil sketch by a Confederate officer reproduced from the original in the Library of Congress

The Lexington of 1861, or the attack of a Baltimore mob upon a Massachusetts regiment. Reproduced from a contemporary lithograph by Currier & Ives

Under these circumstances it is my solemn duty to inform you that it is not possible for more soldiers to pass through Baltimore unless they fight their way at every step.

I therefore hope and trust and most earnestly request that no more troops be permitted or ordered by the Government to pass through the City. If they should attempt it the responsibility for the bloodshed will not rest upon me

with great respect
Your obedient servant
Geo. Wm. Brown
Mayor

To His Excellency
Abraham Lincoln
President of
The United States

I have been in Baltimore City, since Tuesday evening last and co-operated with Mayor G. W Brown in his untiring efforts to allay and prevent the excitement and suppress the fearful outbreak as indicated above; and I fully concur in all that is said by him in the above communication.

verry respectfully
yrob[t]Servt
Tho.H. Hicks
Gov of Maryland

To His Honor A. Lincoln
President of the United States

For the President.

I am (placed between many fires—Fort Monroe, Harpers Ferry, Gosport Navy Yard, &c &c—) much embarrassed by the non arrival of troops. Monday, the 15th instant, Senator Wilson had the quota of Massachusetts doubled, & on the ground of being entirely ready (as I understood) got permission that it should be, at once, pushed (farthest) to the South. Tho' equal to any volunteers in the world, the preference of being in the advance must have been given on that ground. In reply to Governor Andrew's telegram, I said (tuesday night, the 15th)—"Send first regiment which is ready by "rail, here. The second by rail or sea, as you prefer to F^{t} Monroe." (I had but an hour before pointed out the route *via* Baltimore & the Chesapeake)

When I sent those telegrams (late in the night) I did not know that the War Department had already telegraphed the Govr for one of his regiments to take a fast steamer to Fort Monroe, & to send the other three here, by rail.

Two & $\frac{1}{2}$ o'clock, P.M.— I have not heard anything farther respecting the Massachusetts quota.

At this instant the War Department has a telegram, from Philadelphia, saying that "the Massachusetts troops are here, this afternoon. Leave tomorrow (friday) morning early." Also another telegram to this effect tell General Cameron (we) think that troops must go thro' from here to Washington, by day, in number of about 2,000 at a time, so as to be ready to meet any emergency on the way."

The Philadelphia does not say whether three or four regiments are there. I hope but *three* & that the fourth will be, to night in Fort Monroe.

Last night I received a telegram from Major Genl Sandford (of the city of N. York) saying that "under the orders of the Governor the 7th regiment (a crack corps) is ready to report to" me. "How shall it be sent?" I instantly replied by rail & added "telegraph me the hour of departure"— I have, as yet, heard nothing further from Genl S.

In respect to Harpers Ferry & the Gosport Navy Yard, both of which are in great peril, I can do nothing before the arrival of troops, beyond the instructions given this morning to send the third regiment that might arrive, at Baltimore, to Harper's Ferry—the first & second to continue on to Washington.

(Here a report reaches me that the rail-road bridge (over the Gunpowder) 28 miles beyond Baltimore has been burned.)

Col. Delafield, whom I intended to send to Fort Monroe & the

Gosport Navy Yard, has not arrived. If he comes to night, I shall send him tomorrow—hoping that he will find a Massachusetts regiment in position.

If land batteries should be planted on the Potomak to cut off our water communications we must send an expedition & capture them.

Respectfully submitted.
Winfield Scott.

Ap! 18, 1861.

[Endorsed in Mr. Lincoln's hand:]
Gen. Scott's daily report
N°. 16

[Endorsement on envelope otherwise blank in Mr. Lincoln's hand:]
No report from Gen. Scott
this 19, April 1861.

New York April 19th

I have just read to a friend my letters from Georgia—from those who *were strong Unionists* & who now *go with the current*—"Will fight to the death" for the "confederacy"—

This friend (with whom I have just had a [*long &*] most interesting conversation) is a man of much character—cool & thoughtful—very intelligent—very conversant with affairs of moment to the republic—He is of a *well known* Virginia family & passed his youth in that state—His early manhood was passed in the successful practice of Law in Alabama—He is a man of fortune & was a slave holder—Now in middle life he has resided some not very long time in New York—

He [*says*] tells me now that, speaking from no "report" but from an intimate personal knowledge, "*knowing*" just what he asserts, that a plan has long existed & has been carefully nursed & matured, *not* known to the multitude, but *well resolved on* by *the few*—of whom Jefferson Davis has [*ever*] been the soul & master spirit for some years—

It is by every act & measure for that end (by *any* & *all means*) to establish a military despotism—to make it *firm* & *central*—to render its arm flexible, its servants *sure* & *prompt*—& then to *conquer*—not as many deem Mexico & its neighbors chiefly—but to sweep *northword*—to subdue this broad land—not even to leave out the "contemptible, mean, Puritan New England"—to conquer & compel submission on the part of the "Yankees" themselves——They mean to *rule the land*—& with a *strong hand*—Their plans, he says, all tend to *that*—the plans of the *leaders*—of Jefferson Davis—tho' the mass of his subjects know it not—

He adds that if the government, *our government* does not comprehend *this* & understand with *what* it has to deal, & how it *needs* to stop at *no measure* to meet *them* it will find itself surprised & outgenerated—

I would not write this on any light authority—*He* protested—& withdrew from THEM—denounced their scheme as ruinous to [*freed*] free [*institut*] States (free government), as in its probable recoil destructive to the south—& now a "strong southern man" would gladly aid *you* in the contest with *them*—

His *word may be relied on*—He assures me *he, individually, knows*—

Tellula

The writer of this, a woman, is *not* a "literary lady,"—*never* writes for "print" or for "the public"—
But *does* write, [*today*] this letter in a New York "down town" office—

A riot broke out in Baltimore on April 19th, when Pennsylvania and Massachusetts militia, on their way to the defense of Washington, were attacked by mobs. Four soldiers and twelve civilians were killed; many on both sides were wounded.

THE MAGNETIC TELEGRAPH COMPANY

Dated Balto Apr 19 1861.

Rec'd, Washington,________1861,________o'clock,____min. M.

To The President of the

U. S

Sir—a colision between the citizens & the Northern troops has taken place in Baltimore & the excitement is fearful—send no troops here we will endeavor to prevent all bloodshed. A public meeting of citizens has been called and the troops of the State in the City have been called out to preserve the peace—They will be enough—

Respy

Thos H Hicks

Gov

Geo Wm Brown

Mayor

THE MAGNETIC TELEGRAPH COMPANY

Balto

Dated Camden Station. 19th 1861.

Rec'd Washington,________1861,________o'clock,____min. M.

To His Excellency, A. Lincoln

The Governor of Maryland & Mayor of Baltimore have sent you a highly important despatch for fear you may not receive it promptly, we have sent a special Express Engine & messenger to deliver it to you

W. P. Smith

Master of transportation

B & O. R R

DH .

University of Michigan
April 19th 1861

To Abraham Lincoln
Prest of the United States:
Sir

My heart impels me at the risk of appearing impertinent to write you a few words. The heart of the great West—the heart of the entire North is with you in the defense of our beloved country. You cannot ask of us too much. We are ready to give ourselves and all that we have to this great work. The 700 young men committed to my charge are ready to march in a body if need be, & I am ready to march at their head. The country will give you 750,000 instead of 75000 if you ask it. Men and money without limit are at your disposal.

The long repressed enthusiasm breaks forth like a volcano. We are no longer democrats and Republicans—We are under one flag—the flag of our glorious Union. We feel that the stronger the demonstration, the more rapid the movement, the more mighty & decisive the action, the better. Let the traitors see, let the whole world see that we are strong enough to make our cause good, to preserve the integrity of the Union without the loss of a single inch of our domain. We are ready to blockade every Southern port, to protect Washington, to retake Sumpter, to scatter the enemy at Pensacola, to send an army to Texas, to send another down the Mississippi. Why should not five great armies of 100,000 each—move to the grand points and finish the work?

Honored President!

As if the God of our fathers spoke to me, I feel constrained to say that God & our Country are with you in the mightiest effort you can make. The more we put forth our strength, the more united and stronger we would be. Thus, all true patriots will be stirred up to the highest zeal; all the vacillating will become decided; the timid will become strong; those who are looking for the strongest side will know where to go; the Union men in the Border States will dare to put their hand to the work; and the overawed patriots in the Seceding states will be called forth to speak and to act. I may add to that according to Napoleonic tactics one great battle won is worth a thousand skirmishes—

Pardon me this letter—my apology is that it gushes from my heart. Without being accounted presumptuous may I not say these few words while I subscribe myself with sincere and profound respect and earnest love

Your Ob^t Sv^t
Henry P. Tappan
Prs^t of the Un. of
Michigan

STATE OF MARYLAND

Executive Chamber
Annapolis, April 20th 1861

Hon. Simon Cameron. Secretary of War
Sir,

Since I saw you in Washington last, I have been in Baltimore laboring in conjunction with the Mayor of that city to preserve order, but I regret to say with little success. Up to yesterday there appeared promise, but the outbreak came, the turbulent passions of the riotous elements prevailed, fears for safety became reality, that which they had endeavored to conceal, was no longer concealed, was made manifest, the rebellious elements had control. We were arranging and organising forces to protect the city and preserve order but want of organization, and arms prevented success. They had arms, and the principal part of the organised Militia forces and we were powerless under the circumstances. I think it prudent to decline (for the present) acting upon the requisition made upon Maryland for four regiments.

With great respect
Tho. H. Hicks
Gov . of M^d

MAYORS OFFICE
CITY HALL

Baltimore April 20 1861

To His Excellency,
The President of the United States:

Sir: I have had the honor to receive your communication of this date, directed to Gov. Hicks & myself, through Messrs. Bond, Dobbin & Brune.

The especial duty of the authorities of Baltimore being to protect the people & preserve the peace of the City, their official obligations will, of course, be answered, if they are able to obtain assurances from you that no more troops will be brought through the City, or so immediately into its neighbourhood as to provoke the uncontrollable feeling of its people. Should such assurances be given, as I personally hope they may be, the City authorities will use all lawful means to prevent their fellow citizens from interferring with any of the Northern Militia who may pass at a distance from their jurisdiction. Further than this, they have no authority to speak for the people of Maryland, and no means of keeping any promise they might make. They do sincerely & earnestly trust that the government will be warned by the melancholy occurrences of yesterday, & avoid precipitating further disastrous results, which it can serve no earthly purpose to provoke.

I have the honor to be,
Your obedient servant,
Geo Wm Brown
Mayor

Apl 20 1861

If the Baltimore committee is at the "White House," I will be glad to meet them if you will allow me.

Please drop a line by the Messenger, if they are with you. I am at the Dept.

Simon Cameron
Friday night

The President.

For the President.

I furnished no *bulletin* yesterday, having had nothing to say which had not been, by others, reported.

There is no truth in the rumor that men are, or have been engaged in fortifying the neighborhood of Arlington, & it is believed that the rumor of yesterday that a body of armed men were landed on this side of the Potomak, some few miles below this city is equally unfounded.

To meet the troops expected today, at Annapolis, I have sent a Quartermaster to provide for their wants, & to bring them to this city—1. By Baltimore cars, if they can be obtained, to go to Annapolis (the gage now being known to be the same;) 2. If those cannot be hired to go to Annapolis, then to bring the troops to the *Junction* in some eight or ten trips of the small Annapolis cars, & thence to this city, in the Baltimore cars, or 3. If the latter refuse this service, then to march the volunteers here, accompanied by hired wagons.

I have telegraphed General Patterson that if the Pennsylvania quota of militia be insufficient to stud the two rail-roads—from Wilmington to Washington, & from the Pennsylvania line, on the Harrisburg road, to Baltimore—that the quotas of New York & New Jersey should make up the deficiency Gen[l]. Patterson will quicken those measures of protection. The same Quarter Master has my further instructions to consult the Naval commander at Annapolis, and if a guard of two or three companies be deemed necessary to the security of that Harbor, then to request the volunteers to leave a temporary guard of that strength.

I believe that even without the volunteers coming *via* Annapolis (today or tomorrow) that we are in advance of all preparations for an attack upon us.

Several smart & trusty men offer to visit the principal towns in Virginia & Maryland to collect & report on matters important to the defense of this Capital. Such services are always costly, & require discreet management. I, however, am without funds applicable to this use.

Respectfully submitted,
Winfield Scott.

Head Qrs. of the Army
Washington, Apl. 20, 1861.

[Endorsed in Mr. Lincoln's hand:]
Gen. Scott's daily report
No. 17.

CONFIDENTIAL

Chicago April 21st 1861

To His Excellense
A Lincoln
Prest of the U–S
Dear Sir

When I saw you last I said that if the time should ever come that I could be of service to you I was ready—If that time has come I am on hand—

I have in my Force from Sixteen to Eighteen persons on whose courage. Skill & Devotion to their Country I can rely. If they with myself at the head can be of service in the way of obtaining information of the movements of the Traitors, or Safely conveying your letters or dispatches. or that class of Secret Service which is the most dangerous. I am at your command—

In the present disturbed state of Affairs I dare not trust this to the mail—so send by one of My Force who was with me at Baltimore—You may safely trust him with Any Message for me—Written or Verbal—I fully guarantee his fidelity—He will act as you direct—and return here with your answer

Secrecy is the great lever I propose to operate with—Hence the necessity of this movement (If you contemplate it) being kept *Strictly Private*—and that should you desire another interview with the Bearer that you should so arrange it—as that he will not be noticed—

The Bearer will hand you A Copy of A Telegraph Cipher which you may use if you desire to Telegraph me—

My Force comprises both Sexes—All of Good Character—And well Skilled in their Business—

Respectfully yours
Allan Pinkerton

It will be noticed that in Allan Pinkerton's cipher, "nuts" was the unbecoming code word for President and "prunes" the code word for Vice-President.

[Allan Pinkerton's Code]

[April 21, 1861]

Must	*Candles.*	Cavalry	*Sperm.*
Will	*Car Oil.*	Stationed	*Sperm Candle.*
Secessionist	*Coal Oil.*	Station	*Sperm Oil.*
Conspiracy	*Engine Oil.*	Union	*Whale Oil.*
Conspirator	*Head Light Oil.*	Constitution	*Neats-foot Oil.*
Military	*Lamps.*	Rob	*Kerosene.*
Drill	*Hand Lamp.*	Steal	*Tallow.*
Drilling	*Arm Lamp.*	Drink	*Rose Oil.*
Horse	*Oil.*	Drunk	*Lard.*
Foot	*Rosin Oil.*	Wine	*Grease.*

Man	*Sweet Oil.*	Bridge	*Lumber.*
Woman	*Olive Oil.*	Bridges	*Plank.*
Boy	*Cylender.*	Track	*Scantling*
Girl	*Driving Wheel.*	Crowbar	*Shingles*
Old	*Car Wheel.*	Combustible	*Timber.*
Young	*Eccentric.*	Train	*Square Timber.*
Explode	*Axle.*	Trains	*White Wood.*
Explosion	*Pump.*	Express	*Wood.*
Match	*Bolt Spikes.*	Money	*Ash.*
Watch	*Chairs.*	Valuables	*Oak.*
United States	*Cut Spikes.*	Powder	*Elm.*
Elect	*Frogs.*	Ball	*Hickory.*
March	*T. Rails.*	Muskets	*Iron Wood.*
Feby.	*Spikes.*	Firearms	*Bass Wood.*
April	*Ties.*	Revolvers	*Pine.*
Committee	*Rivets.*	Locomotives	*Yellow Oak.*
Congress	*Copper Rivets.*	Cars	*Hard Wood.*
Senate	*Large Rivets.*	Passengers	*Hard Ware.*
Destroy	*Small Rivets.*	Soldiers	*Mahogany.*
Hide	*Brass Rivets.*	Volunteers	*Walnut*
Dangers	*Iron Rivets.*	Troops	*Spruce.*
Quiet	*Anvil.*	Cannon	*Tamarac.*
Safe	*Axe.*	Come	*Maple.*
Police	*File.*	Go	*Beech.*
Train	*Grindstone.*	Send	*Ebony.*
Trains	*Hatchet.*	Sent	*Box Wood.*
Rail	*Hammer.*	Disguised	*Logs.*
Signal	*Saw.*	Letters	*Bar Lead.*
Light	*Sledge.*	Dispatch	*Blistered Steel*
Dark	*Maul.*	Package	*Block Tin.*
Lantern	*Spike Maul.*	Box	*Tin.*
Night	*Wrench.*	Immediate	*Blooms*
Day	*Boards.*	Haste	*Blooms Iron.*
A.M	*Fencing.*	Slow	*Boiler Iron*
P.M	*Flooring.*	Steady	*Brass.*
Disguise	*Joists.*	Easy	*Sheet Brass.*
Burn	*Wheel.*	Caution	*Cast Iron.*

Cautious	*Cast Steel*	Fireman	*Soft Coal*
Quick	*Charcoal Iron*	Trackman	*Tar.*
Fiery	*Copper*	Express Messenger	*Turpentine*
Reliable	*Sheet Copper*		
Unreliable	*Round Copper.*	Treacherous	*Waste*
Probable	*Square Copper*	Terachery	*Rope*
Movement	*Bar Copper*	Coward	*Cord*
Movements	*Hammered Iron*	Shall	*Round Iron*
Tardy	*Hoop Iron*	Black	*Scrap Iron*
Bold	*Hot Iron*	White	*Sheet Iron*
Determined	*Iron*	Indians	*Square Iron.*
True	*Lead*	Secede	*Hawser*
Believe	*Malable Iron.*	Seceded	*Ladder*
Belief	*Pig Iron*	Secession	*Shovel*
Concentrate	*Pig Lead*	Slate	*Spade*
Concentrating	*Pike Lead*	Plunder	*Spermacetti*
Mail	*Willow.*	Reward	*Palm Oil*
Telegraph	*Sumac.*		*Yellow Ochre*
Stage	*Band Iron.*		*Ochre*
Carriage	*Bar Iron.*		*Lard Oil*
Negroes	*Sheet Lead.*		*Chrome Green*
Spy	*Sheet Tin.*		*Green*
Spies	*Wrought Iron*		*Blue*
Grade	*Nail Iron.*		*Red*
Grading	*Brooms.*		*Olive*
Saloon	*Buckets.*		*Brown*
Hotel	*Charcoal*		*Litharge*
Interfere	*Chard Wood*		*Whiting*
Interupt	*Coal*		*Spanish Brown*
Stop	*Coal Dust*		*Venetian Red*
Obstruct	*Egg Coal*		*Paris Blue*
Hazard	*Hard Coal*		
Adams	*Hose*	Philadelphia	*Wheat*
Conductor	*Pipe*	Baltimore	*Corn*
Baggageman	*Rosin*	Cowardice	*Twine*
Brake'sman	*Sills*	Sunday	*Turkey*
Engineer	*Sleepers*	Monday	*Gobler*

Tuesday	*Goose*	Havre DeGrace	*Pumpkins*
Wednesday	*Gander*		
Thursday	*Chicken*	S. M. F.	*Pears*
Friday	*Hen*	W. S.	*Fruit*
Saturday	*Rooster*	G. S.	*Apples*
Wilmington	*Squash*	A. P.	*Plums*
Newyork	*Millet*	T. W.	*Peaches*
Boston	*Sugar*	A.C.	*Gooseberries*
Richmond	*Coffee*	C. W.	*Berries*
Albany	*Molasses*	H. L.	*Cranberries*
Chicago	*Syrup*	M. B.	*Raisins*
P. W & B. RR	*Maple Sugar*		
B. & O. R. R.	*Cotton*	Stans.	*Figs*
B. & W. RR	*Tobacco*	Sct.	*Dates*
N. C. R. R.	*Ham*	Lin.	*Almonds*
North	*Bacon*	Prest.	*Nuts*
South	*Pork*	Vice Prest.	*Prunes*
West	*Beef*	P.M. Genl	*Filberts*
East	*Lamb*	Cameron, Sec of War	*Peanuts*
	Venison		
	Veal	N. B.	*Currants*
	Mutton	E.S. Sanford	*Walnuts*
	Onions	G. H. B.	*Hickory-nuts*
	Beets		*Beech-nuts*
Washington	*Barley*		*Citron*
Back River	*Hops*		*Melons*
Stenomer's Run	*Oats*		*Pine apple*
Rush River	*Malt*		*Oranges*
Gun Powder	*Peas*		*Lemons*
Perryman's	*Beans*		*Potatoes*

Quincy, Apl. 22, 1861

My Friend

I think it likely you will be glad to be kept advised of current events at this extreme western point of the free states.

I will not apologize for writing, for, if my letters are troublesome, you can easily throw them in the fire without reading.

The traitors must be astounded at the unanimity of feeling in the North.

Lying editors and letter writers in the free states have led them to expect very different demonstrations from those which are being made. There, where we had as much reason to expect disaffection as any where else, the sentiment in favour of the government, and the determination to stand by the stars and stripes, is almost unanimous, and altogether overwhelming. The very few who have treason in their hearts, are, in outward act, simply sulky. They dare not utter a word of condemnation of the administration, or of sympathy with the traitors. Now that the fray has begun the universal sentiment is that it shall be pushed vigorously and powerfully on, until the quarrel is settled once, and forever, if it costs the last man, and the last dollar in the free states to do it. Nothing must be left for our posterity to quarrel over—The settlement must be a final one.

On Saturday night we had another immense meeting of the citizens, which was presided over by a leading democrat of the city, who is an Irishman and Catholic. The enthusiasm was unbounded. We organized, and officered a Regiment of home guards, consisting of about a thousand men divided into seven companies.

Yesterday, Sunday, Capt Ben Prentiss left with his command for Springfield.

At 12 M. all the pastors of the city, with their congregations, met the gallant Capt. and his loyal company, in Washington Square, to give them a parting benediction. Six or seven thousand persons were present. A banner was presented, a hymn was sung, prayer was made, and the soldiers addressed by one of the clergymen and myself. We then marched with them to the depot where the star spangled banner was sung, many thousands joining in the chorus.

The scene, altogether, was the most sowlemn and impressive I have ever witnessed and showed unmistakeably how intensely the fires of patriotism are burning in the hearts of our people.

Richardson has not attended any of our meetings. A great crowd went to his house on Friday night and called for him, but he did not appear—He was loudly called for again at the meeting on Saturday night, but did not show himself. His influence is gone. Morris always meets with us, and cooperates fully in all our measures.

We are constantly threatened from Missouri, but have no fear of an attack—will endeavor to be prepared should one be made. They are becoming very violent over there, and our friends on that side of the river will probably soon need protection. When more urgent and important matters are disposed of, and you can turn your attention in this direction, think of the propriety of making this a military station. I am of opinion it will become a military necessity.

Every body is delighted with the measures you have adopted, and the vigor with which you are pushing them. Many are fearful for the safety of Washington. I cannot say that I either am, or have been myself. I am sure the fall of Sumter has been of great advantage to us. The fall of Washington would be most disasterous. Communication ought to, and must be kept open to Washington. Baltimore must not stand in the way. It should be seized and garrisoned, or, if necessary to the success of our glorious cause, laid in ruin.

No city or state can be allowed to interpose between the government, and the final and triumphant termination of this quarrel, and if they get in the way give them up to their doom.

I have not had time to examine to what extent you have power to act in the present emergency, but if the power exists it would be well to exercise it to lay an embargo on trade on the Mississipi and place an adequate force at Cairo to enforce it. All supplies of provisions and munitions of war should be cut off from the South.

Be assured the people are with you in all your efforts to push this war to the uttermost extremity. We hope you will yet get possession of the traitors who have precipitated the country into this fearful strife, and give them up to the death that traitors deserve. God bless, and guard, and prosper you. Truly your friend

O. H. Browning

STATE OF MARYLAND

Executive Chamber
Annapolis, April 22nd 1861

To His Excellency, A. Lincoln.
President of the United States
Sir,

I feel it my duty most respectfully to advise that no more troops be ordered or allowed to pass through Maryland and that the troops now off Annapolis be sent elsewhere, and I most respectfully urge that a truce be offered by you so that the effusion of blood may be prevented. I respectfully suggest that Lord Lyons be requested to act as mediator between the contending parties of our Country.

I have the honor to be
Very Respectfully
Your obt. Servant
Tho. H. Hicks

STATE OF MARYLAND

Executive Chamber
Annapolis, April 22nd 1861

To Lieut Genl. Scott
Sir,

I have feelt it to be my duty to advise the President to order elsewhere the troops now off Annapolis and also that no more may be sent through Maryland, and that Lord Lyons may be requested to mediate between the Contending parties of our Country.

I have the honor to be
Very Respectfully
Your obt. *Servt.*
Tho. H. Hicks

For the President.

I have but little that is certain to report, viz; 1. That there are three or four steamers, off Annapolis, with volunteers for Washington; 2. That their landing will be opposed by the citizens, reinforced from Baltimore; 3. That the landing may be effected, nevertheless, by good management, & 4. That the rails, on the Annapolis road (20 miles) have been taken up.

Several efforts to communicate with those troops today, have failed; but three other detached persons are repeating the attempt—& one or more of them, will, I think succeed. Once ashore, the regiments (if but two, & there are probably more) would have no difficulty in reaching Washington, on foot, other than the want of wagons to transport camp equippage &c. The Quarter Master that I have sent there (I do not know that he has arrived) has orders to hire wagons, if he can, & if not, to impress &c—

Of rumors, the following are probable, viz; 1. That from 1,500 to 2,000 troops are at the White House (4 miles below M[t] Vernon—a narrow point in the Potomak) engaged in erecting a battery, 2. That an equal force is collected or in progress of assemblage on the two sides of the river to attack Fort Washington, & 3. That extra cars went up, yesterday, to bring down from Harpers Ferry, about 2,000 other troops to join in a general attack on this Capital—that is, on many of its fronts at once. I feel confident that with our present forces, we can defend the Capitol, the Arsenal & all the executive buildings—seven, against ten thousand troops not better than our District Volunteers.

Respectfully submitted

Ap[l] 22, 1861. *Winfield Scott.*

[Endorsed in Mr. Lincoln's hand:]
Gen. Scott's daily report
N[o] 18.

THE MAGNETIC TELEGRAPH COMPANY.
Dated Annapolis Junction Apl 24 1861.

Rec'd, Washington, Apl 24 1861, ___ o'clock, ___ min. M.

To Marshall Geo. P. Kane

Balto.

I have acted on your advice but am disappointed about the troops for Balto. who were to come here. The Northern troops are still in Annapolis and those from Washington have left here. I am informed by a messenger from Prince Georges that five thousand (5000) Virginians are near Bladensburg but dont believe it possible. Send me some word or advice.

Frank A. Bond
Capt . United Rifles

For the President.

There is reason to hope that the volunteers which arrived Sunday last at Annapolis are now advancing, in detachments, by means of 4 small cars, over the partially broken road, to the Junction-house, whence they may, with less difficulty, be brought to Washington, as we are, as yet, masters of the road & the cars this side of the Junction. A pioneer train, of a few cars, is about to advance to gain information & to give comfort to the volunteers, & assistance.

The Secretary of the Navy has kindly engaged to send down a war vessel to pilot up a fleet of transports, with N. York volunteers, supposed to be waiting at the mouth of this river for such assistance.

The arrival of that fleet could enable me to detach a force sufficient to occupy the Junction & two posts on this side, & release the troops hemmed in at Annapolis. At present, I cannot make any considerable detachment without endangering the defences of this city.

I have this moment learned that of the three locomotives, seized yesterday, only one is fit for service, so that my order to send a second & a smaller number of cars to support the pioneer train, & to prevent the rails from being taken up in its rear, cannot be executed. Nevertheless, the pioneer train will advance, at least, a part of the distance, cautiously, under a most judicious officer—Capt—Franklin.

Respectfully submitted.

Winfield Scott.

Apl. 24, 1861

[Endorsed in Mr. Lincoln's hand:]
Gen. Scott's daily report—
No 19

For the President.

Some 1600 volunteers have arrived today but I cannot give, as yet the precise States to which they respectively belong. One of the regiments is from R. Island, & that, by permission, is gone to lodge in the Department of the Interior.

Another regiment is known to have arrived, from Annapolis at the Junction-House, & will be here by the second (next) train.

The hopeful news is, that the directors of the rail road between Baltimore & Washington, will send here, tomorrow, an agent to ask for protection to a re-establishment of trains between the two cities & there is other evidence of a return of good feelings in Baltimore; & the report, thro' very respectable channels, that Virginia is opposed to invading this District & wishes to maintain an armed neutrality.

This seems to be contradicted by the preparations for erecting a battery (to command the Potomak) at the White House, 4 miles below Mount Vernon. I believe that such preparations were commenced the day before yesterday & I have earnestly solicited that the work might be delayed, if not prevented, by a war vessel, like the Pawnee with a heavy broadside throwing shots & shells among the workmen. By means of a certain agency, I shall to night or in the morning know something about the progress of the construction at the White-house, but the sooner it is attacked by the Navy the better. The day after tomorrow or even tomorrow it may be in a condition to repel the Pawnee.

Respectfully submitted.
Winfield Scott.
Ap! 26, 1861.

[Endorsed in Mr. Lincoln's hand:]
Gen. Scott's daily report
No 20.

Superintendent Kennedy's report of April 27 is reminiscent of the recent work of the War Manpower Commission.

Census Office, Dept: of the Interior.
Washington, April 27th 1861.

His Excellency
The President.
Sir,

I trust I may not be deemed intrusive in venturing to transmit for your examination the accompanying table—prepared from the population returns of the Census of 1860.

This liberty I take in view of the important bearing upon the public interests of the facts presented at the present juncture. It will be perceived that the results are given in round numbers, as time has not admitted at this early moment of such an examination as would insure perfect accuracy. The figures may, however, be relied on as sufficiently exact for all practical deductions.

With sentiments of unaffected respect, I have the honor to be
Your Excellency's Obedient Servant
Jos. C. G. Kennedy
Superintendent

NUMBER OF WHITE MALES BETWEEN THE AGES OF 18 AND 45 INCLUSIVE.

Census of 1860.

FREE STATES		BORDER SLAVE STATES	
California	76,000	Wisconsin	211,000
Connecticut	92,000	North Carolina	132,000
Illinois	342,000	Tennessee	167,000
Indiana	270,000	Virginia	221,000
Iowa	135,000		1,124,000
Kansas	21,000		
Maine	125,000	SECEDED STATES	
Massachusetts	246,000	Alabama	106,000
Michigan	150,000	Florida	16,000
Minnesota	32,000	Georgia	119,000
New Hampshire	65,000	Mississippi	71,000
New Jersey	134,000	Louisiana	75,000
New York	778,000	South Carolina	60,000
Ohio	468,000	Texas	84,000
Oregon	10,000		531,000
Pennsylvania	581,000		
Rhode Island	35,000	TERRITORIES	
Vermont	63,000	Colorado	6,000
Wisconsin	155,000	Dakota	1,000
	3,778,000	Nebraska	6,000
		Nevada	1,000
BORDER SLAVE STATES		New Mexico	13,000
Arkansas	65,000	Utah	8,000
Delaware	22,000	Washington	2,000
Kentucky	186,000	Dist. of Columbia	14,000
Maryland	120,000		51,000

TOTAL 5,484,000

Fugitive Slaves:

Free States	3,778,000	By the Census of 1850, it appears that in the Border Slave States, one slave escaped to each 2,527 held in bondage. In 1860 one escaped to each 3,276.
Border Slave States	1,124,000	
Seceded States	531,000	
Territories	51,000	
	5,484,000	

COLEMAN'S EUTAW HOUSE,

Baltimore, April 28th 1861

Hon A Lincoln
Washington D.C.
My dear Sir,

Some three weeks ago I wrote an old friend and classmate, who now resides in Mobile, Ala On my arrival here last evening I found a letter from him. I learn from it that it is the settled policy to attack the capital by the Southern Confederacy. It is to be done by foes within as well as without. He says there is not a department at Washington that is not well filled with friends of Jeff Davis. And they are ready to strike at any moment. He further states that a large number of the citizens of Washington will be prominent in the move, and that desperate men dressed in citizens garb will infest your city to take their part in the contest against you. This information comes from a high source. It is imparted in that manner that I cannot betray the name, or expose the letter. I give it to you only at its market value. You can place any estimate upon it you please.

Devotedly yr friend
A. M. Hancock

With secession, Mr. Lincoln's old adversary, Senator Douglas, became one of his most loyal and important supporters. At the inauguration he conspicuously held Mr. Lincoln's hat.

Springfield
April 29th 1861–

My Dear Sir

This letter will be delivered by J. M. Cutts Esq. the only brother of Mrs. Douglas, whom you may remember to have met some years ago at Chicago. He is a lawyer by Profession, a man of talents & worthy of your confidence. He goes to Washington to take a hand in the defense of the Capital and the Government. He will be able to give you any information you may desire in regard to the public sentiment and condition of things in this State, as well Saint Louis where he resides. I found the state of feeling here and in some parts of our State much less satisfactory than I could have desired or expected when I arrived. There will be no outbreak however and in a few days I hope for entire unanimity in the support of the government and the Union.

I am very respectfully your obedient servant

S.A. Douglas

Executive Department
Nashville Te. Apl. 29. 1861

To His Excellency The President of the United States.
Washington City. D.C.

Sir;

On the 26th inst. the Steamboat C. E. Hillman on its passage from St. Louis to Nashville was seized and taken possession of by an armed force on the Steamboat Swallow. This seizure was made on the Mississippi River, a short distance above Cairo Illinois. The boat Hillman was owned by citizens of Tennessee, and its cargo was the property of this State and her citizens. It is beleived that the force employed in this work is a part of the force recently called into the service by the proclamation of the President.

This interruption of the free navigation of the Mississippi river and the seizure of property belonging to the State of Tennessee and her citizens, is aggressive and hostile, and without commenting upon the character and lawlessness of the outrage, it becomes my imperative duty to inquire by what authority the said acts were committed, I have therefore respectfully to request that the President shall inform me whether the same was done by or under the instructions of the Federal Goverment, or is approved by said Government.

Very respectfully,
Isham G. Harris
Governor of Tennessee

[Endorsed:]
Important Letter to the President.

Department of Annapolis
April 30. 1861

To the President

This will be handed to you by R. H— Hare who has rendered good service in getting open the Annapolis line of Communication. He is a gentleman of the strictest loyalty and of capacity for affairs. A native of Philadelphia a large owner of real estate in Baltimore he is most zealous in his efforts to preserve the integrity of the Country. He will in a word give you his plan. I believe it practicable. A loyal Maryland Regiment would be worth 5000 other troops in in its moral effect .

We have the means of furnishing the arms in the north, if that should be difficult

I have the honor
to be. Your obt Servt
Benj. F Butler

The President

April 30 1861

Sir:

I deem it my duty to state formally—

1st That the chief of police at the Capital Mr . Dunnington is a disunionist. Having the civil command of the Capital the importance of that post is apparent.

2nd Many of the Officers as well as nearly all of the "Bosses" or Head men at the Navy Yard are disunionists and it is understood that any attack upon the city will be made at that point for the above reasons.

3rd I have been requested to to state that the appointment of Strangers to the Local Offices is likely to create greater disaffection than now exists and it is feared that a continuation of the present officers such as Commissioner of Public Buildings, Postmaster etc will if trouble ensues be the cause of success by the insurgent which otherwise might not ensue.

Respectfully
Geo. Harrington

Hon S.P.Chase

For the President.

I doubt that I have any thing material to report, today, not already well known to the President.

We have been annoyed every a day or two by reports of hostile batteries at or near Arlington, across the river & at the White-house &c below Mount Vernon.

Confidential reports reached me last night, worthy of entire credit, to the effect that not a gun had been mounted, nor a breast-work commenced, on the opposite side of the river yesterday morning, from Aquia creek—to the northern terminus of the Virginia railroad —55 below, up to the Georgetown aqueduct.

Colonel Mansfield, the immediate commander of the Washington Department came to the conclusion the day before yesterday that we wanted from 17,000 to 20,000 troops to give security to this Capital against the forces of the enemy known to be within 24 hours of us. A small abatement from the larger of these numbers, may be made on account of the favorable change said to have taken place in the temper & purposes of Maryland. We, however, still estimate that some nine or ten [*regiments*] additional northern regiments to be necessary to give us the required security.

I instructed Genl. Patterson yesterday to withdraw the call he had made upon the Gov. of Pennsylvania for 25 additional regiments.

Respectfully Submitted—

Winfield Scott

[Endorsed in Mr. Lincoln's hand:]
Gen. Scott's daily report
No. 21

To His Excellency
The Hon A Lincoln.
Washington
D C

Sir

Desirous of contributing my mite to the present war in defense of the union I have entered upon the work of publishing a weekly war

Journal, the entire profits of which I shall appropriate to the fund for the maintenance and support of the wives and families of our brave and loyal volunteers.

Your countenance and patronage would materially add to the success of the Undertaking, and ensure a wide circulation & bring in thousands of dollars to the Fund.

Taking the liberty of requesting your inspection of the first number of the Naval & Military Path Finder

I am, Sir
Yrs. respectfully
John F. Whitney

List of officers I wish to remember, when I make appointments for the officers of the regular Army–

Maj– Anderson
Capt[t] Doubleday
Capt Foster–
Maj. Hunter
Lieut. Slemmer–His pretty wife says a major or first Captain.

[In Mr. Lincoln's holograph]

5 O'Clock
Saturday evng.

My Dear Sir.

I go to dine to day with the French Minister at Georgetown.

It seems proper to let you know where I may be found, as the times are a little revolutionary, if you should have need of me.

Very truly yours
William H Seward

The President

For the President

I have received a letter from Governor Hicks who has learned that Colonel Ellsworth, at the head of a N. York regiment, called *The Zouaves* is coming on resolved to cut his way thro' Baltimore, which threat, the Governor fears, may check the change now rapidly going on thro' out Maryland, & particularly in Baltimore, in favour of the Union. That this change of sentiment will soon become almost universal I learn, also, thro' a special agent.

My request that Major General Patterson might withdraw his call upon the Governor of Pennsylvania for 26 regiments in addition to the quota of sixteen required by the Secretary of War, was the result of the expressed disapprobation of the Secretary.

Forts Washington & McHenry were reinforced yesterday, & are considered as secure. So I also consider this city, as our means of defence are still ahead of the enemy's means of attack, & additional volunteers may be expected, daily, for a week.

The four companies of the 2d Cavalry, from Texas, sent to Carlisle to be remounted, will be here, in the saddle tomorrow or the next day, which will give us six companies of that regiment. The remaining four that arrived, a few days ago, at N. York, from Texas, will, in a week, be remounted at Carlisle & follow.

Respectfully submitted—
Winfield Scott

[Endorsed in Mr. Lincoln's hand:]
Gen. Scott's daily report
No
No 21–1/2

NY. MAY SCD. TO ABRAHAM LINCOLN. PRESIDENT OF THE UNITED STATES. WASHINGTON. FOR GODS SAKE. DONT PUT YOUR TRUST IN THE UNION MEN OF MARYLAND. AS SOON AS IT WILL BE SAFE FOR THEM TO RUSH TO THE STANDARD OF JEFF. DAVIS. THEY WILL DO SO. OLIVER DYER.
FOUR PINE ST. NY.

Pellham Tavern May 2d. 1861

President Lincoln

Dear Sir:

I can see in the future that an untimely death awaits Jefferson Davis, and his band of traitors, it is not his destiny to destroy our nation, the bones of his people will rise from the ground and curse him as he passes into eternity.

Thank God, that might have been, but is not to be your fate, notwithstanding our flag is on the verge of ruin, our country bent by discord, and cruel war staring us in the face, and even Maryland turned traitor to our most glorious cause, and thus made her countrymen her foes by spilling their precious blood in her streets.

I am delighted to see that you have taken steps to place them under the heel of the law without bloodshed.

I cannot help feeling assured that you are now on the right path, and that the stand you have taken is the only one that justice and a sense of right would dictate, you have now repudiated the past, and stand forth the President of the United States, You are the man I like, because you have thrown off the trammels of your cabinet, and taken the advice of your best friend Mrs. L. and are now acting as plain common sense, and your own noble judgment dicatates.
The spontaneous gathering around you, plainly indicates how the Nation feels. Thousands of bold and brave hearts respond to your call, and sally around the star spangled banner held in your hand, heaven bless it and you.

They are willing and anxious to fight for their country, and their Gov. *But it must not be'*

Your cry for arms has been responded to from the East and the West, from the North, and even from the South, for there are brave southern hearts that beat with the fire of patriotism and who will stand undivided for their Country's flag.

Be assured that the one foolish act of the Southern States, has been firing upon the American flag. It has aroused the hearts of men, from Pennsylvania to the distant land that contains your home, and the martial cry has resounded from North to South; from hill and dale thousands are flocking to your banners; women have given up their husbands and sons like the heroines of old, and told them to begone, and return with honour, or not return atall, and if necessary, bravely will they accomplish their task. Hearts would be made sad, homes desolate, were it not that God has watched over you, and through you will bring forth our beloved land from under the cloud that now hangs over it.

If war should by any unforseen accident be inaugerated, it would raise the evil in mens hearts, and make them wish for blood.

Dear Mr. Lincoln you now are safe, you can defend the Capitol from all assaults, and are master of the Country, and can conciliate the South on your own terms, and with honor to yourself, without treading upon Southern rights.

Oh think of this in the name of humanity, and all you hold sacred, then in after ages, your name will be honhoured and beloved, let your own reason and judgment hold the sway, and you will never regret it. Give up frt Pickens, if any opportunity offers, which will show the South that you do not intend to invade their land, and stand by justice, and act on the defensive. If they attack you, which they will not do, exterminate them if you can. And you may count upon me, my sons, and my fortune to aid you. Take your own counsel, I know you wish this trouble settled without bloodshed, you have the matter in your own hands, let it be done quickly, call to your aid all the soldiers that are now prepared for war, so as to let the Southern people see you are invincible.

Then a bright and glorious future will beam upon you, and our flag will float once more, over all our land, and not be dimmed by the loss of a single star, and will ever remain the harbinger of victory; having been born before the present generation of men flourished. In olden times, when tyrants hand sought to crush it, it floated on the plains of Maryland, and summit of Bunker hill, whenever it was unfurled the fight was victorious, remember this, and though for a time it may be banished from some states, it only rests for you to show them the way, and they will most willingly come back, now they think they have right on their side, and rest assured, if you coerce them, they will fight for those rights step by step, until the whole southern race white and black are exterminated.

You know what war can do, if once commenced, how it desolates the land, Commerce, Science and learning are hushed. Its messengers like vultures and tygers but look for prey. They will not only desolate and plunder those that are opposed to them, but when the war is over, fight each other, for when blood is once shed, it becomes a mania that few can resist, then do not let this war proceed, we of the North are safe, you have placed us by your pacific policy beyond the reach of the South.

Men have freely given their lives, their wealth, their all to aid you, there is not a craven heart so base as not to respond to your call for help; but it is past, be firm as you have already been, and you will step forth into the light of day uncontaminated by those around you, let your policy be your own, give us peace instead of war, and millions will bless the name you bear, and acknowledge you the Saviour of the greatest Country on the face of earth.
No man has ever lived, possessed of the power that you now have, of becoming immortal.

I am with great respect.
Your Obedient Servant
Robt L Pell

Head Quarters, O.V. M.
Columbus, Ohio, April 27, 1861

Lieut. Genl. Winfield Scott
Comdg. U. S. Army,
General:

Communication with Washington being so difficult, I beg to lay before you some views relative to this region of country, & to propose for your consideration a plan of operations intended to relieve the pressure upon Washington, & tending to bring the war to a speedy close; the region North of the Ohio, and between the Mississippi and the Alleganies, form one grand strategic field in which all operations must be under the control of one head, whether acting offensively or [*defensively*] on the defensive—

I assume it as the final result that hostilities will break out on the line of the Ohio.

For two reasons it is necessary to delay this result by all political means, for a certain period of time.

1st To Enable the North West to make the requisite preparations now very incomplete.

2nd That a strong diversion may be made [*to*] in aid of the defense of Washington, & the Eastern line of operations—

First urging that the General Govt. should leave no means untried to arm & equip the Western States, I submit the following views.

Cairo should be occupied by a small force, say 2 Battalions strongly entrenched, & furnished with heavy guns, & a gun boat to control the river. A force of some 8 Battalions to be in observation at Sandoval (the Junction of the Ohio & Miss, & the Illinois Central Railway) to observe St. Louis, sustain the garrison of Cairo, & if necessary re-inforce Cincinnati. A few companies should observe the Central below Vincennes. A Division of about 4000 men at Seymour, to observe Louisville & be ready to support Cincinnati or Cairo —A Division of 5000 men at or near Cincinnati. Two Battalions at or near Chillicothe—

Could we be provided with arms, the North West has ample resources to furnish 80000 men for active operations, after providing somewhat more than the troops mentioned above for the protection of the frontier.

With the active Army of operations it is proposed to cross the Ohio at, or in the vicinity of Gallipolis, & move up the valley of the Great Kanawha on Richmond; in combination with this Cumberland should be seized, and a few thousand men left, at Ironton or Gallipolis to cover the rear & right flank of the main column. The presence of this detachment & a prompt movement on Louisville, or the heights opposite Cincinnati would effectually prevent any interference on the part of Kentucky. The movement on Richmond should be conducted with the utmost promptness, & could not fail to relieve Washington, as well as to secure the destruction of the Southern Army if aided by a decided advance on the Eastern Line. I know that there would be difficulty in crossing the mountains, but would go prepared to meet them. Another plan would be in the event of Kentucky assuming a hostile position, to cross the Ohio at Cincinnati or Louisville with 80,000 men; march straight to Nashville and then

act according to circumstances. Were a battle gained before reaching Nashville, so that the strength of Kentucky & Tennessee were effectually broken, a movement on Montgomery, aided by a vigorous on the Eastern Line, towards Charleston & Augusta, should not be delayed. The ulterior movements of the combined armies might be on Pensacola, Mobile & New Orleans. It seems clear that the forces of the north west should not remain quietly on the defensive, & that under present circumstances, if the supply of arms is such as to render it absolutely impossible to bring into the field the numbers indicated above—then offensive movements would be most effective on the line first indicated; but if so liberal a supply can be obtained as to enable us to dispose of 80,000 troops for the active Army, then the 2nd line of operations would be the most decisive
To enable us to carry out either of these plans, it is absolutely necessary that the Genl. Govt. should strain every nerve to supply the west with Arms, Ammunition & Equipments.

Even to maintain the defensive we must be largely assisted. I beg to urge upon you that we are very badly supplied at present, & that a vast population, eager to fight, are rendered powerless by want of Arms—the nation being thus deprived of their aid—

I have the honor to be, General,
Very respectfully yours,
Geo. B. McClellan
Maj. Genl. Comdg. O.V.

A true copy—
Interlineation of omitted paragraph Page 4. made before
Certifying
Schuyler Hamilton

[General Scott's report to President written on last sheet of this letter]

CONFIDENTIAL

Head Quarters O.V.M.
Columbus, Ohio,
April 27, 1861

Geo. B. McClellan
Maj. Genl. Comdg
To the Genl-in Chief, relating to movements in the West.
Remarks &c—

As the date of this letter Genl. Mc. knew nothing of the intended call for two years' volunteers, he must have had the idea of composing his enormous columns of three months' men for operating against Nashville & Richmond—that is, of men whose term of service would expire by the time he had collected and organized them. That such was his idea appears from a prior letter, in which, altho' the Ohio quota is but 10,000 men, the general speaks, I think, of having 30,000 & wants arms &c. &c. &c. for 80,000.

2. A march upon Richmond from the Ohio would probably insure the revolt of Western Virginia, which, if left alone, will soon be, 5 out of 7, for the Union.

3. The general eschews water transportation by the Ohio and Mississippi, in favor of long, tedious & break-down (of men, horses & wagons) marches.

4. His plan is to subdue the Seceded States, by piecemeal, instead of enveloping them all (nearly) at once, by a cordon of posts on the Mississippi to its mouth, from its junction with the Ohio, & by blockading ships of war on the sea-board—For the cordon a number of men equal to one of the general's columns would, probably, suffice; & the transportation of men & all supplies by water, is about a fifth of the land cost—be-sides the immense saving in time—

Respectfully submitted to the President
signed *Winfield Scott.*
a true copy May 2. 1861.
Schuyler Hamilton
Lt.Col & Mily.Secy.

[Endorsed in Mr. Lincoln's hand:]
Gen. Scott's daily report
No. 22—

Will the President please receive the Gentlemen, who hand this? They come from Richmond and have valuable information.

Simon Cameron
May 3, 1861

Head Quarters 8th Regt. Mass.Volts.
Washington May 3/61.

His Excellency The President

Will please accept the compliments of Col. Munroe & Staff, together with the Commissioned officers of the 8th Mass. Regt. and their regrets that official business of an extraordinary character, compels them to forego the pleasure of keeping the appointment with His Excellency, at the Executive Mansion this day—

For the officers of the 8th Mass. Regt.

Very Respectfully
Your Obt. Servt.
I. T. Coe
Secy

For the President.

It being ascertained that the President's square & all the western part of this city, with Georgetown are within the reach of heavy gun batteries on the Arlington heights, I gave instruction yesterday to Col.o Mansfield not to lose a moment in anticipating the enemy by occupying those heights, with redoubts, sufficient to hold them. They will render an addition of several regiments to the force estimated for the defence of this Capital in my *bulletin* (report to you of the 30th ultimo.

Perceiving, in a news-paper, that the Legislature of Maryland has appointed commissioners to wait upon the President, with certain propositions, I fear that, after all, we shall be forced to reopen free communications with the north, thro' Baltimore, by our troops.

Respectfully submitted.
Winfield Scott.

Head Qrs. of the Army
Washington May 3, 1861.

[Endorsed in Mr. Lincoln's hand:]
Gen. Scott's daily report
No. 23.

For the President.

I have authorized commanders of Departments, Butler & Mansfield, to interchange two regiments, so that the former may have two of his brigade with him, at Annapolis. The movement will be made without an expence to the U. S.

Brig. General Butler has my instructions to send, from Annapolis to the Relay-house, 8 miles this side of Baltimore, a heavy regiment to hold that important point;—control the B. & Ohio Rail Road, & at the same time influence the legislature, at Frederic, & the population of Baltimore. The same regiment will be at hand in case we should soon be obliged to take possession of Baltimore by the force of arms. And, for this enterprise, Major General Patterson, Brig. Genl Butler & Lieut. Col. Porter (on the road leading from York) are all instructed to hold themselves prepared. On the other hand—with the amicable acquiescense of Baltimore & Maryland—Major General Patterson is instructed to send, thro' Baltimore, to this place, a battalion of 7 companies of regulars now under his command, at, & on this side of, Elkton—(If expedient, this battalion may be halted in Baltimore, to support law & order.)

Besides the forces designed to occupy Arlington Heights, to retake Harper's Ferry, & to threaten, from Fort Monroe the Gosport Navy Yard, & other important points on the navigable waters falling into the Chesapeake, I deem it inexpedient to make other aggressive movements with three months' levies. Out of these, & for the purpose indicated, I shall add some 5,000 men to [*the*] necessary garrison of Fort Monroe, to be encamped about it.

Possibly, I may—tho' like other old soldiers, chary of detachments—recommend the occupation of Alexandria, if our forces here should seem to justify the movement.

Respectfully submitted.
Winfield Scott.

Head Qrs. of the Army,
Washington, May 4, 1861.

[Endorsed in Mr. Lincoln's hand:]
Gen. Scott's daily report
N° 24

Brooklyn May 9th. 1861.

Respected Sir,

It is with feelings of sadness, I have just noticed in a papers, that Our Flag, floats not upon, or over Our Presidents Mansion. This should not be, it shall not be any longer, if you will allow me the privilege, the honor, the glory, of presenting one that will be suitable and appropriate for the place. I most respectfully ask your permission and consent to furnish one, as a slight expression of my feelings and sympathies for the honor and welfare of our country in this her hour of trial and trouble. If you will permit me that privilege, I will forward one immediately, upon hearing from you what sised one will be proper, for the place you intend to hoist it. Please forward me a few lines, to the care of Messrs. Wm. C. Bryant & Co. New York Evening Post. N.Y.

I remain with great respect
Yours most truly
Robert G. Thursby

"PERSIA"

"PRIVATE"
Liverpool 10 May 1861

Sir,

The merchants of this Town deeply and warmly sympathise with you at the present moment because they feel that you are acting with energy & determination to put down an unjustifiable rebellion, they feel also that although they as merchants will be great sufferers, still that your energetic acts will be the means of abolishing the curse of your land—Slavery—which it is impossible can exist with a republican government, they also see clearly that the greatest blow you can inflict is to issue a proclamation declaring that all slaves in your United States are free & they must anxiously expect by every mail to hear that such a proclamation has been issued.—

Wishing you God speed
I have the honour to be
Your most H— servant
Joseph Aspinall

To
Abraham Lincoln

(P–S– If there is any difficulty in the law—Congress could make the remedy on July 4 *CMC*)

Off Ireland
May 11. "61

His Ex—A. Lincoln
Pres— DC"
Sir,

When I spoke to you last, I felt it to be my duty to my family to discourage the idea of my being made a general. But reflection and the sentiment of very distinguished gentlemen in N. York and elsewhere have caused me to change my mind. Volunteers *must* have confidence in their leaders—they press me on all sides—make me a general in the regular service (which must hereafter be large) and Ill return home at once upon notice.

I think my talent is military and that I will not fail the public expectation. God defend the Union.

Your most obt svt.
C. M. Clay

Sandrague 13th May–61

Sir

We the Irishmen on the other side of the Atlantic feel very much for the Americans at the present Crisis—prayers are offered up in their behalf every where.

Now it occured to me a scholar, politician & historian, that a termination might be put to the war without striking a blow.

Let the slave holders pay a tax on account their privilege And altho' it would be a retrograde movement in the work of civilization & refinement; any thing is better than war, civil war devastating the empire weakening its resources.

"Homo sum nihil humani alienum a me puto." I have the honor to be Sir your obt servt

Sir H. A. Montgomery

Washington D. C.
May 13. 1861.

To the
President of the United States:

It is thought proper that you should be informed that a large number of the Citizens of this place propose complimenting you with a Serenade this evening, at about 11 o'clock, as a token of their appreciation of the favor bestowed upon them by your appointing our fellow-citizen Mr. L. Clephane to office of Post Master of our city—

Hoping that the same may meet with your approbation,

I am, yours
Very Resp'l'y
A. C. Richards

P.S.

The Band attached to the Rhode Island Regiment now in this city has been engaged for said purpose—

A.C.R.

New York May 14th 1861

To his Excellency Abraham Lincoln)
(
President of the United States)

On behalf of the members of Empire Fire Engine Co. No. 42 of this city, I beg leave to offer the services of the company with their steam fire engine, for duty in the city of Washington.

Hoping to receive a favorable response to our offer, I remain,

Very Respectfully
Joseph D. Costa
Foreman Engine Co. 42

New York
May 18th 1861.

My dear Sir,

There are two things that worry people in this town, a good deal; one of which it certainly is in your power to modify, if not reform altogether—

1. The first is, fear that the government will not feed the troops as they ought to be fed, and keep their spirits up, without which feeling, they will be good for nothing, however patriotic they may be at the start:— but it may not be in your power to regulate that thoroughly, while it cannot too quickly receive the notice of Mr Cameron and his Department—

2— The second source of worriment is your own personal manners—your drawing-room receptions will take care of themselves— In them you are not particularly found fault with, but when you come to the receiving of military citizens (as all the volunteers are) it becomes a serious question enough, whether you please them or not—

Now then, soldiers write home to their friends in this town with reference to their disappointment in your bearing and manners when reviewing them—

They say when you are on horseback, and platoons of men marching by you, that you lean about and turn your head to talk with people behind you, when they claim that you should sit erect & talk to nobody and look straight at the saluting soldiers—that you ought to assume some dignity for the occasion even though your breeding has not been military. It makes but little difference whether the demand is reasonable or not—it dont require half so much sacrifice on your part to rectify it as it does of the men to go from their homes for the hardship they undertake—

And when you are passing lines of soldiers, reviewing them, afoot, they say you take your boys along, and straddle off as if you were cutting across lots, to get somewhere in the quickest time you can, and pay a good deal more attention to your own getting along, [*that*] than to the soldiers whom you start out to review.

These things dont sound well at all—The influence is bad here—The complaint may be frivilous and based on a mistake; but such things are written home here and fortify Raymond in his position of advertising for a "Leader"—He has got over that, rather, but there is no need of your being so infernally awkward, if these things are true—For God's sake consult somebody, some military man, as to what you ought to do on these occasions in military presence—Nobody will volunteer advice, probably, and if you are arbitrary and conceited on these little things, as Webster used to be, you will alienate your friends and go where he went and John Tyler too, towit where a man has no party—I dont mean a political party, but a great and universal body guard of men who speak well of you and will do anything to bear aloft and above reproach your administration.

The people here care a mighty lot about the volunteer soldiers—

They feel that unless the spirit and loyalty of the soldiers are kept up and encouraged in every way, the country is to suffer immeasurably before these troubles are disposed of—and you, thought you were autocrat, can never be popular with the army unless you try your best to lead them to think you appreciate their evolutions by addressing yourself to the business in hand when you are amongst them; and your manner is full as important as your talk—A lawyer in his office can put his feet on a table higher than his head, if he wishes to, but he cant come any such performance as Commander in Chief of the Armies of the United States in their presence—Then he must pretend to be a soldier even if he dont know anything of talking at all—

You had better let some officer put you through a few dress parades in your leisure moments, if you can get any, and get some military habit on you so you shall feel natural among military men—Dont let people call you a goose on these *very very* important relations to the Army—

Mrs Lincoln is growing popular all the while, because people say she is mistress of her situation—She aptly fits herself to the times—The dinner service she bought at Houghout's makes people think she is "in town"—they like to talk about her and say she has a good deal of sense and womanly wit about her—she is coming into excellent reputation in this naturally prejudiced city against you and her both—

My impression is that you will do well by paying more attention to your manners and make less effort at wit and story telling—All well enough in private but publicly it is a nuisance—Your talent is conceded—be a gentleman and courtly in your manners when you ought to be———now I dont care whether you take this well or ill—I voted for you and have a desire to be proud of your administration and I dont wish to see yourself over slaughed by these damaging stories when you could prevent it so easily—

I take it for granted that your temper is as clever as when you fought Douglass in the great campaign, and if it is, you wont be very mad at my writing you these things—Your position is a trying one, and when, on leaving Springfield you asked the people to pray for you, you did well, and millions do pray for you every day, and God is with you, on general principles, I really believe; but it wont do for you to be careless about any thing, not the least thing—

I am doing as I would be done by—In the general administration of your affairs up to this time none but fools and traitors, I imagine, find much fault—I think you have done wonderfully well—

If the stories I hear about Nicolay, your private secretary, are true, you ought to dismiss him—If he is sick, he has a right to be cross and ungentlemanly in his deportment, but not otherwise—People say he is very disagreeable and uncivil—That is wrong—

and I dont think the amenity and popularity of the White house ought to be left too much to your wife—It is said that clergymen and women are the getters up of secession in the South—Women and clergymen and every day people who have not much to do but criticize, are the people that make or unmake popularity—more than representatives in Congress or statesmen in the cabinet—And you know it—

You and I will probably never have any thing to do with each other personally, for we never have met and may never meet, and the greatest fault you can ever find with me, I imagine, is telling you what I think is true—to wit, you need more dignity.

I hope to gracious, you will take care of yourself in a way worthy your position—

That is all I ask—

Robert Colby
47 Wall St

President Lincoln
Washington—

P.S. There is one other thing conceded by every body but the secessionists, to wit: that you are a very warm hearted, honest & patriotic man—I give you a good deal of credit in this "Soverign" communication, after all—

Washington May 18. 1861

To His Excellency
Ab. Lincoln
President—U. S.
Dear Sir

The ladies of Washington desirous of giving expression to their fealty to the government, their strong sympathies for the Cause of their Country, and their devotion to the flag of the Union as well as to testify their high respect and admiration for you as the Chief Executive Officer—respectfully request your permission to raise a National flag over the Executive Mansion that yourself and family may be sheltered under its folds, and that all loyal citizens shall know it flies from the White House first under your administration.

Very Respectfully
Yours
Eugene Frean
No. 448–13th St.

New York, N Y 19, 1861.

Dear Sir:

The intelligence that the war for the Union is to be prosecuted with emphatic vigor, and that the traitors are to be thrown back from Washington in every direction causes general rejoicing here. We feel that the struggle thus prosecuted, cannot be of long duration. All are confident that the result will justify our fondest hopes.

The one drawback on the general satisfaction is the existence of wide-spread complaint and heart-burning with regard to the acceptance of this regiment and the rejection of that and the other.— These men have volunteered to defend the country on its own terms, they cannot be made to see why they should not be taken. The report that *all* who are efficient and ready are henceforth to be accepted, rejoices every loyal heart. I trust that report is well-founded; if it is not, I pray you to make it so at the earliest moments, and thereby gratify millions beside

Yours,
Horace Greeley

Hon. A. Lincoln, Washington.

Paris, France.
May, 22.1861.

Sir,

I left Boston on the 1. inst on the Cunard line steamer Niagara: and reached Liverpool on the 13.inst. at 12–1/2 P.M. I went on the same afternoon to London, where I was persuaded by Americans to have a frank talk with members of the H.Commons and House of Lords, and also with Lord Palmerston: which I did, as our affairs were were not at all understood in London and on the Continent. I had a full conversation with Lord Palmerston at his House in London, through the kindness of Mr. Motley the Historian (who is a warm and zealous Republican and having the association of the first men in England, greatly advances our cause,) whom I would recommend to your and the President's consideration for the first vacant mission. Lord P^{er} received my remarks in a very kindly spirit: so did Lord Brougham and others. I was also persuaded to write a popular article for the Times on the American question: [*which*] which was next day copied into the Galignani here: and translated and put into the French papers also. I sent you a cut from the Times—I hope the letter will meet your approbation. It is received with great enthusiasm by the Americans here. I have been requested by our friends here to stay and help make a public sentiment for our cause—among others by Mr. Marsh. This brings me to the purpose of my letter, for upon declaring that I must set out as I was drawing no salary until I could get to St. Petersbrug—he told me that he and others drew their salary from *the time of setting out upon their mission.* You have drawn my letter of credit so that I cannot get my salary till I get to "my post of official duty." So that here I am in the midst of my journey *without means*—the very railroad and boat fares having exhausted my advanced $1000— I left home on the 11 day (11) of April on my mission, and have not spent a day which was not absolutely necessary since on the way—as I was detained partly in Washington by you: and then by the blockade of the City.
I trust therefore you will send me and the Baring Brothers & Co. a new letter of credit giving me pay from the 10th of Apr. on till now: and till I get to St. Petersburg. I shall go on then in a few days: borrowing money of friends till I hear from you there. I have a wife

five children and nurse (8 of us) and am compelled to hire a private secretary who can speak French, at a high rate: and the Russian Court is the most expensive one in Europe. Under all the circumstances I earnestly ask you and the President to urge upon Congress at it's next session on the 4th July to raise my salary to 17–1/2 thousand dollars; as is the case in England and France. As I do not believe the Government desires me to live in a worse style than the poorest Ministers here: and then not have a dollar after four years service in the cause of the Country, in my still more advanced years. I am sorry to trouble you with these private matters during the Public Crisis but the necessity with me is urgent and what the department and the President intended to be to me an honour will prove an humiliation.

It will I trust be convenient for you to call the attention of the President to this matter and *show him this letter.* The letter of credit of my secretary, Green Clay, is written as mine. He left home after me on the 16 April ulto. Please change his also to suit the date.

Mr. Dayton has entered upon his duties–presented to the Emperor two days ago. I learn that the Emperor is wholly our friend. I have it from private and confidential sources– England–the Government–*not the people,* probably would rejoice in our calamities.

I have the honor to be your

Ob^{t} Sv^{t}

C. M. Clay

Minn.&c to Russia

Sec. of State &c.
Wash. D.C. U.S.A.

(P.S. The embarrassments in Washington prevented me from reading the statute.)

His Excellency
A. Lincoln
Pres. U. S.

Hon. Sir,

Herewith please find record of the birth of Abraham Lincoln Potter.

Born in the village of LaCrescent County of Houston State of Minnesota on the morning of the 23rd of May 1861—at 8. o.c'lk

Abraham Lincoln Potter. Son of George F. and Mary Anne Potter. The father ardently supported you for the Presidency and knows of no better way to express his satisfaction with your administration than by naming his son after you feeling satisfied that the future will present no cause for regret. The sympathy of the people are with you and hope that this wicked rebellion of the very *"brave" men* who do not dis-dain to poison and murder may soon be effectually crushed out—

Respectfully yours
George F. Potter.

THE MAGNETIC TELEGRAPH COMPANY.

Dated Indianapolis May 24 1861.

Rec'd, Washington ______ 1861, ______ o'clock, ______ min. M.

To Hon A Lincoln

We congratulate you that the campaign is successfully & energetically opened on Virginia soil. We hope that the West will not be long held back but will be permitted to take its part in the contest & push the War to a prompt conclusion

W Dennison
Richd Yates
Lyman Trumbull
O P Morton
G B McLellan

Morley's, Trafalgar Square
London, 24th. May 61

My dear Sir.

In my last I told you that I was endeavoring to procure the means to purchase war material. We have succeeded in acquiring the control of sufficient for [*about*] three or four batteries completely equipped for service and perhaps 10000 rifles. The difficulty which we have encountered, after having obtained command of means, is in getting the guns cast and the rifles made within the time which I can bring myself to pass here. But under all the information which I can obtain, I judge that such a supply of arms and ammunition, of the best quality, wd. be very valuable and I have therefore resolved to complete the contract and if possible bring the arms with me. I trust that you will do all in your power to prevent the delay from operating prejudicially. My object is to render the most direct and efficient service and the most of it that I possibly can. I shall have cartridges put up for the rifles and shot and shell for the guns, which will be of the most approved construction and accompanied with their carriages. If I do not go on to France this evening or in the morning I will advise you tomorrow as to a rifle contract about which I am to have the answer this evening. Nothing can be obtained here from the government which has given the most explicit instructions to its departments not to permit a gun to be furnished (that is government property) to us or even an old one to be recast without the clear knowledge that it is not going to us. I presume the instructions apply also to the other side. Meanwhile I have no doubt that privateers will be sent out from these ports. Out of a crew of eleven discharged yesterday from a returned ship, seven accepted a bounty of five pounds to go to Liverpool and hold themselves in readiness for a service which was not made known & [*my*] is undoubtedly privateer. My informant says that probably 600 sailors will go to Liverpool this afternoon and remain there at the command of the crimps.—By the last steamer the agents of the Southern Confederacy received an increase of credit which enabled them to complete negotiations in which they were engaged for the purchase of steamers. Yesterday they completed the purchase of two screw steamers, one for $75000. These vessels are to sail from Liverpool under English colors and are to endeavor to enter the port of Charleston. They are *not* to have any thing on board contraband of war. Yesterday the former owners were endeavoring to procure underwriters—I shall try to let you know the names of the vessels, how commanded, who the underwriters are, where bound etc.

Yours truly,
J. C. Fremont

The agents for the Southern Govt. are very active here. A prominent worker yesterday offered to bet that in six months this government would withdraw its Diplomatic relations with the Northern States Govt.

Isaac Sherman Esq.

Pray do me the favor to call on Mr. Greeley and explain to him the cause of my delay here. Both himself and Mr. Bennett I see think well enough of me to express themselves very decidedly and are entitled to my very cordial thanks and to explanations besides.

U.S. Marshal's Office
Washington D C May 27 1861

Hon A. Lincoln. President of the United States
Dear Sir

I was born in Frederick County Virginia, within twenty miles from Harper's Ferry and I lived in that section of country until I was twenty one years of age,—since that time I have associated intimately with those that I knew then in my boyhood, and I know that there are thousands of men there who are at heart loyal to the Union and to the Government. Their voices are now silenced by the reign of terror and violence to which they are subject, but give them an opportunity and they will at once manifest their real sentiments. I desire to serve this Government to the best of my humble ability, and in so doing it would be peculiarly gratifying to me to be instrumental in relieving my early associates from their present thraldom, and to rejoice with them in seeing our standard again wave over their heads—with these ends in view, I propose to raise a regiment of one thousand men, from the valley of Virginia for and during the war, of which regiment I propose to take the command—I desire the Government to accept the regiment when raised, and should your Excellency [*and should your*] signify your willingness to do so, I hereby tender my resignation of the office of U.S. Marshal of the District of Columbia

I am with great respect

Your

Obt Servant—

Ward H Lamon

New York, May 27th 1861

Mr Henry B Stanton of Seneca Falls, late & *now* applicant for the office of Surveyor of the Port of New York, is the husband of "Mrs Elizabeth Cady Stanton" President of the "American Woman Rights Convention" and author of *violent* abolition tracts—she badly damaged her own cause ("Woman's rights") last spring by a speech in this city so very *loose* on the *marriage relation* as to call down severe reproof from Wendell Phillips & various female members of the Convention——Mr Henry B. Stanton was still in Washington at the time of the Baltimore outbreak—coming on to New York, he published in the daily papers a letter from his wife announcing that their two eldest sons had *volunteered* & "she only regretted the other three were not old enough to do so"—adding editorial comments [*on*] on the patriotism thus evinced—& went immediately home to withdraw (as *he did*) both sons from the volunteer army—This is a trifling circumstance. Those who know the Stanton know her un-"reliability"—& this letter has another object *than* Mr Stanton whom it only incidentally suggests—Baltimore is pacificated—"order reigns in Warsaw"—Nevertheless order may not always reign there—*One* class of "Secessionists" in Baltimore consists of those by old tradition (family tradition) a part of the state of things *now* best represented [*by the*] perhaps by the *Lloyds* (large planters) on the Eastern shore of Maryland—& by various families west of the Cheasapeake—Old "aristocracy" with old dignified manners & grand hospitality—(with this class General Codwalloder has close & deep *social* sympathies—& tho' doubtless "honorable" as man & soldier is likely to be easily influenced by *certain people* in his LOCAL administration—*sometimes* a *stranger* can most FIRMLY & EFFECTUALLY administer law—) The *other* (commercial) class of Baltimore "Secessionists" who believed their trade to depend on "the South" or their future to be enriched by leading the South, are more easily led (with few exceptions) to take a new view of "interest" when interest takes on urgent shape—The *first* class are *heart & soul deep* in the thing—This too is *incidental*—My *main* point is to come *Mr George S. Brown of Baltimore* is a man of twenty seven to thirty years of age—His wife was a Miss Eaton of this city—a niece of the Mrs Stanton above named—also a niece (& residing with her mother at the house) of Mrs Dr Edward Bayard of New York (brother of Senator Bayard of Delaware) —N.B. The Bayards do *not* fraternize with Mrs Bayard & her connexions—as being a "different sort of people"—& Mrs B. & her connexions *do* assiduously cultivate the Bayards & "their set" as having "aristocracy"—(*Incidental* still—but with its bearing on the main point—) *Mr George S. Brown* is the second son of the late George Brown—The Baltimore member of the great Banking firm of "Brown Brothers & Co"—He had withdrawn from the firm & had his own separate firm before his death—Socially *he* & *his* were unrecognized in *the* "good society" of Baltimore (having no shade of aristocracy & little intellectuality or elegrance—differing therein from the Philadelphia & New York Browns of the same house) until his children were grown up—They knocked at the door of this "good society" & their *millions* gave them ready admission—nevertheless they *do not reach* & *constantly strive after* access to the *intimate inner circle* of this society & its sanctities—proselytes are proverbially in extremes—*new* "aristocrats" have the most *ardent* & *far reaching* sympathy with "their order" & *talk* of "our class."—

Now, to FACTS—Mr George Brown Senior saw fit to leave certain sums *in trust* for the benefit of his eldest son (with reversion to a child) his daughter (childless) & *a million* (trust) to his wife— of these Mr George S. Brown is trustee (possibly not sole trustee) with either a *reversion* or "contingent remainder" in his own favor—To the rest (& largest portion) of his father's estate he was absolute heir & devisee—

His active sympathies *were* & *are* with the southern rebellion—Just before the Baltimore outbreak he brought his wife & child to New York—he also brought two hundred thousand dollars to be placed in safe keeping—He observed in general a discreet silence *after* the Baltimore disturbance, while he remained in New York—He returned to Baltimore—a week or two since he seriously contemplated *joining in person* the rebel army in Virginia—probably he will *not* do this—but "aid & comfort" if he CAN give, he *will*—In *intellect* & in *character* (energy,&c) his ability is very moderate—financially & "material—"ly it is very considerable—He *had* nearly $100,000. invested in a manufactory of arms rifles I think in Massachusetts (perhaps at at Chicopee—I am not sure—) which he could almost wholly control—The works *were* some months since injured by fire—but are probably now in operation—

This letter is written to inform you of the *wishes* of Mr George S. Brown—His *intentions* are for the government to discover—

Tellula—

Louisville 27 May 1861.

President Lincoln

I am informed by letter from Capt. Wm Nelson that the arms intended for the Union men in Ky— have been entirely exhausted—

The distribution of the small number received has had a most salutary influence upon the party in Ky—Giving strength and confidence to our friends—and weakening our foes—We are fast getting them on the hip—The arms are distributed only to such men as we know to be reliable and who will swear to Support the Constitution of the United States—If the good work can go on—without bloodshed or violence we will have Ky all right—So far, we have beaten them at their own game—Thereby hangs a tale—Our Governor—borrowed $60,000 from the Banks and dispatched an agent (Blackburn) to New Orleans to buy arms— He's dispatched to this city that he has made a purchase of Arms—and that they would soon be here— Each secessionist looked to be a foot taller—talked loud and boastfully of what they intended to do—

The arms at length arrived when lo & behold—they were old flint lock muskets altered to percussion—in altering them they had omitted to bore a touch hole—They could load them very well but d——n the one would go off

This was not the best of the joke—it is now known that the Guns belonged to some Yankee and entrusted to George Saunders to sell— who had offered them at $1.25 each & could not find a purchaser— They now sold to our Governor at $8.50 each—the agent I suppose pocketing the difference— The joke was so good a one that the lovers of fun could not keep it.

Let us of the Union party then I pray you be supplied with arms—

If we have them—there will be no necessity for their use—If we don't have them we will in all probability have to run the gauntlet for our lives—

We will elect 10 Union men to Congress in June—and in August carry the Legislature by an overwhelming majority—

Your friend

J. F. Speed

State of California
County of Solano

Oliver B. Powers, being duly sworn, deposes and says that he is and has been, for a period of a year and nine months last past, a resident of Suisun City in said country and state; that he is a proprietor and editor of the "Solano County Herald, a Republican news-paper published in said Suisun City, and that he is a member of the Republican County Committee for said county.

And deponent further says that he was personally acquainted with Lockwood M. Todd for about one year before and up to the time of said Todd's departure for the East; that during the late Presidential campaign he frequently heard the said Todd claim to be a nephew of Mrs Lincoln; that he has repeatedly heard the said *Todd* declare that he considered "Abe Lincoln's connection with the Todd family a disgrace to him," the said Todd, and that he "would not vote for him to save him from hell."

And deponent further says that the evening before the said Todd left Suisun City he declared to this deponent, with an imprecation, that he would not accept an office or position at the hands of a damned Black Republican.

And deponent further says that he knew the said L.M. Todd to be a pro slavery democrat, and a bitter and abusive enemy of the Republican party, its principles, and its members; and it is a matter of public notoriety that the said L. M. Todd did all that he could do in the late Presidential election to defeat the candidates of the Republican party, both State and National: and that he made use of his relationship to Mr. Lincoln to give point to his opposition.

And further this deponent sayeth not.

(Signed) *Oliver B. Powers*

Subscribed and sworn to before me this twenty eighth day of May A.D. 1861.

(Signed) *G. R. Miner*
Justice of the Peace,

State of California)
(SS
County of Solano)

I Perry Williams County Clerk of the County of Solano Do hereby certify that G.R. Miner before whom the foregoing affidavit was made was at the time of the date thereof an acting Justice of the Peace authorized to administer Oaths etc. And that full faith and credit are due to all his official Acts as such and that his name thereunto subscribed appears to me to be his genuine signature

Witness my hand & Seal of the
County Court of said County
this 28th day of May 1861.
(Signed) *Perry Williams*
County Clerk

County Court
Seal
Solano Co. Cal

May 28th
1861

Mr Abm Lincoln—Dr Sir

I send you a hurried sketch of a Military balloon, which if the government thinks proper to adopt may be of essential service in the present campaign. You will see by the drawing the arraingement is simple.The locomotive can be run on railroad or common roads as the case may require. The balloon of this arraingement can be elevated or lowered as circumstances may require, by a cilinder arrainged on the top of the engine to wind up a cable or to be let out, to give the balloon proper elevation, the balloon to answer for an observatory, also to carry a brass gun for siege operations, when it is necessary to lower to balloon, all that is necessary is to put the engine to motion and bring it in—information, may be transmitted from the balloon by signals or by small halyards with a ring and a small weight causing it to traverse the entire length of the cable, worked by the engine in the same way as the cable attached to the Balloon by the balloon arraingement in this way attached to an engine, draw it in you have control of the balloon which will always be in readiness for an emergency, and the balloon is not subject to being lost. as in ordinary cases, with a balloon arraingement of this Kind an enemy occupying difficut positions, might be obliged to retire, giving the attacking party the decided advantage.

If you think proper let the Commander in Chief examine the feasibility of this new military arraingement—

I have transmitted to you this plan for an observatory to be attached to an engine, which is perfectly new in Military tacticks, withou taking a patent out for it. The government are perfectly welcome to any benefit it may derive from it

I have also a new and very effective plan for a steam gun boat for coast and harbour defense to be built of iron, bombard ball proof, which cannot be boarded which I shall take out a pattent for. I have the moddle completed.

Yours
Jno' Merlett
Boundbrook
N J

PRIVATE

Brevoort
May 30th 1861.

To His Excellency
The President.
Sir,

I pray you not to deem me intrusive in that I presume on the kindness you have already shown my husband, when I take the liberty of requesting, that, in filling the Army appointments, you will not forget *Major Anderson.* He has certainly a claim to your *justice,* as well as on your generosity and on the Government which he has served *so* long, *so* faithfully.

Mr President, he would die rather than ask for—or connive at getting—an appointment for himself: and *his Wife* is willing to ask for it for him, only because she knows how gratifying such an acknowledgment of his services, on the part of his Government, would be to him.

She knows too, how keenly his sensitive nature would feel his

Juniors in the Service being placed above him: and she could not *bear,* Mr. President, to see him endure *that* trial, after all he has already borne for the good of his Country.

Whilst other appointments are made for political considerations, I hope it may not be presuming in me to remind you, that Major Anderson has had the good fortune to strike the chord which has reverberated through the whole country with such surprising effect.

You will, therefore, I am sure, excuse and grant the request I make of you.

His whole military career proves him equal to *any* command you may be pleased to confer on him; and, after the very kind manner in which you expressed yourself toward him, when he had the pleasure of seeing you in Washington, I hope and believe that you will give him *such* a position as you, his Wife and his Country deem that the *length* and *nature* of his services entitle him to.

Be pleased to present me to Mrs Lincoln, whom I had the pleasure of seeing when she was in New York, and believe me, Mr. President,

With sentiments of the highest
Respect and Esteem
Your most Obt. Svt.
E. B. Anderson.

UNOFFICIAL

Head Quarters Dept of the Ohio
Cincinnati May 30 1861

His Excellency
Abraham Lincoln
Presdt of the United States
Sir

I avail myself of the return of Lieut Nelson to inform you briefly of what has been said to me by some of the leading Union men of Kentucky, in regard to the recent distribution of arms among them. They uniformly represent that the effect has been extremely bene-

ficial, not only in giving strength to the Union party & discouraging the secessionists, but that it has proved to the minds of all reasonable men that the Genl. Govt has confidence in their loyalty & entertains no intention of subjugating them. I am confidently assured that very considerable numbers of volunteers can be raised in Western Virginia as well as in Ky, & I would most respectfully urge that an ample supply of arms be placed at my disposal to arm such regiments—we shall need in addition equipment, money & clothing. The issue of the arms to Kentuckians is regarded by the staunch men as a masterpiece of policy on your part, & has—if I may be permitted to say so—very much strengthened your position among them.
A very delicate question is arising as to Western Ky—that portion west of the Tenna. River; Lieut Nelson will explain to you that a convention is now being held at Mayfield which may declare the "Jackson position" separate from Ky, its annexation to Penna, & that this will be followed by an advance of Tenna. troops upon Columbus & Paducah. The Union men say that immediately upon this being done they will call upon Gov. Magoffin to drive out the invaders, & that, should he fail to do so will endeavor to find means to cause Genl Pillow to repeat his Cerro Gordo movement without violating the wil of Ky. I am informed that my proclamation to the Western Virginians has produced the happiest effect in Kentucky —it not being possible for me to refer the matter to Washington, I prepared it in great haste & on such a basis as my knowledge of your Excellency's previous course & opinions assured me would express your views—I am confident that I have not erred in this very important matter—if I have, a terrible mistake has been made, for the proclamation is regarded as expressing the views of the Prsdt, & I have not intimated that it was prepared without authority.
I received the information that two bridges on the B & O had been burned, at a late hour on Sunday P.M. & at once made all my arrangements by telegraph—in the hurry I could only endeavor to express your views & shall be very much gratified to learn that you approve of what I have done.
I am now preparing to seige the valley of the Great Kanawha—there are some 1200 secessionists encamped there—I shall go there in person with from three to four rgts & endeavor to capture them—

then to occupy the Granby Bridge & return here in time for any necessary movement on Ky. By occupying Grafton & Granby Bridge we hold the passes thro' the mountains between Eastern & Western Va. It is also possible that I may occupy Guyandotte—a small hot bed of secession. By that means I hope to secure Western Virginia to the Union.

Rest assured that I will exert all my energies to carry out what I suppose to be your policy, & that I will be glad to be informed if I have misconceived your views.

Should it not be in the power of the Govt to send Lt Nelson back to distribute arms, I would be glad to have him attached to my staff, on account of his intimate relations with the Union men of Ky.

I am very respectfully your obd svt
and friend

Geo B McClellan
Mj Genl USA

Paris, May 31.1861

To His Excellency
Abraham Lincoln
President of the United States
Sir

In obedience to the instructions of a large and enthusiastic meeting of American Citizens holden at the *Hotel du Louvre,* on the 29th inst. I have the honor to transmit to you the Resolutions and proceedings of the same.

The occasion, you will perceive was honored by the presence of several of our distinguished Ministers abroad, whose eloquent and patriotic remarks made a deep impression. This meeting was most timely, and will do much to correct the public sentiment of Europe, which had been altogether misled by traitors, some of whom availed themselves of official positions to plot the destruction of their Government.

Rest assured, Sir, that our citizens abroad feel deeply grateful to you for the energetic manner in which you are prosecuting the war, and will stand by you to the end.

I have the honor to be, Sir,
Respectfully
Your Obedient Servant.
Elliot C. Cowdin
President

T. Wallis Evans,)
(Secretaries
Aug. De Peyster.)

PRIVATE

San Francisco
May 31. 1861.

Sir.

I feel compelled to write to you in reard to the appointment of L. M. Todd as Custom House Drayman.

He has not yet arrived here, but it has become known that he expects the appointment, and a formal protest has been sent to me against it, signed by the County Committee, and a large number of the Republicans of Solano County, where Mr T. has resided, representing that he has been a most bitter and violent opponent of the Republican party up to the very day of the election and even longer, and that his appointment to any position of trust under your administration would be regarded as a gross insult and wrong to the Republicans of the County. An affidavit has also been sent to me signed by one of the protestants, a copy of which I take the liberty to enclose to you herewith, and which sets forth substantially the same facts. I am sorry to have to communicate such statements, but they have come to me in so many different ways, that I cannot doubt they are true. Several personal friends living in Suisun where Mr T. has lived, inform me that the statements sent to me are correct beyond question. Such being the case, I shall take the liberty when Mr T. arrives to withhold his appointment unless he can satisfy me that I have been misinformed. Until I can hear from you, and until he can so satisfy me I hope for my credit and that of the party you will not insist upon my giving him the position. Admitting that all which is said of him is true, if still you desire on account of personal kindness or family feeling [*you wish*] to do something for him, permit me to suggest that in giving the drayage contract to another party, I make a reservation of a certain sum to be paid over to Mr Todd from the net profits, without his being known at all in connection with the appointment .

In the midst of your great cares I am very reluctant to trouble you with a personal affair like this, but in justice to you and myself I cannot do less.

General McDougall leaves here in the morning as one of our Senators. He has been known heretofore as a Democrat, and was elected by fusion of the Union Democratic and Republican votes of the Legislature—but in the present exigency you can count on him as a Republican Senator. That is, you will find him, if I do not mistake ready to go as far as the farthest in Sustaining Your Administration in enforcing the Laws, and maintaining the integrity of the Union. A great majority of the people of this State rejoice in the strong measures taken by Government to uphold its authority, and most earnestly hope to see no flinching until treason is effectually quelled. If any call should be made on this State for troops it would be responded to instantly—indeed one Regiment is nearly organized only in the hope of a call.

I have the honor to be
Most respectfully
Your ob[t] svt
Ira P. Rankin

To
His Excellency
Abraham Lincoln
President of the U.S.

THE MAGNETIC TELEGRAPH COMPANY.

Dated Chicago June 3d. 1861

REC'D WASHINGTON

To President of U S.

Hon Stephen A. Douglas is dead

R. T. Merrick

Dear Sir,

I have directed that the State Department be draped in mourning for the death of Douglas.

I did not feel at liberty to propose a general order, because Senators might except to it as a precedent. Perhaps you may think it well to notice the matter in some way.

Very truly yours
William H Seward

Washington June 4. 1861

To His Exclency The President of
The United States

I was introduced to you by Judge James of New York but knowing that your time was fully occupied have not done myself the honor to call since except at your public receptions.

Am please to see that your family pass over our Seventh St. Turnpike and I have given direction to our toll gather to not detain your carriage or to receive any compensation for its passage .

Wishing your administration entire success
I am your Obdt Servant
J. C. Lewis
Hopeton
North of Washington
D.C.

[*June 5, 1861*]

My dear Mr. President:

Nothing can be more kind than your courtesy to me in a matter so exclusively within your own competency as the appointment of a quarter Master general. Col° Meigs has, doubtless, high genius, science, vigor & administrative capacities—every qualification for the office in question—save special experience in that department of the public Service, & this, certainly he would rapidly acquire. Indeed I know of no one possessed of so many positive advantages, or to whom so little can be objected, & if he can win the *cordial* support of the principal assistants in the Department, that little would be *nil* in a month. It costs me nothing, therefore, cordially to support your preference; for, in truth, I have not, from the beginning, had any candidate to present for the office, tho' I would have been willing to accept Waite, but for his giving his parole in Texas, or of C. Thomas, the highest in rank at present, in the Department, merely to give a step in promotion to the more valuable officers below him.

With the highest esteem & consideration,

Yrs. faithfully,

Winfield Scott.

The President

June 8 1861

His Excellency A Lincoln. President of U S of A

Hon Sir

Amid your many cares, vexations & responsibilitys please excuse the intrusion of an old friend for a few moments. I will not weary you with long preliminary remarks; but make my wishes known at once. If it is possible, my dear Sir for you to appoint Mr. Browning to the Supreme Judgeship without doing violence to your feelings, or better judgment; you will gratify a sincere friend, and a devoted wife.

Mr Lincoln I do not ask this, because I am thirsting for distinction, far from it! I ask it, because I know my husband to be one of the *Wisest best* men in the Nation I know him to be, an unselfish Patriot, & not a miserable office Seeker. I ask it, (with pain and mortification I say it) because I know he has never been appreciated, owing in part, to his great modesty, and unselfishness in not pushing himself forward. I ask it at your hands Sir because I know, there has always been a class of cold, heartless Politicians in Illinois, that have left no stone unturned, to defeat him, and prevent his taking that position that his talents and integrity so justly entitles him to. It is truly humiliating to see men, that labored with the Democractic party in Illinois, through all the long, dark days of their corupt reign; now, exalted to high and responsible Situations in the Republican ranks; Men that gave all their talents and influence to demoralizing every department of the Government, at a time, when my husband was devoting all of his energys to the upbuilding of a party, that he believed could alone save our beloved Country from ruin; And this he did Mr Lincoln, not for office but from the purest patriotism that ever warmed an American heart. I could write volumes numerating the Sacrifices Mr Browning has made for his Country; but I know you are sick of such; and I will spare the infliction. I feel a great delicacy even to allude to such things, I mention it merely to remind you that men, that have done more to injure, than to bless our Country, are the very ones, that are the most opposed to Mr Brownings geting the only appointment, he has ever really desired, or asked. He wrote you on the Subject at my earnest solicitations. he said it pained him to do so, for fear it might embarrass you in filling the vacancy. After saying all I have on this subject, I will now tell you in *Confidence* why I feel so anxious for my husband to get the appointment. Two or three years since—whilst he was making laborous political speeches in the open air, he brought on a rupture of the bowels, that gave him great pain, and was considered eminently dangerous by his Physician. By wearing a supporter all the time he is able to attend to business; the difficulty must increase with age; and we have no income, except from his profession. He has property enough to make us independent but that will be valuable only, when we are under the sod. These are a few of the reasons, my dear Sir why I am so anxious you should not allow yourself to be influenced against my Noble husband. I could say many things regarding Mr. Brownings devotion to you, and your illustrious Administration; but that would be an ignominious argument with you; and unworthy your high position. I know Judge Davis wants the appointment & is pressing his claims. I know men in Indiana (that horse leech State always crying, give! give!) want the office. I know men in Ohio (that have had it for thirty years) want it. Now I ask you Mr Lincoln in view of the whole matter, do you *conscientiously* do you, think any of them have Stronger claims that Mr Browning? if so I have not a word to say, I bow submissively— Mr Browning is in Springfield attending Court; I know he would be deeply mortified if he knew I had written you on this subject, but circumstances are such I cannot forbear. I am told his friends are anxious to have him appointed to fill the vacancy in U S Senate; I care nothing about that situation, it would not relieve him from the labor of public speaking. Should he be appointed by Gov. Yates I know he would not wish to be in the Senate longer than the call session. I know he thinks it very important to have warm adherents to the Administration in that Congress; and he might be induced to accept for the one terme. I have occupied more of your valuable time than I intended: please excuse an anxious wife.

May God bless you, and make you
the Savior of our dear, dear, Country
Very Respectfully your old &
Sincere friend
E. H. Browning

Sub ro'sa

COPY

Suisun City, June 10th 1861.

L. M. Todd Esqr.
Dear Sir;

Some of your good friends, for example, the Solano Herald & Cummins &c having been turning hell to break you of your appointment & my impression is Mr R— has been somewhat instrumental in all the mess, as I see he had made another appointment, but Am in hopes it is only temporary. Would it not be you had better go to work & clear up the charges against you. It may be Mr Rankin had some of his own pets for whom he is anxious to provide and is very willing to hear to the charges made against you. Powers of the Solano has certified to some trash;— I think a portion of which is that you went into the Herald Office & called Mr Lincoln a damned Abolitionist,—a disgrace to the family & I presume many other hard things.— They went to Mr Rankin as soon as he came home, with these complaints & he promised to withhold the appointment until they could communicate with the President. You had better write at once by Pony to the President the truth of the matter, also to the ladies, as they may have some influence. Should Mr Rankin have made his appointment permanent, your course will be to throw him if you can, that is, if he has not lived up to his agreement, but be very careful how you approach Mr Rankin as he may be dealing fair with you, & may have made the appointment temporary to see how it sits. Should he have indirectly or positively promised you the place, if possible, hold him to it. I got Waterman to write him some time since whether any notice would be taken of their petition but he did not answer. I think the plan will be that you were not ready, (& by the way you acted very unwise in not being here,) & that he must fill up.

Yrs &c
J.B.L.
[John B. Luman]

NATIONAL CADETS

Fort Corcoran, Arlington Heights, Va. June 14 1861

His Excellency
Abraham Lincoln, President of United States.
Your Excellency

I find it a most agreeable duty to present my most sincere and grateful thanks together with those of our worthy Colonel, and officers of the 69th Regiment, for the clemency and great mercy which you have extended towards James Foley in commuting the sentence of death passed on him, the just penalty of his crime, to that of imprisonment. In this noble act of compassion, you have endeared yourself still deeper in our affections, and poured a stream of consolation into the hearts of many thousand of his sympathizing friends.

We again thank you, and beg to assure your Excellency that nothing will afford us greater delight than at all times to prove ourselves devoted citizens and true patriots of our glorious Union.

Wishing you and your Excellencies family, good health and the blessing of Heaven

I beg to subscribe myself
Your Excellencies Devoted Servt.
Rev. Thos. J. Mooney
Chaplain 69th Regiment
N.Y.S.M.

London
June 15/61

To the Hon. Abraham Lincoln
President of the United States
Sir,

We have taken the liberty to write to you to solicit the favor of advance sheets of Your address to Congress to be delivered on the 4th of July for publication in "The London American"

The great anxiety felt throughout Europe by all classes for the result of the struggle now going on in our beloved country emboldens us to ask this favor of you as our Journal has taken a stand in England & is looked upon as an authority upon all matters connected with America—The great majority of the English papers give to the people but an imperfect knowledge of the true state of affairs and we labor hard to place them in a proper light—We have the satisfaction to know that we are doing so with good effect. Several of the English Government offices having sent for copies containing articles in defence of your Government and upon Mr. Gregory in relation to his motion for the recognition of the Southern Rebels.

Your advices from England will have told you by this time of the signal failure of that gentleman—our humble efforts contributing to his defeat.

We take this opportunity to thank you for your courtesy in reply to our former application of a similar nature and we trust we will not now be too late should your great pressure of business enable you to grant it.

I am
Sir
Yours Very Respectfully
John Adams Knight

THE MAGNETIC TELEGRAPH COMPANY

Dated Balloon Enterprise *1861.*
Washington, June 16 *1861*

To President United States

This point of observation commands an area near fifty miles in diameter—The city with its girdle of encampments presents a superb scene—I have pleasure in sending you this first dispatch ever telegraphed from an aerial station and in acknowledging indebtedness to your encouragement for the opportunity of demonstrating the availability of the science of aeronautics in the military service of the Country

T. S. C. Lowe

[Endorsed in Mr. Lincoln's hand:] First Balloon Dispatch.

Mr. Lincoln's young and warmly admired friend, Colonel Elmer Ephraim Ellsworth, of the Zouaves, was shot and killed by a Southern sympathizer immediately after he had removed a secession flag from a pole on the roof of the Marshall House, a second-class hotel in Alexandria, Virginia. Mr. Lincoln was profoundly saddened by his death, and on May 25 addressed a letter to the young officer's parents, which ranks with his message of condolence to Mrs. Bixby, beginning:

> In the untimely loss of your noble son, our affliction here, is scarcely less than your own. So much of promised usefulness to one's country, and of bright hopes for one's self and friends have rarely been so suddenly dashed as in his fall. In size, in years and in youthful appearance a boy only, his power to command men was surpassingly great. This power, combined with a fine intellect, an indomitable energy, and a taste altogether military, constituted in him, as seemed to me, the best natural talent in that department I ever knew. . . .

Mr. and Mrs. Ellsworth's acknowledgment follows:

Mechanicsville June 19", 1861

Mr Lincoln
Dear Sir

Pardon us the long delay in answering your kind and sympathizing letter. It has not occurred through want of inclination to write, but from the many calls made upon our time. The fact that Elmer succeeded in gaining the love & esteem of those with whom he was associated is to us one of great joy, and the reception of a letter, expressing such sentiments, from one whom we all so much respect is highly gratifying.

It would be useless for us to attempt to describe our feelings upon the receipt of the sad news of Elmers death. Although the blow was severe, how severe God only knows, yet through his goodness and mercy we are enabled to say "thy will not ours be done" The sympathy of all true Christians, and lovers of that country in whose defence he perished has done much to assuage the intensity of our grief We sincerely believe that God has removed him from a life of strife to one of eternal peace.

He was indeed toward us all you represented him, kind loving & dutiful Our present comfort and future happiness always seemed uppermost in his mind. But he is gone and the recollections of his goodness alone is left us. We trust he did not die in vain, but that his death will advance the cause in which he was engaged.

With these few words accept our most grateful thanks for your kindness *to* and interest you have shown *in* our beloved son May it never repent you.

We would always be pleased to hear from you

We are with respect

Yours &c

E.D. Ellsworth

UNITED STATES MILITARY TELEGRAPH

Received June 19 1861

From Williamsport

To Hon A. Lincoln.

President U. S.

If there is any prospect of an attack on Washington telegraph me at Hagerstown. My messenger will wait your answer and I will come immediately.

Ward H. Lamon

Fredonia Chautauqua Co. N.Y.

June 27. 1861

Hon. A. Lincoln

Dear Sir

Having been engaged the last three years in the sale of medicines from Pierpont & Co. of Rochester N.Y. and having witnessed the instant relief, and permanent cure of many of the various ailments for which Dr. E. Cooper's Universal Magnetic Balm is recommended—such as Paralysis, Cramps, Colics, Burns Bruises Wounds Fevers, Cholera Morbus, Camp Disease, &c. &c. &c. I have thought it might be well to send "Our President" a small supply of the Mag. Balm; and therefore sent it, a few days since, via. Pierpont & Co.

Please accept the same and do not fear to trust it as you would a true friend,—administer to your own family and friends, (especially to Gen. Scott) note its effects, and write to me giving the result, and you will much oblige

Yours Respectfully
P. Miller Jr.

P.S.
On receipt of this please write, and let me know if the med. is received

P.M. Jr.

Cochran Indiana June 23–1861
To His honor the president of this United States of America Mr Abraham Lincoln you Will pleas pardon Me for taking the Liberty of Addressing you Apon this occasion Honorable Sir Having had the pleasure of casting my Ballot for you the second father of My Country, I have seen fitt to name my youngest Son, Abraham Lincoln Tudor he Was Born february the 8th 1861 And Was Duly Crisond on the fourth of March of the same Sir you may think it strange of Me taking this liberty but sir lett me asure you, that the Love for My Country And the presant choise of its Cheafe Executiv has induced Me to Take the Corse I have, As A Mechanic And An American I feel that all i can bequeath to him is his good Name And fitt him for his Country to the best of My Ability I have an other Son George Washington With those glorious names recorded in My Bible I feel confident of there success in life hoping dear sir you Will Take No offence of the liberty I have taken or of my remarks hear I have Made And With your Best Wishes for my little Linky, I Remain your humble Servent

Jacob L. Tudor

The Honorable Mr holman the Barer of this Note Will vouch for My sincerity.

FUNERAL OF COLONEL ELLSWORTH IN THE WHITE HOUSE

At the foot of the casket sits Abraham Lincoln, holding his head in grief; to the right, with epaulettes and sword, chin in hand, is General Scott.

Contemporary drawing by Waud

Reproduced from the original in the Library of Congress

Department of State
June 25th 1861

My dear Sir,

I have engaged to present to you tomorrow, at half past eleven o'clock, Dr. Francis Lieber of Columbia College, New York, who comes to deliver to you the diploma conferring upon you the degree of L.L.D.

At 12 o'clock, I have promised to present Lord Lyons, who brings a letter from Queen Victoria announcing the death of her mother.

On neither occasion is any formal speech expected.

Very truly yours
William H. Seward

The President

COMMONWEALTH OF MASSACHUSETTS.
Executive Department.

Boston, June 27th 1861.

To the President:
Dear Sir:

They reproach New England with having no natural products except granite and ice. But I think the list might be somewhat enlarged, and in order to bring you to my own opinion I have sent to you by the Steamer Cambridge which sailed from here yesterday, a cod-fish and a salmon, both fresh and dripping from our New England waters. I hope that their quality may not be *compromised* on their southward journey, and that they may reach their destination in as good condition as when they started. The steamer is due at Washington tomorrow (Friday) evening, and the officer having them in charge is instructed to deliver them immediately.

I am faithfully &
Obediently Yours
John A. Andrew

July 4th

President U States
Hon A Lincoln.
Dear Sir

Will you excuse my daring to address, you, and enclosing this petition for my eldest son, for, your kind consideration It will tell you all I need, and allow me to say a few words. I know you will listen to them for you have a kind *heart,* and my story is a sad one. I am a widow left with only these two sons, who have left, me, to fight, for the good cause and I am proud to send them forth allthough they leave me desolate, and heart broken, as they are all I had, for my support, and are my only hope in this world, but I have given them up, but trust in God's mercy to return them to me, some day. My eldest son is a first Lieut in the 15th Regiment and educated for the Army holds a permanent place in it my youngest son, is a Private Soldier in Gen Duryea's 5th Regiment Advance Guards, now at Fort Monroe. he is a druggist by Profession and almost a Physcian he was my only stay because the youngest—and to have him perhaps forever taken away from me almost kills me. my health is extremely delicate and if he could only have a higher place, than a private in the Regiment, would make me feel better if he could assist in the Medical Staff in the Hospital, perhaps I am wild to ask such things but I know you can do ALL THINGS. As for my family I can refer to Gov Seward who was a old friend of ours. And also a great man. I could refer, but it is useless. Dont dear Mr Lincoln refuse to listen to a Widowed Mother prayer. Will you look favorable upon this petition. Let me ask your forgiveness for trespassing but you will excuse a broken hearted woman—

Cornelia Ludlow Beckman

Hon A Lincoln
President U States,

Martinsburg Virginia
July 4th 1861

Hon A Lincoln—
Dear Sir:

We are now celebrating, here the anniversary of our Independance—the Flag is now waving over the Court house—and in different parts of the Town—Bands are playing—"Hail Columbia" & "Star Spangled Banner and there is a general jollification here—we expect another fight between here and Bunker Hill,—Dr Zeller—one of our best and truest men—starts from here to Washington. I write to say that Johnson has not swung me yet—He says he would give more for my head than for yours—

I particularly desire that my good friend the Rev. Mr. Chas. H. Russell of Williamsport M[d] who is now with me, and sticks by me closer than a brother and who has just climed the steeple of the Court House & tied on the Flag of the Stars and Stripes—be appointed Chaplain—He is a remarkably talented man—(Presbyterian) good—true, & trusty—

We all want him appointed—

I will write you again to-morrow—

Yours as ever
Ward H Lamon

Hon A Lincoln

Should my Deputy Mr. Phillips want any money to run my machine draw on U. S. Treasury—in my name—about this time I expect he wants about 3 or 4000[00] dollars—

I write in haste

Your Obt
Servt
Ward H Lamon
U. S. Marshal
D C

It was on the eighty-fifth anniversary of the Declaration of Independence that the Congress of the Union assembled in extraordinary session to listen to Mr. Lincoln's war message. In it, "the Executive," as he called himself, presented a detailed review of the events which had transpired since his assumption of office, discussed the legal aspects of secession, and called for men and money with which to put down rebellion. The evolution of the text, from the first draft through emended and corrected preliminary printings, may be traced in the Lincoln papers, where one whole volume of one hundred and twenty mounted leaves is devoted to it. Carefully prepared, searchingly and brilliantly phrased, it constitutes, perhaps, the finest, clearest, and most important statement of the Union cause to which Mr. Lincoln ever gave expression. The following extracts have been transcribed from his original manuscript:

Fellow Citizens of the Sen-
ate and House of Representatives.

Having convened you on an extraordinary occasion, as contemplated by the Constitution, I do not ask your attention to any ordinary subject of legislation. You will act on your own judment and pleasure whether you will consider any such.

At the beginning of the present Presidential term, four months ago, all the functions of the Federal Government were found to be entirely suspended within the several States of South Carolina, Georgia, Alabama, Mississippi, Louisiana, and Florida, excepting only those of the Post-Office Department. . . .

By the affair at Fort Sumpter, with its surrounding circumstances, that point was reached. Then, and thereby, the assailants of the Government, began the conflict of arms, without a gun in sight, or in expectancy, to return their fire save only the few in the Fort, sent to that harbor years before for their own protection, in whatever was lawful. In this act, discarding all else, they have forced upon the country, the distinct issue "Immediate dissolution, or blood"

And this issue embraces more than the fate of these United States. It presents to the whole family of man, the question whether a democracy—a government of the people, by the same people—can, or can not, maintain its territorial integrity, against all its domestic foes —It presents the question, whether discontented individuals, too few in numbers, to control administration, according to organic law, in any case, can always upon the pretences made in this case, or on any other pretences, or arbitrarily, without any pretence, break up their Government, and thus practically put an end to free government upon the earth. It forces us to ask: "Is there, in all republics, this inherent, and fatal weakness?" "Must a government, of necessity, be too *strong* for the liberties of its own people, or too *weak* to maintain its own existence?"

So viewing the issue, the administration had no choice left, but to call out the [*military*] war-power of the Government; and so to resist force employed for its destruction, by force for its preservation. . . .

I now ask that you give the legal means for making this contest a short, and a decisive one—that you authorize to be applied to the work at least hundred thousand men, and three hundred millions of dollars—That number of men is less than one twelfth of those of proper ages, within the regions where *all* are willing to engage; and the sum is less than a thirtieth part of the money value owned by the men who are ready to devote the whole. . . . A right result, at this time, will be worth more to the world, than ten times the men, and ten times the money it will cost.— The evidence reaching us from the country leaves no doubt that the material for this work is abundant; and that it needs only the hand of legislation to give it legal sanction, and the hand of the executive to give it practical shape, and efficiency— . . .

It might seem, at first thought, to be little difference whether the present movement at the South be called "secession" or "rebellion" The movers, however, well understand the difference. At the beginning they knew they could never raise their treason to any respectable magnitude, by any name which implies *violation* of law. They knew their people possessed as much of moral sense, as much of devotion to law and order, and as much pride in, and reverence for, the history, and government of their common country, as any other civilized, and patriotic people. They knew they could make no advancement directly in the teeth of those strong and noble sentiments. Accordingly they commenced by an insidious debauching of the public [*morals*] mind.— They invented a single ingenious sophism which, if conceded, was followed by perfectly logical steps through all the incidents to the complete destruction of the Union. . . .

This is essentially a people's contest—On the side of the Union, it is a struggle for maintaining in the world that form, and substance of government, whose leading object is to elevate the condition of men—to lift artificial weights from all shoulders—to clear the paths of laudable pursuit for all—to afford all an [*even*] unfettered start, and a fair chance in the race of life—Yielding to partial, and temporary departures, from necessity, this is [*I hold to be*] the leading object of the government for whose existence we contend. . . .

Our popular government has often been called an experiment. Two points in it, our people have already settled—the successful *establishing*, and the successful *administering* of it—One still remains —the successful *maintenance* of it, against a formidable attempt to overthrow it. It is now for them to demonstrate to the world that those who can fairly carry an election, can also suppress a rebellion —that those who can *not* carry an election, can not destroy the government.— that ballots are the rightful, and peaceful successor of bullets; and that when ballots have fairly, and constitutionally, decided, there can be no successful appeal, back to bullets. Such will be a great lesson of peace, teaching men that what they can not take by an election, neither can they take it by a war—teaching all the folly of being the beginners of a war. . . .

It was with the deepest regret that the Executive found the duty of employing the war-power, in defence of the government, forced upon him. He could but perform this duty, or surrender the existence of the government. No compromise could, in his judgment, be a cure; but, at best, could only be a little more lingering death to our popular institutions. No popular government can long survive a precedent, that those who have carried an election, *must*, on pain of death to the government itself, surrender the point upon which the people gave the election—As a private citizen, he could not have consented that these institutions shall perish; much less could he, in betrayal of so vast, and so sacred a trust, as these free people had confided to him. He felt that he had no moral right to shrink—nor even to count the chances of his own life, in what might follow—In full view of his great responsibility, he has, so far, done what he has deemed his duty—You will now, according to your own judgments, perform yours. He sincerely hopes that your views, and your action, may so accord with his, as to assure all faithful citizens, who have been disturbed in their rights, of a certain, and speedy restoration to them, under the Constitution, and the laws—

And having thus chosen our course, without guile, and with pure purpose, let us renew our trust in [*the justice of*] God, and go forward without fear, and with manly hearts.

Phil^a. July 6th, 1861.

President Lincoln,
Dear Sir.

Would it not be a grand idea to strike off hundreds of copies of your noble message and let Mr Lowe ascend in his balloon and scatter them in Southern camps and all over the South—Depend upon it, if the poor deluded beings who cannot see a Northern paper were to read your address the South would be electrified, and Union would triumph—They know not what they do, many of them are held in ignorance by the greatest villians the world ever knew, light would in many cases prove a blessing, but alas! I know too many glory in the wrong—Pardon the liberty I take, but a woman's mind is full of inventions—

Yours respct—
Union

Index

[Question marks in brackets indicate partial or doubtful identification.]

INDEX

INDEX

INDEX

INDEX

INDEX

INDEX

INDEX

INDEX

INDEX

INDEX

INDEX

INDEX

INDEX

INDEX

INDEX

INDEX

INDEX

INDEX

INDEX

INDEX

INDEX

INDEX

INDEX

INDEX

LEE COUNTY LIBRARY SYSTEM
3 3262 00147 2064